STUDIA
ARCHAEOLOGICA

155

1 - De Marinis, S. - La tipologia del banchetto nell'arte etrusca arcaica, 1961.
2 - Baroni, F. - Osservazioni sul «Trono di Boston», 1961.
3 - Laurenzi, L. - Umanità di Fidia, 1961.
4 - Giuliano, A. - Il commercio dei sarcofagi attici, 1962.
5 - Nocentini, S. - Sculture greche, etrusche e romane nel Museo Bardini in Firenze, 1965.
6 - Giuliano, A. - La cultura artistica delle province greche in età romana, 1965.
7 - Ferrari, G. - Il commercio dei sarcofagi asiatici, 1966.
8 - Breglia, L. - Le antiche rotte del Mediterraneo documentate da monete e pesi, 1966.
9 - Lattanzi, E. - I ritratti dei «cosmeti» nel Museo Nazionale di Atene, 1968.
10 - Saletti, C. - Ritratti severiani, 1967.
11 - Blank, H. - Wiederverwendung alter Statuen als Ehrendenkmäler bei Griechen und Römern, 2ª Ed. riv. ed. ill., 1969.
12 - Canciani, F. - Bronzi orientali ed orientalizzanti a Creta nell'VIII e VII sec. a.C., 1970.
13 - Conti, G. - Decorazione architettonica della «Piazza d'oro» a Villa Adriana, 1970.
14 - Sprenger, M. - Die Etruskische Plastik des V Jahrhunderts v. Chr. und ihr Verhältnis zur griechischen Kunst, 1972.
15 - Polaschek, K. - Studien zur Ikonographie der Antonia Minor, 1973.
16 - Fabbricotti, E. - Galba, 1976.
17 - Polaschek, K. - Porträttypen einer Claudischen Kaiserin, 1973.
18 - Pensa, M. - Rappresentazioni dell'oltretomba nella ceramica apula, 1977.
19 - Costa, P. M. - The pre-Islamic Antiquities at the Yemen National Museum, 1978.
20 - Perrone, M. - *Ancorae Antiquae*. Per una cronologia preliminare delle ancore del Mediterraneo, 1979.
21 - Mansuelli, G. A. (a cura di) - Studi sull'arco onorario romano, 1979.
22 - Fayer, C. - Aspetti di vita quotidiana nella Roma arcaica, 1982.
23 - Olbrich, G. - Archaische Statuetten eines Metapontiner Heiligtums, 1979.
24 - Papadopoulos, J. - *Xoana e Sphyrelata*. Testimonianze delle fonti scritte, 1980.
25 - Vecchi, M. - Torcello. Ricerche e Contributi, 1979.
26 - Manacorda, D. - Un'officina lapidaria sulla via Appia, 1979.
27 - Mansuelli, G. A. (a cura di) - Studi sulla città antica. Emilia Romagna, 1983.
28 - Rowland, J. J. - Ritrovamenti romani in Sardegna, 1981.
29 - Romeo, P. - Riunificazione del centro di Roma antica, 1979.
30 - Romeo, P. - Salvaguardia delle zone archeologiche e problemi viari nelle città, 1979.
31 - Macnamara, E. - Vita quotidiana degli Etruschi, 1982.
32 - Stucchi, S. - Il gruppo bronzeo tiberiano da Cartoceto, 1988.
33 - Zuffa, M. - Scritti di archeologia, 1982.
34 - Vecchi, M. - Torcello. Nuove ricerche, 1982.
35 - Salza Prina Ricotti, E. - L'arte del convito nella Roma antica, 1983.
36 - Gilotta, F. - Gutti e askoi a rilievo italioti ed etruschi, 1984.
37 - Becatti, G. - *Kosmos*. Studi sul mondo classico, 1987.
38 - Fabrini, G. M. - Numana: vasi attici da collezione, 1984.
39 - Buonocore, M. - Schiavi e liberti dei Volusii Saturnini. Le iscrizioni del colombario sulla via Appia antica, 1984.
40 - Fuchs, M. - Il Teatro romano di Fiesole. Corpus delle sculture, 1986.
41 - Buranelli, F. - L'urna «Calabresi» di Cerveteri. Monumenti, Musei e Gallerie Pontificie, 1985.
42 - Piccarreta, F. - Manuale di fotografia aerea: uso archeologico, 1987.

Continued at page 314

Dorothy M. Thorn

THE FOUR SEASONS
OF CYRENE

The Excavation and Explorations in 1861 of Lieutenants R. Murdoch Smith, R.E. and Edwin A. Porcher, R.N.

«L'ERMA» di BRETSCHNEIDER

Dorothy M. Thorn
The Four Seasons of Cyrene
The Excavation and Explorations in 1861
of Lieutenants R. Murdoch Smith, R.E. and Edwin A. Porcher, R.N.

Copyright 2007 © «L'ERMA» di BRETSCHNEIDER
Via Cassiodoro, 19 – 00193 Roma
http://www.lerma.it

Progetto grafico:
«L'ERMA» di BRETSCHNEIDER

Thorn, Dorothy M.
The four seasons of Cyrene : the excavation and explorations in 1861 of lieutenants R. Murdoch Smith, R.E. and Edwin A. Porcher, R.N. / Dorothy M. Thorn. - Roma : «L'ERMA» di BRETSCHNEIDER, 2007. – 319 p. : ill. ; 25 cm. (Studia archaeologica ; 155)
ISBN 978-88-8265-446-7

CDD 21. 939.75

1. Cirene – Scavi archeologici – 1860-1861 – Documenti
2. Smith, Robert Murdoch – Spedizioni archeologiche – Cirene
3. Porcher, Edwin Augustus - Spedizioni archeologiche – Cirene

This book is respectfully dedicated to the memory of Lidiano Bacchielli, former Head of the Italian Mission in Cyrene

*and also to my parents,
Irene May Bolwell (née Ford)
4.5.1909-22.6.1983
and
Maurice Bolwell
30.4.1915-11.2.2006*

CONTENTS

ACKNOWLEDGEMENTS

I owe a great debt of gratitude to many people, as follows:

James Copland Thorn for involving me in his project at Cyrene, and for enthusiastically encouraging my interest in Smith and Porcher; Rodger Harvey-Jamieson, the great grandson of Robert Murdoch Smith, for his delighted interest and kind permission to use Smith's written and photographic material, which is owned by his family and housed in the National Library of Scotland, and for making available Smith's 1856 photograph; Sheila Mackenzie (National Library of Scotland) for providing copies of original photographs and for making it possible for me to correspond with Murdoch Smith's descendants; Christopher Date (British Museum) and John Ward (Science Museum) for their help and advice regarding the 'photographic apparatus'; the Trustees of the British Museum, Janet Wallace, Kim Overend, Paul Roberts and Kate Morton (Central Archives and Department of Greek and Roman Antiquities) for making available the contemporary records in their care; Kelly-Ann Nolin (Royal British Columbia Museum) for the photograph of Edwin Porcher; Susan Kane (Oberlin College) and Donald White (Pennsylvania University) for their encouragement; John Miles for his expert ornithological advice; Beverley Williams and Maggie Magnusson (Royal Engineers – Museum and Library) for producing the 1861 Dress Regulations; Kate Manners (archivist, Royal Botanic Gardens) for delving in search of Porcher's 'silphium'; Brenton C. Wood in Adelaide for assistance in tracking down some of this elusive naval officer's earlier activities around the world, and especially for obtaining a photocopy of his Australian journal; and all the members of the Department of Antiquities at Cyrene for their constant help and generous hospitality.

PREFACE

Robert Murdoch Smith was born at Bank Street, Kilmarnock on 18th August 1835, the second son of Dr. Hugh Smith and his wife Jean Murdoch. He was educated at Kilmarnock Academy and Glasgow University, after which he joined the Royal Engineers in October 1855, obtaining his commission by passing first out of 380 candidates in open competition. Based at Brompton Barracks on the hill above Chatham Dockyard, overlooking the wide sweep of the River Medway, he studied drawing and planning, architecture, chemistry, fortification, meteorology, astronomy, civil engineering, knotting and splicing, pontooning, escalading, traversing, reconnaissance, night tracing, surveying and theodolite work. Mastering all these subjects within a year, he became a Lieutenant at the age of 20, and, not surprisingly, came to the notice of Lieut. Gen. Sir John Fox Burgoyne as a promising young officer.

On Wednesday 8th October 1856 he was *ordered on Special Service with Mr Newton & H.M.S. Gorgon at Boudroum (Halicarnassus)'* and he left Chatham the following day to bid farewell to his family in Scotland. Here he received a telegram with instructions to be on board on Monday, so on Sunday 12th he *'posted to Glasgow'* and took the express to London, joining 'Gorgon' on Monday afternoon. The ship sailed via Malta and Smyrna for Asia Minor, where Smith worked as an executive officer for three years with Charles Newton's excavations, organising the digging and photography, drawing plans and sections, writing reports and regular letters to Burgoyne and maintaining discipline. It was not all work – he attended a Greek marriage, went wild boar hunting with the Turks, and, on the day when 'Gorgon' sent the paddle boat to collect the first marble column, he spent an evening *'escorted by Turks with torches, drums &c'* at a 'Palivan' held in an open space *'illuminated by torch fires'*, where a horde of men watched a contest by muscular stripped wrestlers, the women crowding on the walls and house-tops to get a view. On a visit to Rhodes he walked over the ramparts and saw the effects of a recent terrible explosion, and while H.M.S. 'Swallow' was at Boudroum there was a *'cricket match between Swallows and Gorgons'*. Smith also explored the countryside, and one of his favourite places seems to have been the Mylassa road, where he liked to walk over the hills or through a beautiful valley which he found. Letters from home must have been eagerly awaited, but on 2nd January 1857 the mailboat brought news of the death of his father. It was Smith who discovered the mausoleum at Halicarnassus, and on 23rd May he began writing his report on it, which he finished on 4th June, sending it with the drawings, a letter and other papers to Sir John Burgoyne on 9th June, with copies of the report to Lord Clarendon and Lord Stratford. In July he recorded that it was *so hot that the photographic chemicals evaporated greatly*. Not until September 15th did he discover that his report had never reached England. A bitter blow – but he rewrote it and sent it off in two days.[1,2]

Between February and June 1857 the ship's log for 'Gorgon' records the arrival on board of the expedition's growing harvest of marble statues of various subjects including horses and lions, and cases containing an entire mosaic pavement. These were stowed in the main hold, but as the collection grew the cases and casks spilled into the bread room, the spirit room and the fore troop deck. Old hammocks, 106 of them, were provided for packing Newton's statues, a method also to be used at Cyrene. H.M.S. 'Supply' relieved 'Gorgon', and on 25th June, with portions of colossal marble horses secured on deck, 'Gorgon' got up steam for passage to England.[3] Later, at Cnidus, Smith had the task of engineering the removal of the nine-ton marble lion from its site high on a hill. It was transported to the coast for shipment to England, entailing the construction of a special zig-zagging road down to the edge of a 100ft cliff and its lowering to a raft in the sea – the entire operation providing excellent experience for his later work at Cyrene.

In June 1859 Smith was appointed to garrison duty at Malta, where during the following eighteen months he planned, and then put into operation, his excavations in the Cyrenaica. After the expedition in Libya he returned to England and obtained a post in the War Office, and later spent many years in Persia, where officers of the Royal Engineers were laying the telegraph cable in connection with the Indo-European telegraph system. He became Director of the Museum of Science and Art in Edinburgh in 1885, and during his period of office he made negotiations with the British Museum about the figure of Young Dionysus from his Cyrene excavations, which at that time was not on display (see pp. 178, 180, 224).[4] Due to his

[1] DICKSON (1901), 107-142.

[2] Journal – Sir R. Murdoch Smith Papers, Department of Greek and Roman Antiquities, British Museum.

[3] Public Record Office ADM 53/5759.

[4] The Museum of Science and Art in Edinburgh was designed by Royal Engineer Francis Fowke in the 1850s.

efforts this statue is now displayed in the collections of the National Museum of Scotland, together with those found by Warrington.[5] His biographer, who was also his son-in-law, had access, not only to Smith's collection of copies of both private and official letters to General Burgoyne, but also to the draft despatches covering his exploits at Cyrene,[6] which were then in the family's possession, but are now housed in the National Library of Scotland, referred to here as the Edinburgh drafts.[7]

Edwin Augustus Porcher was born in 1824, the second son of Rev. George Porcher and his wife Frances Amelia of Maiden Erlegh, near Reading, Berks and Bryanston Square in London. The genealogical records state that both parents were christened in India on 8th January 1792 at Fort St George, Madras. Porcher had the sea in his blood on both sides of the family. His paternal grandfather was Josias Dupré Porcher, now settled in Devon after several years in India, and M.P. for the rotten borough of Old Sarum. Josias was descended from a French Huguenot family which fled to England in the late 17th century, and had married Charlotte, the daughter of Admiral Sir William Burnaby.[8] Edwin Porcher's uncle on his mother's side was Frederick Chamier R.N., who entered the Navy when he was 13 aboard 'Salsette', serving mainly in the Mediterranean, although he became involved in the American War of 1812. Leaving the Navy as Commander in 1833, he proceeded to publish, between 1833 and 1839, five books on naval history and he was given the rank of Captain in 1856.[9]

Young Edwin also entered the Navy at the age of 13 in 1837 aboard 'Donegal' as a Volunteer 1st Class, being made up to Midshipman after two of his three years on that ship. He then joined 'Britannia' for a year, after which he served for three weeks on 'Powerful', five weeks on 'Tyne' and was paid off in November 1841 after a total of four years, two weeks and six days.[10] After about three months leave his true career at sea began under Lieut. Francis Price Blackwood aboard the survey ship 'Fly', which left England in 1842 for a four-year mission in Australian waters, including New Guinea, Malaysia and the islands of Indonesia. He was the artist on board for this voyage which circumnavigated the Australian continent, and during the surveying of the coastline and most of the offshore islands such as the Whitsunday group, originally discovered by Cook, he kept an *articulate dia-*

---

[5] THORN (1993), 57-76 Figs. 1-14.

[6] Op. cit. no. 1, 21, 150-162.

[7] NLS ACC 9569, no. 2 fol. 82.

[8] Information Dr. Bailey; O'BYRNE (1849).

[9] Commander, later Captain FREDERICK CHAMIER (1796-1870) was the author of: 'The Life of a Sailor' (1833); 'Ben Brace: the last of Nelson's Agamemnon' (1835); 'The Saucy Arethusa: a Naval Story' (1836); 'Jack Adams: the mutineer' (1838); and 'Tom Bowling: A Tale of the Sea' (1839).

[10] PRO ADM 107/75 Certificates of Servitude.

ry interspersed with sketches', [11] which is a blue-covered quarto book, annotated inside: *'Private Journal, E.A. Porcher, HMS Britannia, Jany 20th 1841'*. It was a document he would have to produce, together with certificates asserting *'his diligence and sobriety'*, when he was examined on his seamanship skills. Porcher chronicled the movements between January 1842 and October 1844 of 'Fly', her tenders 'Bramble' and 'Midge' and the cutter 'Prince George', some of the happenings on board and ashore, and gave descriptions of the Australian birds, animals, plants and trees which were all new and strange to him, and represent knowledge gleaned from joining Jukes, the naturalist on 'Fly', in excursions on shore. It was five days after Sulivan, the troublesome Mate on 'Fly', tore up his certificate in the Captain's face, that Porcher passed his Lieutenant's exam, on 8th June 1844, and was himself awarded the rank of Mate. [12] His journal, together with the log books he kept and a collection of early Porcher watercolours painted during this tour of duty are now housed in the Australian National Library, Canberra. [13] After departing from the Great Barrier Reef and returning to England in 1846 for four months on leave after obtaining his commission on 9th November, Porcher joined the 'Sidon' steam frigate in November under Captain William Honyman Henderson to serve in the Mediterranean until March 1848. He returned to the East Indies for a spell on 'Cleopatra' in 1849-52 as 2nd Lieutenant under Captain Thomas L. Massie, and in early 1854 he joined the 'Majestic' screw steam ship under Captain James Hope to serve in the Baltic Sea. This must have been a horrific experience, as reflected in the Ship's Log is some form of epidemic – possibly cholera, which ran rife in the crowded living conditions among the ship's crew, peaking in mid July with 163 men on the sick list, and on four occasions three bodies in a day being consigned to the sea. In November the sick list

[11] Information: Ray Blackwood and Brenton C. Wood, Adelaide.

[12] At this time Porcher had been among a group of officers and men which landed on Raines Islet, with a party of convicts brought from Sydney for the purpose of erecting a beacon on this small island, to warn shipping of its existence and to act as a depot for provisions, should any shipwrecked mariners land there. The foundation stone was laid on 16th June, with a procession of the Captain, officers and men led by the head mason, and one of the men playing 'Rule Britannia' on the flute. Porcher's role there was to make 'Astronomical observations' and register the tides. During his leisure time he assisted in making a garden on the island, planting *'Radishes, Turnips, Cabbages, Lettuces, Beetroot, Peas, Scarlet runners, Indian corn, Potatoes, Onions, Sweet Potatoes, Melons, Pumpkins'* and some *'cocoanuts'*. The soil he described as *'beautiful'* and they had their first crops, a plate of radishes, on 30th June. The beacon was completed by 12th September, and left inside it by the order of the Captain were bread, spirits, salt beef and salt pork for any who landed in distress. In 1994 there was a programme of restoration by the Raine Island Corporation to repair the beacon, as it had suffered over the years from lightning strikes and weather.

[13] National Library of Australia MS 4602.

16

still stood at 50, and Porcher must have felt relieved to join the 'Esk' screw steam corvette as 1st Lieutenant under Captain Thomas Birch, again in the Baltic.[14] This vessel was awarded battle honours in 1855 for her services during the Crimean War. He was later based in Malta on H.M.S. 'Hibernia' which he joined in 1857. The latter vessel, a first rate launched in 1804, spent most of her active life as flagship of the Mediterranean Fleet, based from 1855 until 1903 in the Grand Harbour at Malta, where she was eventually broken up.[15] While on this tour of duty Porcher became involved in archaeological excavations at Carthage, which were being carried out between 1856 and 1859 by Nathan Davis.

Smith and Porcher's initial meeting may have been when 'Gorgon' called at Valetta on 3rd November 1856. It is not known if Porcher was on board 'Swallow' when she visited Boudroum, but this vessel was also based at Malta. Whatever may be the case, the two like-minded gentlemen were already friends when Lieutenant Smith, fresh from his exploits at Halicarnassus and Cnidus and full of enthusiasm, devised the idea of an expedition to the Cyrenaica, and naturally brought Porcher into his scheme. A letter written in Malta on 18th May 1860 to Charles Newton at the British Museum outlined his intentions: *'I have formed a project of going to examine Cyrene and the Pentapolis and hope to be able to carry it out. The only information about it is Captain Beechey's book ... I should like to go and make plans of the principal sites between Cyrene & Bengazi but chiefly Cyrene itself. The country is covered with beautiful architectural Greek tombs. I should make plans of the principal ones and take photographic views of them & of any architecture or sculpture that I might find.'*[16]... *'Porcher the First Lieut. of the Hibernia whom you remember meeting here would be very glad to go. He would be very useful as he takes great interest in these things and is besides a good surveyor & draughtsman.'*.[17] Newton, according to his letter to Antonio Panizzi on 14th March the following year, recommended Smith's project to General Burgoyne, and the ponderous wheels of officialdom began to turn. The intention of Smith and Porcher was for an investigative visit at their own expense, using a small ship as a base offshore, to be followed at a later date by a season of excavations. However, the Admiralty decided that the idle schooner 'Kertch' attached to the 'Hibernia' on which the pair had fixed a speculative eye was not, after all, available and the original plan had to be altered. The Admiralty was prepared to offer passage to and from Libya for the two officers and transport for any items of archaeological interest which were to be

[14] PRO ADM 53/532; 53/3246-3248; 53/4247-4252; 53/5675-5676; 53/4900-4902.
[15] ELLIS, WARLOW (1989) I, 28-29, 104.
[16] Brit.Mus.G.R.Dept. Ph.Album II, 19-25.
[17] Brit.Mus.G.R.Dept. Orig.Lett. II (1861-1868) fol. 705.

removed, they were granted indefinite leave and Lord Russell arranged for their documentation and a Firman from the Turkish Government giving them authority to dig, but apart from these concessions they were left to fend for themselves within the country. After the first news reached England of the antiquities that were being discovered, the Trustees of the British Museum awarded the expedition £100 towards its expenses, and later a further £500 which made it possible for the number of workmen to be multiplied by five and for more extensive excavations to be carried out.

The vessel which eventually transported Smith and Porcher to Libya was H.M. Gunboat 'Boxer' – according to Smith *the most incommodious vessel in the Fleet'*. They landed first at Tripoli, where they met the Consul General, Colonel Herman, who had visited Cyrene himself in 1849 and afterwards wrote a definitive description of the ancient city and its surrounding necropolis. [18] They sailed on to Benghazi and stayed with Vice-Consul Frederick H. Crowe, who had excavated a subterranean tomb which he discovered while out horse-riding a few months before. He took them to see it, and must also have described the details of its layout and contents to them in the course of conversation. [19] In Benghazi they acquired horses, camels, four workmen, a guide and an escort, including a man appointed by the local Sheikhs to look after them. He was later referred to as Amor, but in Smith's first letter to Newton he was likened to 'Mehemet Chisoux', probably meaning 'Mehemet Chaoux', a landowner at Halicarnassus. With this party, Mr Gregoris Cesareo, Chancellor of the Consulate and two Maltese servants, they eventually set out on the journey to Cyrene.

Some of the photographs produced during their ten-month stay until 14th October 1861, which are housed in London and in Edinburgh, are the earliest photographic views of the Necropolis, showing the eastern slope of Wadi Haleg Shaloof, close-ups of the archaic tombs, and those in Wadi bel Ghadir. No photographs exist of the city, other than general views of the Apollo Sanctuary and its acclaimed Fountain and external views of the Tomb of Residence, which also features as a background to some of the statuary. There are also no photographs of Smith and Porcher's excavations in progress, only miscellaneous posed views of their guide, three unidentified Arabs and a group of workmen. [20]

Porcher's excellent draughtsmanship skills provided the basis for the publication on Cyrene, but the full extent of his work remains not in the printed engravings, but in a portfolio of unpublished views and plans, still clear and fresh, which he presented to the British Museum in about 1865. [21]

---

[18] Brit.Mus.Cent.Arch. Orig.Lett.Pap.XLII (March-Oct 1849) fol. 13.
[19] BAILEY (1972), 1-11 Pls. 1-4; (1988), 87-94 Figs. 1-6.
[20] WANIS, THORN (1995), 27-33 Fig. 2.
[21] Brit.Mus.G.R.Dept. Porcher Watercolours.

Tracing the despatches and letters

The majority of the official despatches to Lord Russell were subsequently passed by the Foreign Office to the British Museum, where they were traced in the Central Archives Department. The official Despatch No.5 was not found, but a letter of the same date to Antonio Panizzi has been substituted here, as Smith stated that he was sending a near duplicate of it to Lord Russell.

Draft copies of the first four despatches were found among Smith's papers, now housed in the National Library of Scotland at Edinburgh. These provided an insight into how the letters had been altered, usually in minor ways, when a fair copy was made for transmission to Lord Russell. The official despatches and drafts differ mainly in matters of punctuation and capitalisation, although some rephrasing occurs. *'Arabs'* can be altered to *'Bedouins'* and vice versa, and in some places *'I'* has been changed to *'we'*. Some phrases appearing in the drafts are missing from the final copy, and conversely an entire paragraph in one despatch is completely missing from the draft. The spelling of place names was sometimes changed and on occasions surplus words are crossed out on the draft, although they are present in the official despatch; it seems probable that Smith was using the drafts when compiling the publication after the expedition's return home. Only the more significant or informative differences will be indicated in the following text. Among the Edinburgh papers were some personal letters to Smith from General Burgoyne, the Foreign Office and a friend in Malta – also a letter from Admiral Codrington to Porcher, enclosing a telegram.

Further material in the British Museum Central Archives incuded letters to and from Newton, Panizzi and Burgoyne; Smith and Porcher's letters from Cyrene to Newton, Panizzi and Burgoyne; letters within the British Museum; letters to the museum from the Foreign Office, the War Office and the Admiralty; and letters within the Navy. Several of Smith's letters to Newton are now in the British Museum Department of Greek and Roman Antiquities.

Another cache of material is in the Foreign Office papers, now housed in the Public Record Office at Kew, which consists mainly of letters to and from the Consul at Tripoli and the Vice-Consuls at Benghazi and Derna. A letter from the War Office to the Foreign Office encloses an extract copied from a letter by Smith to Lord Herbert, although the original letter has not been found. Judging by references in the correspondence to other letters, there are at least forty pieces from various sources which remain untraced, and may not survive. Only one letter of a personal nature was found, that from Smith's friend in Malta, but there would have been letters to and from the families of both men, which have not gone into the national records. A letter must have been written to Porcher informing him of the marriage on July 25th of his only surviving sister, Madelina Louisa, to Penton Thompson Esq. at St George's, Hanover Square,[22] while he was excavating the Zeus Temple – the *'large temple near the Stadium'*, but no letters seem to have been received at Cyrene after the batch brought in mid-June by the 'Scourge', so the two officers probably met a considerable pile of mail or, as Smith termed it, *'a budget'*, when they returned to Malta.

[22] Gent.Mag.N.S.Vol.11 July-Dec 1861, 317.

I. THE 'SCIENTIFIC EXPEDITION' – THE CURTAIN RISES

It was the spring of 1860, the clear waters of the Mediterranean lapped around the fortress island of Malta and the great harbours and docks were bristling with masts and funnels, and full of the pervading smell of tar. Every day the busy pilots escorted shipping in and out – frigates and sloops, supply ships and troop carriers, steam packets and the survey vessels working on the Alexandria-Malta telegraph cable-laying project. Their crews, on leave, spilled joyously on shore, threading their way past shipwrights and chandlers, to where the bright sunlight gleamed on the domes of churches and illuminated sharply the stone tracery on the terraces of balconied houses which climbed steeply away from the water. People thronged the thoroughfares, going about their business, and donkeys negotiated the streets of steps as easily as if they were level. The whole scene was one of bustle, merchants and businessmen, tradesmen and shopkeepers, men with lopsided blue Spanish style caps, women in their hooded cloaks of black silk, priests, schoolboys, groups of soldiers and strings of sailors all passing hither and thither. The markets were full of vegetables, early fruit, fish, colour, smells and noise, and watching over all this kaleidoscopic activity from above was the impregnable fort of St Elmo, hewn from the solid rock of Malta itself.

Cooling his heels on the island was Lieutenant Robert Murdoch Smith of the Royal Engineers, who was stationed there on garrison duty as part of his foreign service. Life probably seemed rather tame, as for the past three years he had been working with Charles Newton on his archaeological excavations at the ancient sites of Halicarnassus and Cnidus in Turkey. It had been demanding work, requiring all of Smith's planning and engineering skills, but the young man had obviously thrived on it and now, during the aftermath of this period, he found himself thirsting for more activity. Three months after his arrival in Malta, news had come through of the outbreak of the Chinese War, and he immediately wrote to his elderly friend and patron at the War Office, General Sir John Fox Burgoyne, to request that he and his company should be sent on active service to China. His suggestion was refused, however, as the troops for China were being drawn from those already serving in India, who were more readily available.

Thwarted, but determined to make his military career an interesting one, he began to think in terms of further archaeological involvement. He knew there were many promising sites in the countries around the Mediterranean, and was influenced and encouraged by Captain Spratt of the survey ship 'Medina', who was himself immensely interested in the archaeology of the area and its antiquities. Gazing out to sea from his island base, Smith realized that the most promising classical site of all was in Libya, practically on his doorstep, and this led him to study his copy of the book by the Beechey brothers on their expedition nearly forty years previously and also the more recent account by Hamilton, and to devise the project which was to colour all future exploration at Cyrene.

This city, founded by Greek settlers in 630 B.C., had lain in ruins for well over a thousand years before coming to the notice of early 18th century European travellers, and was now under Turkish rule. Smith's primary intention was to conduct a prospecting expedition, at his own expense, to be followed at a later date by an excavation if the Foreign Office allowed it, and ways and means were turned over in his head and discussed with his friend, Lieutenant Edwin Porcher of H.M.S. 'Hibernia', who had become keenly involved in the project.[1] They both frequented the Malta Union Club, and one can imagine the animated speculation and planning which must have taken place in the long, cool lounge or on the terrace overlooking the sea. Just a few days away, across this stretch of green and deep blue, lay the land of promise. An eager letter from Smith to Newton at the British Museum emanates enthusiasm:

SMITH to NEWTON – May 18th 1860

My dear Newton,

I sent you some extracts by last mail which I hope reached you. I write now inclosing a tracing of part of the Admiralty map of the country near Cnidus. Before sending this off I will call at the Palace and see if the thing is finished that I mentioned in my last letter, the Copy of an old book. If it is finished I will send it, if not it will go by next weeks mail. I hope you are getting on satisfactorily with the Book.[2]

---

[1] S & P (1864) Chap. II, 7-8.
[2] NEWTON (1861-63).

I have formed a project of going to examine Cyrene and the Pentapolis and hope to be able to carry it out. The only information about it is Captain Beechey's book[3] which from treating of the whole country from Tripoli to Cyrene is not at all detailed. I should like to go and make plans of the principal sites between Cyrene & Bengazi but chiefly Cyrene itself. The country is covered with beautiful architectural Greek tombs. I should make plans of the principal ones and take photographic views of them & of any architecture or sculpture I might find. Captain Beechey says that there are many Greek statues above ground. From them and the ruins I could form a pretty correct report on the expense & feasibility of an excavating expedition. This I could do without any expense to Government. In the harbour here there is a small sailing vessel the Kertch that is never made use of. She was built here during the war and in fact they do not know what to do with her. Her sister vessel the 'Azoff' Admiral Codrington[4] makes use of as a yacht.[5] Porcher the First Lieut. of the Hibernia[6] whom you remember meeting here would be very glad to go. He would be very useful as he takes great interest in these things and is besides a good surveyor & draughtsman. We could get say eight men from the Hibernia as a crew.

I should have spoken to the authorities here to get the thing done but Captain Spratt[7] whom I consulted on the subject told me not to do so, as any application of the sort would be quite hopeless. He recommended me to do what I in fact always thought the right thing viz. to write to you and get you to set it before the higher authorities at home. I have written by this mail to Sir John Burgoyne & Captain Fowke,[8] who in their way would I am sure do everything. The place is quite at one's door here, the means are ready and would cost nothing, there is a long summer before me, in fact such a coincidence of favourable circumstances may never offer itself again. The French will probably in a few years extend their conquests in Africa so as to exclude us altogether. Porcher & I may be ordered from Malta any day. I think it w^d be a great pity not to do it. I

---

[3] See Dramatis Personae.

[4] Rear Admiral W.J. Codrington C.B., based on his flagship 'Hibernia' at Malta.

[5] 'Kertch' and 'Azoff' were schooner-rigged gunboats, ordered to be built at Malta in 1855 by Admiral Stopford, and possibly even designed by him. In spite of Smith's doubts on the matter, 'Kertch' was indeed converted to a Gibraltar water tank vessel. As he mentioned, 'Azoff' was used as a yacht, and in 1897 was described as *'slow and leewardly, steers badly in light winds'* and was sold two years later.

[6] 'Hibernia' was launched at Plymouth in 1804, classed as a 120 gun ship, and hulked in 1855, becoming a guard and receiving ship in Malta until she was sold in 1902.

[7] See Dramatis Personae.

[8] See Dramatis Personae.

sh^d be much indebted to you if you favour & forward the scheme in whatever way you think best, such as writing to Panizzi &c.

> *Hoping you are well*
> *Believe me, Yours very truly*
> *R.M. Smith*

P.S. Captain Spratt desired me to remember him kindly to you. He took great interest in our work. He showed me a beautiful Venus about 2¹/₂ ft high he got some where, he w^d not say where. ⁹ It is <u>quite perfect</u> and the surface in Excellent preservation. The attitude I never saw before. She is nude coming from the bath, with one hand passing across the body drying the opposite foot, thereby covering the pubenda quite naturally. He says he does not show it to profane eyes, but w^d like to show it to you, although afraid if you saw it that you w^d like to steal it – Mrs Graves here has been asking about Capt. Graves's coins. I promised to ask you as you w^d probably know. Will you let me know about their fate when you write – R.M.S.

Source: [Brit.Mus.Dept. of G & R Antiquities, Orig.Lett. 1860 fol. 705]

In England, Newton must have acted almost immediately upon receipt of this letter, by writing to Antonio Panizzi, Principal Librarian at the British Museum and following up Smith's own letter to General Burgoyne. The authorities typically reacted more slowly, but it was still only mid-July when the British Consul in Tripoli was informed of the undertaking. Smith, on his part, kept Newton informed of the activities at his end.

SMITH to NEWTON – June 8th 1860

My dear Newton
Many thanks for your letter of last week which I received two days ago. I am much obliged to you for writing to Panizzi & Sir John Burgoyne. Both Porcher & I would be very glad if you w^d write to Lord Clarence Paget, ¹⁰ as he is the very man to get the expedition started.
Two or three days after I wrote to you an order came out from the Admiralty to send the 'Kertch', the vessel I wanted, to Gibraltar, there to be converted into a water tank. Fortunately, however, this is not yet done. Porcher was sent

---

⁹ The origin and whereabouts of this piece are unknown, but considering that Spratt was exploring in Crete from 1851-1853, there is a possibility that it may have originated from there.

¹⁰ Lord Clarence Paget of the Admiralty in London.

*with her yesterday to the neighbourhood of Tunis to inspect some wood said
to be good for shipbuilding. [11] I suppose he will be away about a fortnight or
three weeks. This will give time to the Admiralty to postpone the tank till after
we have made our expedition to Cyrene. There can be no immediate necessity
for sending her to Gib, as they have gone on hitherto without her. Besides, the
fleet, for the use of which she was intended, left Gib long ago.*

*Spratt has just left, to proceed with his Survey so that I have not seen him
to deliver your message. I hope to hear from Sir J. Burgoyne by next mail. I
will write to let you know the result.*

> *Yrs most truly*
> *R M Smith*

Source: [Brit.Mus.Dept. of G & R Antiquities, Orig.Lett.1860 fol. 706]

It is to be presumed that the following letter from General Burgoyne at
the War Office in Pall Mall, London is the one hoped for by Smith, although
about a month later than expected, as emphasised by the writer:

GENERAL BURGOYNE to SMITH – July 16th 1860

My dear Mr Smith
*After much trouble and delay, the various authorities sanction your pro-
posed excursion in Africa – I hope it is not too late in the season.*

*I have directed copies of my letter to the Foreign Office and the answer to
be sent to you.*

*You will perceive the Admiralty can not detach the <u>Kertch</u> but propose
some other arrangements.*

*In some notes from the higher Powers, it was repeated that you were not on
any account to make excavations or remove objects without full and distinct
authority.*

> *Yours faithfully*
> *J. F. Burgoyne*

The Foreign Office will send out to you a Photographic apparatus. [12]

Source: [NLS ACC 9569 no. 2 fol. 81]

---

[11] The Navy was always looking for fresh sources of timber – in 1827 George Warrington,
son of the British Consul at Tripoli, was instructed to report to his father on a large forest
which was said to exist at that time a day's ride from Cyrene (**PRO FO 160/48**).

[12] Fig. 17.

Smith was familiar with the use of photography on archaeological sites. In a letter from Cnidus to General Burgoyne in November 1856 he stated that *'Before we left Malta we got the Photographic Apparatus which had been sent by the Indus'* and described how *'One of these rooms we have set apart as a photographic one, fitting it up with a dark chamber, shelves etc., for the use of Corporal Spackman'*, who was kept busy in Turkey as Newton's site photographer, and recorded a large mosaic floor at Halicarnassus from a scaffold erected above it. While he was based at Chatham before leaving for Asia Minor, Smith had his own portrait taken by a London photographer, and described in a letter how the image was *'taken on glass, then printed off the glass upon paper and lastly painted and finished by an artist'.* [13]

The Admiralty, in refusing to allow 'Kertch' to be used as a base, had altered the whole concept of the proposed expedition. Transport to the coast of Libya was to be provided – but from there the lieutenants were on their own. Gone was the exploratory visit – instead the project became the full-blown excavation that Smith had envisaged for a later date. The Foreign Office began, on July 18th, to pave the way for the expedition after its arrival in Libya, by informing the British Consul in Tripoli, Major Herman, of the intended proceedings, and instructing him to take any steps in his power 'to promote the Exploring Expedition' that was to be undertaken. [14]

Herman in turn alerted his Vice-Consul in Benghazi, Frederick H. Crowe on October 8th, transmitting *'a letter from the Gov: Gen to the Caimacam of Your District to afford to them all the aid and assistance in his power – and I likewise beg of you as far as the limited means at Your disposal may admit of to strenuously promote the object of their expedition. I transmit likewise to you enclosed Copy of the Vizierial letter to the Gov: Gen setting forth the conditions under which the Sublime Porte* [15] *has granted permission to these officers to make Archeological Researches in the Cyrenaica.'* On November 19th he contacted G. de Fremeaux, whom he had recommended to Lord Russell to succeed Antonio Aquilina as Vice-Consul at Derna, where he entertained Smith and Porcher on their two visits to that town. Herman asked him to cooperate *'with Mr Crowe in promoting the objects of the Archeological expedition which has been sent for the exploration of the Cyrenaica.'* [16] H.M.S. 'Boxer' arrived in Tripoli Harbour with the expedition on November 21st, where Commander Gulliver sent a message to the Consul and received the following reply:

---

[13] NLS ACC 9569 no. 1 fol. 43; ibid fol.–, March 13th 1856. The miniature, which can be seen in [Pl. 1], is still in the possession of Smith's descendants, and reproduced with their kind permission.

[14] PRO FO 160/78.

[15] Constantinople, the seat of Ottoman Government.

[16] PRO FO 160/18 fols. 55, 59.

I have the honor to acknowledge the receipt of your despatch of this morn-
ing's date reporting your arrival last night from Malta, with the expedition des-
tined for the exploration of the Cyrenaica which you inform me that you have
it in command to convey with the least possible delay to Benghasi and
Derna. [17]

As it is necessary to make with H.E. the governor General some prelimi-
nary arrangements for the purpose of furthering the objects of the expedition
in question I deem it advisable that you should defer your departure until
Monday morning. In the meantime I take the liberty of observing to you that
from the advanced season of the year and as there is no British Authority at
Derna that it would be only necessary to proceed as far as Benghasi, which
being the best port on the Eastern District of this Regency will in every respect
be the most eligible point for the disembarkation of the expedition.

I have &c
G F Herman

Source: [Public Record Office FO 160/18 fol. 59]

Herman's advice was heeded, and the expedition was taken to Benghazi,
after spending four days with him and his wife at the Tripoli Consulate. On
their last evening the Turkish Pacha was invited to dine, and was found to
play *'a fair game of billiards'*.

Samuel Birch, Orientalist at the British Museum, had been examining
the history of nineteenth century Cyrenaican excavations when he wrote to
Antonio Panizzi at the end of November, [18] but it seems he was under the

---

[17] S & P (1864) Chap. III, 10.

[18] Original Letters and Papers Vol. LXVIII July-Dec 1860 (B.M.stamp P.10328 1 Dec 1860).

Dear Panizzi   *November 28th 1860*
From all I can gather of the present state of Cyrene, and the Pentapolis it appears that an excava-
tion in the Cyrenaica would be probably attended with very successful results. The two Beecheys'
who visited that Country in 1821 & 1822, mention the numerous statues, inscriptions and archi-
tectural fragments found in the vicinity of Benghazi and the probability of finding objects of conti-
guity within the radius of half a mile, and also in the early tombs of Teucheira.
In 1848 M. De la Porte the French Consul & M. Vattier de Bourville made some excavations at
Benghazi which were rewarded by the discovery of Vases and some remarkable rare ones with the
names of Athenian archons contemporaneous with Alexander the great [Musée du Louvre MN
704-706]. *M. Bourville speaks of many promising tombs but was unable to undertake much exca-*
vation owing to a want of Funds. In 1854 Mr Werry H.M.Consul undertook some extensive exca-
vations in the ruined cities of the Pentapolis & was successful in finding many interesting vases
and terra cottas, a selection of which was made by the Museum. These excavations were however

impression that Lieut. Smith's excavations at Cyrene were already under way. Far from it – in fact, after delays which swallowed up the *'long summer'* Smith had envisaged, the expedition was at sea, still two days' sailing from Benghazi, on the very day Birch was writing.

The 'Boxer', after crossing the immense Gulf of Sirte, approached the rust-red coastline of the Cyrenaica, and on the last day of November the two lieutenants went ashore at Benghazi. The vessel returned to Malta the next day, and Vice-Consul Crowe looked after the welfare of Smith and Porcher by giving them hospitality at the Consulate and helping them to obtain further necessary equipment. Some essential items were *'girbehs'*, whole goat-skins with the hair still on them for holding water and keeping it fresh and cool, a leather bucket and *'another bag of biscuit and a large bag of onions'*. What seems to have been a chance purchase were a dozen 'Barbary mats' of reed, for which they found a thousand uses. They also bought grey and white striped burnouses for keeping out the chill of winter on the Jebel Akhdar, and various items to use as *'bakshish'*.[19] Crowe helped them to acquire camels, which would have to be brought in from distant grazing lands, for carrying equipment, horses were bought by auction, and he eventually sent the expedition on its way, as he reported in his Consular Letter No. 28 of December 17th: *'The arrival at Benghazi, three days previous to the departure of the Expedition, of Sheikhs Amor Gelaf, Mussa, and others who live in the vicinity of Cyrene was a most fortunate event, inasmuch as I was thus enabled to introduce Lieuts Smith and Porcher to them. The Sheikhs have very kindly furnished them with letters to their respective Tribes, and have, in addition to the guards dispatched by the Caimacam, sent two of their own followers as Guides. They moreover, have promised me, that as soon as they return, they will not fail to call on Lieuts Smith and Porcher and place at their disposal all they may require.'* The letter ends: *'Under such favourable auspices, I have every reason to hope that success will attend the Expedition.'*[20]

The party set out in the afternoon of 12th December and travelled only four miles, halting for the night at the 'Garden of Osman', a traditional stop-

subsequently given up, but lately excavations were I understood going on by Lieut. Smith R.E. who assisted Mr. Newton in the excavation of Bodrum, but whether he has found any thing as yet I know not; my impression however is that Lieut. Smith has been assisted or sent by the Government a point desirable to be known before commencing a fresh excavation in the same part of the world, as another excavation in that case would be unnecessary.

As the greater part of these cities are of late origin, subsequent to the Ptolemaic epoch it is desirable that sarcophagi and other sculptured remains should be carefully selected, those most remarkable for artistic excellence being chosen.

Believe me to remain, Yours very truly

    S Birch

[19] S & P (1864) Chap. IV, 15.
[20] PRO FO 160/78.

ping place for caravans where the well water was sweet, in contrast to the brackish water of Benghazi, which is still a great problem today. During the next few days they crossed the plain, ascended the hills which marked the edge of a plateau and eventually reached the Castle of Merdj where a garrison of Turkish cavalry was quartered, all the while beset by wet weather which made the going difficult and at times prevented them from moving on. They sheltered for two days there, entertained by a great raconteur, the jovial Mudir of Merdj, until the ground dried out a little, and describe how the castle was built of blocks of reused stone from a much earlier edifice on the site, including four marble pillars used to adorn the Mudir's single room. When the weather improved they crossed the fertile plain of Merdj and climbed the wooded hills to the upper plateau, a landscape of hills and valleys which, during the course of their journey, became ever higher, deeper and more rugged.

This was Jebel Akhdar – the Green Mountain.

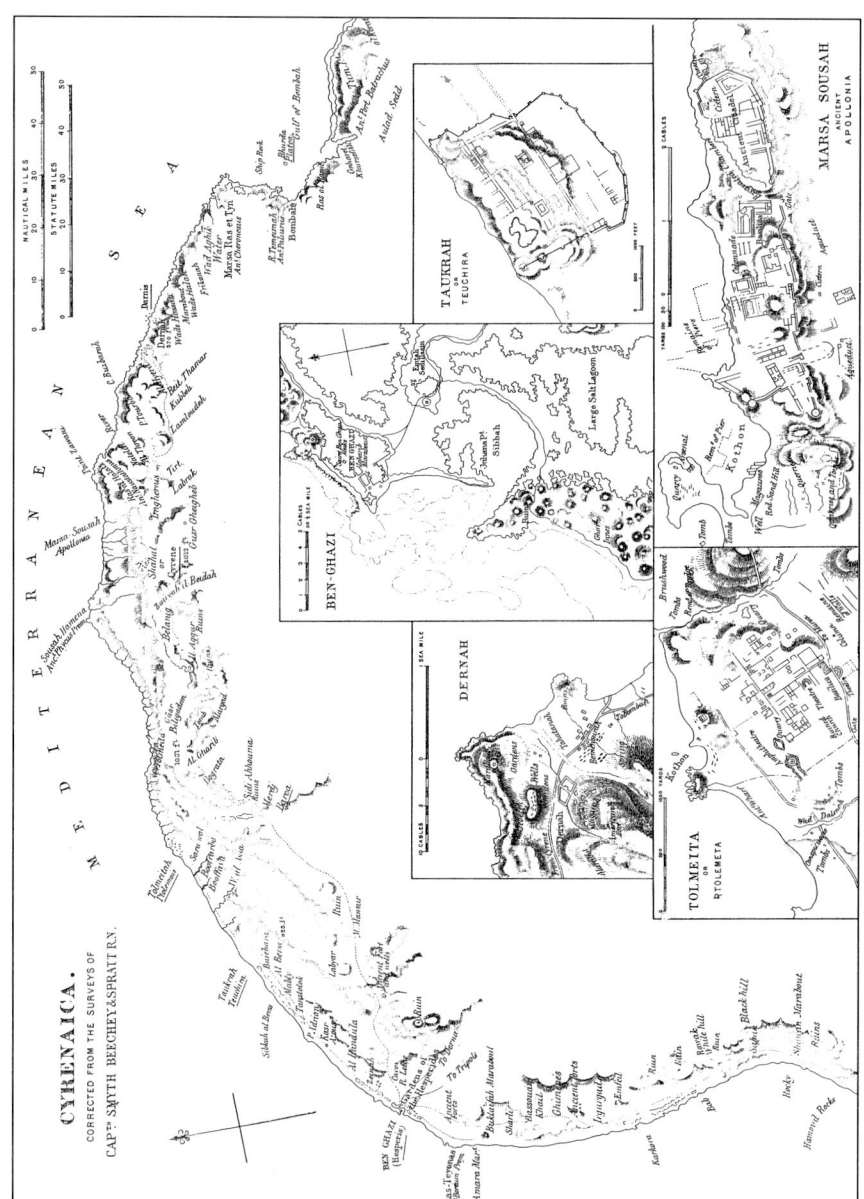

Fig. 1 – General Map of the Cyrenaica.

30

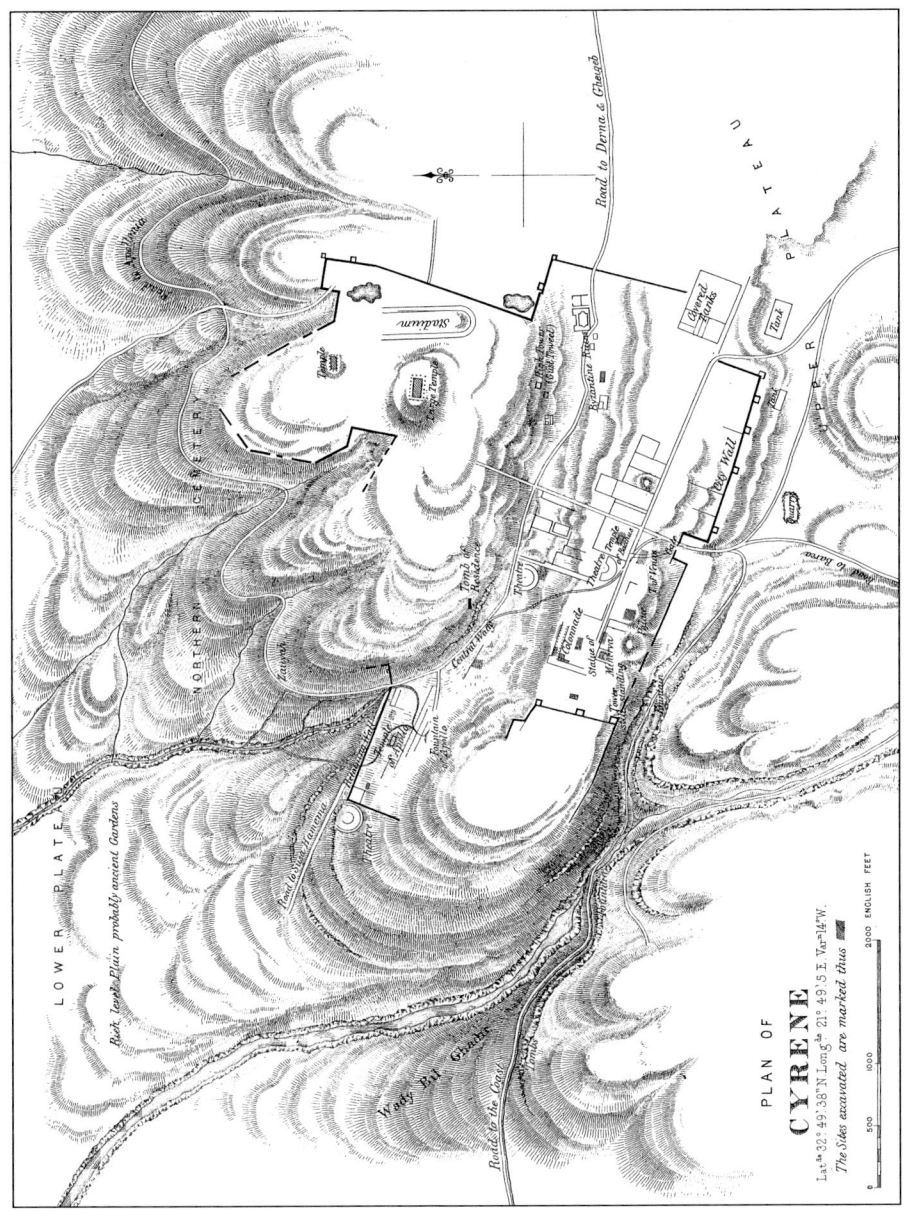

PLAN OF
CYRENE
Lat.ᵈ 32° 49′ 38″ N Long.ᵈ 21° 49′.5 E Var=14° W.
The Sites excavated are marked thus ■

FIG. 2 – Plan of the City of Cyrene.

31

II. FIRST NEWS: THE YOUTHFUL BACCHUS

The arrival of Lieutenants Smith and Porcher in Cyrene on Sunday 23rd December 1860, a cold, overcast, misty winter's afternoon, coincided with a violent seasonal storm driving from the direction of the Mediterranean. After they had crossed the open, desolate ancient city and started to descend the track which runs down the valley towards the Apollo Sanctuary, an ideal place to camp with its copious supply of fresh water, the lashing rain and biting north-west wind funnelling up the valley into their faces forced them to take shelter in a dry rock-cut *'tomb'* beside the road.[1] Smith must have remembered how, because of the remote situation of Cnidus, the Turkish workmen had their quarters in rock-cut tombs[2] and, realising the comfort which could be obtained from these initially unpromising premises he and Porcher began, when the rain eased a little, to clear out the earth and debris inside. A few hours later the slower baggage caravan arrived, with the camels' feet slipping on the wet ground, and their drivers were so anxious to be off again that all the sodden boxes and bags were unloaded and left in the mud for their owners to get under cover. Although Smith and Porcher had been shooting game along the way, and during the previous days had bagged hares, partridges and plovers in order to conserve their emergency supply of

[1] WELD-BLUNDELL (1896), 123-124 Fig. 2. The Tomb of Residence can be clearly seen in Weld-Blundell's Fig. 2, taken 34 years after Smith and Porcher's expedition.

[2] DICKSON (1901), 107. It was a known custom for European gentlemen to take up quarters in tombs. In the late 1820s John Gardner Wilkinson established an extremely comfortable home in a frescoed tomb at Qurna on the west bank of the Nile against the prismatic backdrop of the Western Mountains, facing Luxor and Karnak. This he embellished and extended, making partitions and walls of mud brick to create additional rooms where he entertained numerous visitors, his kitchen stove fuelled by coffin wood (SILIOTTI (1998), 218-223). At Cyrene in 1825 Jean-Raimond Pacho (see Chapter III) had taken residence in a vast, distinctly unwelcoming tomb cut in the rockface below the Apollo Sanctuary. The Arabs themselves inhabited many of the Cyrene tombs until recent times, when they were turned out by the authorities. Nevertheless, I know of two which are still used domestically – both very comfortable, one with its limewashed walls decorated with painted Arab designs.

preserved food, there was no fire that night on which a meal could be cooked, so their first evening in Cyrene was cold, damp, cheerless and supperless.

However, the following day, in true naval fashion, they spent in making things shipshape, and used the *'tomb'* for the next ten months as their *'Tomb of Residence'*, and the range of rock-cut chambers on the terrace above as kitchen, stables and storerooms, all cut in an area of extremely friable sandy limestone. [3] The engraving of the Tomb of Residence, with the afternoon sun flooding into the chamber, shows some of the items of luggage listed in the publication and carried by the camels, such as their portable wooden beds with pillows and blankets and cork mattresses which could be rolled up. Smith is sitting on his bed, reading one of his three books, Shakespeare, Schiller or Molière, while something in a large cooking pot simmers gently. Nearby, Porcher, also deep in a book, is seated on one of their iron-framed folding chairs, which also appears in a photograph with the head of a statue laid on it [**Pl. 24**]. Their tools and equipment are stacked in orderly fashion behind the door which they constructed and in the two deep recesses, or hung on the walls. There appears to be a third bed made up and covered with a Union Jack, probably that of Mr Cesareo, who left in mid March to return to Benghazi. The large camera on its tripod, provided by the Foreign Office, stands at the foot of Smith's bed, and leaning against the wall by the bedhead is his gun.

On Christmas Eve they also received their first visitor, an influential Arab named Mohammed el Adouli – Frederick Crowe's landlord, in fact – who had learned of their arrival by letters sent from the Sheikhs in Benghazi, and turned up with a camel-load of milk and butter for the lieutenants. He was to be of considerable help to them in many ways during their stay.

After arriving in pouring rain and thick mist which blotted out everything but the immediate vicinity, it must have been unbelievable, on the first clear day after the damp curtain had risen, to look out from their eyrie near the top of Jebel Akhdar and see the immensity of the plateau rolling away beneath them like a huge rug in reds and greens, with the *'abrash'* of the great passing cloud shadows, and the line of the sea beyond.

The first letter to arrive on Newton's desk in the British Museum must have come like a bolt from the blue, with its striking news of success and its emotive address:

> *Ruins of Cyrene*
> *Jan. 9.1861*

My dear Newton
  Here I am living in a tomb near the Fountain of Apollo. Coming here not-

---

[3] S & P (1864) Chap.V, 20-23 Pls. 9,18,40.

withstanding the orders of the Foreign Office Admiralty &c, was no easy matter as the Admirals in the Mediterranean jealous I suppose, of an interloping Army Subaltern would not or could not find a vessel in their enormous fleet to convey us to Benghazi.

The orders were dated I think July 19th. We left Malta exactly <u>four months</u> after in the worst season of the year in the Boxer [4] the most incommodious vessel in the Fleet. The voyage and journey here were however very pleasant. We went first to Tripoli where our stay of four days was made quite delightful by the kindness of the Consul General Colonel Herman with whom we lived. At Benghazi we were detained 12 days waiting for escort, Camels &c. There we lived at the Consulate with Mr. Crowe who did every thing for us in his power. As I had a Firman from Constantinople giving me Authority to dig I brought four men for that purpose with me from Benghazi. The Sheikhs also gave us a man acquainted with this district to look after us and see that we got plenty of grub &c. He is in fact our Mehemet Chisoux. Mr Cesareo the Chancellor of the Consulate [5] came with us & remains with us. As he knows the language and the people his presence is of great service. With these different people, two Maltese servants, a guide and an escort we formed our caravan and started from Benghazi on the 12th December. [6] Porcher & I bought horses before starting. Our caravan consisted altogether of 17 men, 10 camels & 7 horses. I brought tents & a few tools from Malta. The journey was delightful great part of the country resembling park scenery in a hilly part of England more than any thing else & abounding in game. After twelve days travelling we reached this place and established ourselves in the tomb we still inhabit.

As I have been here only a fortnight I cannot tell you very much yet about the Antiquities. I have come to the conclusion however that the Cemeteries which seem to have been the places most visited by Beechey Hamilton [7] & Bourville are not the places in which to look for sculpture or any thing else. They are exceedingly beautiful on the steep slopes of the hills looking toward the sea. Very many have architectural facades hewn out of the rock, others are partially built, but all are thoroughly ransacked. They have I think been robbed in the Early Christian times as I dug down to one a depth of five feet before coming to the top of the doorway & found it as empty as the others. The roof was so covered with long stalactites that I had to clear them away before I could enter. This & the depth below the surface convinced me that it must

---

[4] S & P (1864) Chap. III, 10; Chap. IV, 13.

[5] S & P (1864) Chap.IV, 15: 'a merchant of Benghazi'.

[6] S & P (1864) Chap.V, 18.

[7] James Hamilton, who visited Cyrene in 1852, the author of 'Wanderings in North Africa' (1856).

have been rifled Centuries ago, & consequently that the chances of finding any thing in the Cemeteries were very few. [8]

Having given up the tombs, which I commenced with simply because I had only four men, I turned my attention to the City itself. After examination I chose a place I took for the Site of a temple. After digging four days I found a most beautiful and perfect statue within the Cella. It is a youthful Bacchus. It is rather more than life size. The upper part of the body is naked, the drapery hanging from the left shoulder down the back across the front below the loins & gathered up falling over the left hand which holds a bunch of grapes. On the feet are sandals. When I found it the head, the right fore arm and the left hand were wanting [Pls. 4-5]. Next day however I found both the head and left hand. The head is quite perfect without a scratch. It is crowned with grapes & vine leaves. I can barely trace remains of a pinkish tint about the eyes. The head & in fact the whole statue I am certain you would say are excellent. It is highly finished and the drapery very much undercut. The head (which I fitted on to try) is slightly turned toward the right and bent a little downwards [Pls. 2-3]. How to move it was the great difficulty. It could not be left there as the Arabs would certainly have smashed it to pieces, this being one of the forms their fanaticism breaks out in here. To prevent that for the time I had a tent pitched on the spot & made the four workmen live there. Next day I went into a neighbouring wood and cut down a tree with three prongs to use as a sledge. By a series of backbreaking heaves I got the statue packed in a mat & placed on the improvised sledge. Yesterday our four blacks, Cesareo, Porcher, myself & our attendants commenced hauling it down. We got on better than I expected but long before evening I had scarcely a bit of whole skin on my hands. Today therefore I yoked a camel in and brought the sledge down in grand style. I have deposited the statue in one of the chambers of our tomb and I am happy to say he is not a bit the worse of his half mile's journey.

Near the statue I found an animal not in marble of a nondescript character more nearly resembling a goat than any thing else. It has a collar of vine leaves. I found also the head of another animal half dog half serpent also with a collar of vine leaves. There is also a small head of an animal exactly like a Walrus. As I have only cleared out a corner of the cella in my four days digging I hope to find something more in what in want of a better name I shall call the Temple of Bacchus. [9] *The temple itself is small but the peribolus very large.*

---

[8] S & P (1864) Chap.VII, 39.

[9] S & P (1864) Chap. VII, 39-40; The small Temple of Bacchus stands in the middle of the great colonnaded Caesareum, which was largely restored under the Italian Caputo between 1938-40. Smith and Porcher gave a fuller description of the temple in Despatch 1. Their surveying was checked in 2000 and found to be accurate, the metric measurements being: 14.25m (46ft 9in) from the exterior of the rear wall to the riser of the top step; 7.80m (25ft 7in) across the cella to the exterior faces; 6.60m (21ft 8in) across the cella to the interior faces. The isodo-

I cannot quite make out the plan till I have dug more but it is something like this.

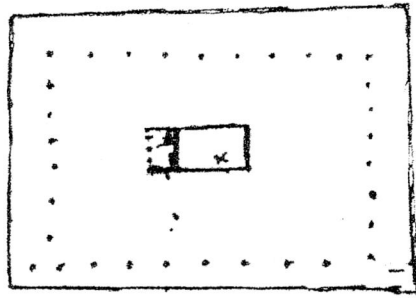

The outer line is a massive wall with a gateway still standing. The dots are columns in situ. The temple itself seems to have had a colonnade only in front. The statue I found at the letter X.

There are many statues above ground in the City but most of them I think of a late date. I must say I cannot quite subscribe to Beechey's glowing description of some of them. The Greek City is probably for the most part underground, and must be dug for. This however is I think an advantage from the fact that things buried are generally in good condition. The city I am sure is full of things but I cannot hope to do a great deal with four men and I cannot afford more as I have one way & another to provide for a perfect mob. Two or three months will enable me however to form a pretty correct idea of what can be done in the way of Excavations. I shall take an early opportunity of going to Mersa Souza to examine the road &c with reference to means of transport. I have not written to the Foreign Office yet but will do so by & bye when I can give accurate information about transport &c.

The people here, all wandering Bedouines are not very easy to deal with. The other day we very nearly came to powder & bullets. We have settled them however by getting the Mudir of Gaigeb to send two of them to Benghazi to be dealt with by the Pasha. One cannot move out of doors without a revolver. At present we are all quiet again & now that they see we have all the soldiers at our disposal, I hope we may continue so.

When you last .... [the rest of the letter is missing]

Source: [Original Letters and Papers Vol.LXIX Jan-May 1861 (B.M.stamp 2760 14 Mar 1861)]

mic blocks of the cella are long and low, L.1.14 (3ft 9in), W.0.56 (1ft 10in), H.0.30 (1ft 0in). The statue base at the western end was probably more than one course high, L.2.06m (6ft 9in), W.1.07m (3ft 6in); the present height above the floor is 0.26m (10¼in). The marble veneer of the floor is thin, having a thickness of 12mm, and consists of tile-like sheets 0.37×0.39m. (Information James Thorn). See also Chapter III note 19.

The effect of Smith's news was like a thunderclap which, on its arrival in March, woke those in authority, and excited letters flew between Government offices and the British Museum. Suddenly, because of the discovery of Bacchus, Smith and Porcher could do no wrong, and all departments were anxious to give them every form of assistance. Newton passed this initial letter to Lord Herbert, who wrote from his home at Wilton House, Salisbury to Panizzi on March 17th: *'I enclose two letters which Mr. Newton left with me yesterday to read, and have interested me much. The last page of one of them was missing when Mr. Newton gave it me. We will send orders for an extension of leave for Lt. Smith R.E. & Admiralty will no doubt sanction our sending the stores required to Cyrene.'* [10] The missing page must have been detached at some point between the arrival of the letter on 14th March and its being handed to Lord Herbert two days later. Although its loss is frustrating, it probably contained only trivialities or personal enquiries, which would be the reason for its not being passed to His Lordship. However, another letter originally accompanied this one, as Herbert refers to *'two letters'*, and a shadow of it can be seen in the resulting correspondence. It must have contained Smith's recommendation that an artillery drag could be used to transport the statues, a conclusion he came to after visiting Marsa Sousa a few days after writing the letter of 9th January, and he probably also gave a provisional list of stores which would be needed, as well as privately expressing his worries to Newton on the financial state of the expedition.

Smith and Porcher's visit to Marsa Sousa, once Apollonia, the port of Cyrene, on 14th-15th January was their first exploratory journey. [11] Following the ancient road down from Cyrene they passed a sea of sarcophagi, barely visible through the undergrowth, and the half-buried façades of hundreds of tombs, the limestone pitted and dimpled by centuries of extreme weather and, in the places most exposed to the elements, eroded into a jagged mass of deep holes that gave shade and shelter to geckos and snails. They crossed the lower plateau, which was then partially covered by dense woods and cut by wadis, and descended via the *'Augubah'* to Marsa Sousa where they saw, but only briefly described, the city walls, theatre and *'two temples'* with their beautiful fallen columns, known now as the Christian churches. A rock-cut tomb formed their camp for the night, and they lay down to sleep wrapped in their burnouses. After a while they were alarmed by the sound of rustling from the dark depths behind them, and thinking instantly of assassins they grabbed their guns – but were astonished when *'a huge porcupine suddenly emerged from an inner chamber of the tomb, rushed*

---

[10] Original Letters and Papers Vol. LXIX Jan-May 1861 (B.M.stamp P.2760 18 Mar 1861).
[11] S & P (1864) Chap. X, 57-58.

through the smouldering fire that was burning in front, and made his escape amid a cloud of sparks and flame'.

Charles Newton was doing some hard thinking on what would be needed by the expedition, based on his own experiences in a similar terrain. He realized that an excavation which had begun so auspiciously would require more time if it were to be carried out properly, and had applied to Lord Herbert for an extension of Smith's leave and for the necessary stores. He also pressed for a vessel to be arranged immediately for the transport of the statuary.

Newton to Panizzi – March 14th 1861

My dear Panizzi

I enclose a letter from Lieut. Smith R.E. who was, as you know, employed with me in the Bodrum expedition and is now exploring the Cyrenaica with Lieut. Porcher R.N. under the auspices of the Foreign Office.

You will perceive from his letter that he has already, in the course of a very few days at Cyrene, discovered a statue of Bacchus in a temple probably dedicated to that god.

Lieut. Smith describes this statue as in very perfect condition, the head being without a scratch, one forearm only wanting [**Pls. 2-5**]. *He also states his opinion that it is finely sculptured. Lieut. Smith was so long associated with the Bodrum expedition and in the course of it had so much opportunity of studying ancient sculpture of the best period that I do not think his judgement would be very far wrong in deciding on the merits of a statue such as he describes.*

Conceiving as I do that his discovery is one of great importance, I trust that the Foreign Office will take important steps for the transport and shipment of the statue from Cyrene so that it may be secured uninjured for the National Collection. I would also draw your attention to the fact that Cyrene is a most promising field for excavation from the circumstance that it was a most flourishing Greek city in the best period of art, but became insignificant under the Romans, a circumstance which leads me to hope that its Greek remains are still intact in the soil.

You will see by Lieut. Smith's letter that his means are of the slenderest, he has only four workmen and none of the means and appliances which so much economise and shorten labour in expeditions of this kind. A subsidy however small in money, say £50 and a few stores from the arsenal at Malta, would at once place him in a position to follow up his discovery in an effective manner. It must be borne in mind that if he is forced from want of means to abandon his discovery, it will in all probability be immediately taken up by the French.

I may add in conclusion that in the first instance I strongly recommended Smith's project to Sir J. Burgoyne from a conviction that Cyrene was most likely ground and that Smith had a practical knowledge of excavations, an energy and intelligence which are rarely combined in one man.

Yours very truly
C T Newton

Source: [Original Letters and Papers Vol.LXIX Jan-May 1861 (B.M.stamp P.2639 14 Mar 1861)]

The possibility that the French would move in to make discoveries at Cyrene and elsewhere in the Cyrenaica had been present for many years. Franco-British enmity was, of course, traditional, and nowhere was it more apparent than in faraway diplomatic outposts, where the British and French consuls prowled warily around each other like suspicious cats, and none more so than Colonel Hanmer Warrington of Tripoli with his gold braid and ostrich plumes and his French counterpart, the dastardly Baron Rousseau – pantomime characters, larger than life. Back in 1826, the fiery Welshman Warrington had warned the Under Secretary of State that, if England did not take advantage of the privilege granted several years earlier by the Bashaw of Tripoli, to extract antiquities from the area, then that gentleman would consider himself at liberty to *'bestow it elsewhere'*. This Grant of Privilege may have stemmed from the Bashaw's gift to the Prince Regent of marble columns from Leptis Magna (Lebida) in 1817, in which both Warrington and Captain W.H. Smyth [12] were instrumental. Warrington wrote *'I have good reason to believe the French wish to excavate both at the Cyrenaica as well as Lebida'*. He would like to go to Cyrene himself with a view to obtaining the *'antiques'*, even at his own expense, as he *'would be truly sorry to see another Nation derive advantages which were originally designed as a Mark of favour to our Great Nation.'* He intended sending someone to mount guard over the antiquities at Grenna (Cyrene) while he awaited a reply to his letter. [13]

Over twenty years later, in 1848, the British Consul G.W. Crowe at Tripoli wrote to Viscount Palmerston *'the French Vice Consul at Benghazi has been employed, under direction, as it appears, from his Government, in collecting and removing the remains of Greek and Roman Art, which are to be*

---

[12] Captain, later Admiral William Henry Smyth, was a charismatic personality, deeply interested in science, astronomy, meteorology, mathematics, geography, poetry, the English language and all matters nautical. Apart from numerous other papers dating from 1824, he published his book *'The Mediterranean'* in 1854, and in 1867 *'The Sailor's Word-book: an Alphabetical Digest of Nautical Terms'* appeared.

[13] PRO FO 160/47.

found among the ruins of the Cities of the Cyrenaica. For this purpose he has made excavations, and has opened many of the ancient tombs at Ptolemeta and Cyrene. I am informed that he has succeeded in finding, besides a great number of Antique Vases, lamps and Fresco paintings, many marble statues which he is now endeavouring to ship on board a Greek vessel hired for the purpose'. [14]

Six years after the expedition by Smith and Porcher, the subject of the marble columns was raised yet again, this time by George Dennis, the Vice-Consul at Benghazi. In a letter to Henry Layard of March 15th, 1867 he mentions Apollonia and *'the monolithic columns of cipollino lying on that site'*, also the similar columns *'lying on the beach at Lebdah'*, which were those left behind in 1817, fifty years previously. These, he says, *'might be useful in adorning the new Foreign Office or the National Gallery.'* [15] Dennis's idea must have fallen on stony ground, for the abandoned columns at Leptis Magna are still there, while those at Apollonia were photographed on the ground in 1915 by Ghislanzoni and erected by the Italians before the Second World War. [16] During this conflict they suffered some damage, and were subsequently re-erected by the British.

On receipt of Newton's note Panizzi must have been galvanised into action, requesting Newton's recommendations as to the most effective way of providing practical help to the expedition.

NEWTON to PANIZZI – March 15th 1861

My dear Panizzi

In reply to your question in what manner Lieut. Murdoch Smith R.E. and Lieut. Porcher R.N. can be best assisted in following out the interesting researches which they are making in Cyrene, and in securing the valuable fruits of their discoveries, I would suggest that the most effectual mode of rendering assistance would be to send a ship of war at once from Malta or elsewhere to Mersa Souza the ancient port of Cyrene on the Coast of Barbary, with instructions to the Captain to render every aid in his power to Lieut. Smith in the removal and shipment of such marbles as he had discovered.

Mersa Souza, the ancient Apollonia, is a small town of which the situation is marked in the Admiralty Chart of the coast of Barbary and which is described by Captain Beechey in his account of the Survey – p. 490.

---

[14] Original Letters and Papers Vol. XLI Oct 1848-Feb 1849; G.W. Crowe was the father of F.H. Crowe.

[15] Brit.Mus.MS Dept. 38993 fols. 390-393; the *'new'* Foreign Office was built in 1868.

[16] GHISLANZONI (1915), 39 Figs. 46-47; Jowett Archive C.C.84 (photo taken before re-erection)

I do not know whether there is any anchorage there but, as it is only three hours distance from Cyrene, the scene of Lieut. Smith's labours, a ship calling at Mersa Souza could at once communicate with him and make further arrangements.

The road from Cyrene to Mersa Souza Lieut. Smith considers practicable for an artillery Drag, but it would be desirable to send out in the Ship, some plank, say 50 three inch deals and 50 two inch deals, which could be used to make good the road in rough places, and also for packing the sculptures. Some rod iron would also be needed for bolting the cases.

I trust that the Admiralty will not refuse to spare the services of a ship of war for the purpose I have suggested, because the discoveries already made by Lieut. Smith are of very great importance and no time should be lost in securing the statues which he has found, one of which I should infer from his description to be of very great value.

Yours very truly
C T Newton

Source: [Original Letters and Papers Vol. LXIX Jan-May 1861 (B.M.stamp P. 2709 16 Mar 1861)]

As promised, Lord Herbert recommended in a letter of March 19th that Smith *'should be granted an extension of leave for six months, for the purpose of making discoveries on the site of the ancient Cyrene situated on the coast of Barbary, in company with Lieutenant Porcher of H.M.S. Hibernia'.* [17] Panizzi was also busy, writing to the Duke of Somerset on March 16th to enlist the assistance of the Lords Commissioners of the Admiralty, who replied two days later: *'Vice Admiral Martin has been instructed to render Lieuts. Smith & Porcher such assistance as may be in his power to facilitate the removal of the statue of Bacchus and other Marbles from the District of Cyrenaica'.* [18]

Summing up the progress of the expedition, an undated British Museum Minute stated:

Lieut. R. Murdoch Smith R.E. who was employed in the Bodrum expedition with Mr. Newton went from Malta to Benghazi in December last in the company of Lieut. Porcher of the Hibernia for the purpose of exploring the ancient Cyrenaica. Lieut. Smith was furnished with a Firman from Constantinople & sent over by the Admiralty to Benghazi in the "Boxer". He proceeded at once to Cyrene and by a letter to Sir John Burgoyne of February last [19] *it appears that immediately after his arrival he explored the site of a small temple in*

---

[17] PRO WO 55/1056 fol. 45.
[18] Original Letters and Papers Vol. LXIX Jan-May 1861 (B.M.stamp P.2764 19 Mar 1861).
[19] Letter untraced (see Smith's Despatch 1 of 23rd February).

which he found a statue of Bacchus rather above life size [**Pls. 2-5**]. *The head detached, the statue perfect all but the right hand. The sculpture very fine, the piece has not a scratch. He found in the same temple several nondescript sculptured animals. He then found two more statues near the theatre, and at the date of his letter the beginning of February was digging in the temple of Apollo where he had found three inscriptions, one of which contained a dedication by Mark Antony to Apollo. He describes the Arabs of the district as very fanatical and fears that unless the statues are speedily removed and shipped he will be unable to protect them. Mr. Newton recommends that Lieut. Smith's leave should be extended and a ship of war sent to assist him. He has submitted to Lord Herbert a small list of stores which could easily be supplied from the arsenal at Malta and which would much facilitate the operations in which he is engaged.*

Source: [Original Letters and Papers Vol. LXIX Jan-May 1861 (B.M.stamp P. 2759 18 Mar 1861)]

III. FIVE MEN AND A CROWBAR

It is noticeable that, in general, nineteenth century explorers passing through striking landscapes gave very little description of the scenery surrounding them. The exception to this is contained in the book by the Beechey brothers, which some readers consider excessive. Nevertheless, although it may be a little flowery in places, their record of the environs of Cyrene is amazingly accurate. Similarly, Jean-Raimond Pacho may be suspected of having used considerable artistic licence in his drawings, but in fact, using his views of the tombs in Wadi bel Ghadir as an example, one can see exactly the same vista as portrayed in 1825, and it is sheer delight to realize that the identical varieties of trees and bushes – small pines, figs, oleanders, junipers and carobs – are growing today in the same position where Pacho drew them. [1]

Smith, in his official despatches and in other correspondence, gave a very perfunctory glimpse of the Cyrenaican landscape, although in the publication his style is more relaxed, with more detail woven into it about their surroundings, but from the time of their arrival Porcher's paintbrush gave its own comprehensive account without the need for words, showing the complete range and depth of colour of sea, sky and land in all lights, right through to the end of the summer.

The Foreign Office passed the originals of the first two official despatches, both dated February 23rd, to Panizzi on April 4th requesting that *'if the Trustees desire to possess the Antiquities adverted to by Lieut. Smith they will communicate with the proper departments of Her Majesty's Government in order to attain that object: – but His Lordship will be glad to know the decision at which the Trustees may arrive, in order that he may inform Lieut. Smith of it.'* [2]

---

[1] Jean-Raimond Pacho, the talented French artist and botanist who explored Egypt and Cyrenaica, published in 1827 a fully illustrated account of his travels in *'Relation d'un voyage dans la Marmarique, la Cyrénaïque et les oasis d'Audjelah et de Maradeh'*.

[2] Original Letters and Papers Vol. LXIX Jan-May 1861 fol. 373 (B.M.stamp P. 3318 5 Apl 1861; copied 13 April 1861).

Lieut. Smith's Despatch 1 – February 23rd 1861

My Lord,

In accordance with Your Lordship's desire expressed in Lord Wodehouse's despatch [3] *of July 19th I take this opportunity of a courier's going to Benghazi to give your Lordship a short account of our proceedings up till the present time in the Cyrenaica.*

Lieut. Porcher R.N. and myself left Malta in H M's Gunboat "Boxer" on the 19th November last. As the Vizieral letter which your Lordship was kind enough to obtain from the Porte was addressed to the Pacha of Tripoli, we went there in the first place to get the necessary orders from His Excellency to his subordinate, the Kaimakam of Benghazi. Colonel Herman [4] *H M's Consul General had however already presented the Firman, and sent the Pacha's orders to Benghazi.* [5]

We left Tripoli on the 25th, and proceeding under sail, reached Benghazi on the 30th. Our original intention was to have gone to Derna & landed there after calling at Benghazi. Mr Crowe H M's Vice Consul advised us, however, to land at Benghazi and make it our starting point inasmuch as we should find considerable difficulty in procuring Camels, Horses &c at Derna in the absence of the English Vice Consul who it seems is nearly the only European there. Besides this there was the danger of taking a vessel to such an exposed anchorage in Winter. [6]

We accordingly landed at Benghazi, and the "Boxer" left for Malta the following day. [7] *We were detained twelve days getting horses + camels during which time we were the guests of Mr Crowe, whose kind hospitality made our detention very pleasant.*

Having procured the means of conveyance for ourselves, servants and Baggage, the next subject of consideration was that of escort. By order of the Pacha of Tripoli the Caimacam was obliged to provide for our safety by furnishing us with a proper guard. Mr Crowe, however, advised us not to take soldiers with us because their presence would only provoke the hostility of the Arabs without being of any service in case of a real attack. He recommended us on the contrary to

---

[3] Letter untraced; see Dramatis Personae.

[4] Edin.draft: *'(formerly of Foreign Legion)'.*

[5] S & P (1864) Chap. III, 10.
Under the direct rule of the Ottoman government was the Pacha of Tripoli (Governor-general of Barbary), who in turn controlled the Kaimakam of Benghazi, under whom were the Mudirs of Merdj, Ghegheb and Derna. Answering to each Mudir were the principal sheikhs of the local tribes. There was no Mudir at Cyrene in 1861, but this post had been created at some time before the visit of Hogarth in 1905.

[6] S & P (1864) Chap. IV, 13.

[7] Ship's Log, Dec 1 1860 PRO ADM 53/7101; S & P (1864) Chap. III, 10.

go as independently of the Turkish Authorities as possible, and to rely rather on the protection afforded by the English name.

Before we started he sent for a number of the principal sheikhs who happened to be at Benghazi at the time. When they came to the Consulate he introduced us and told them the object of our visit, adding that he entrusted our safety to them. In reply they stated they were glad of the opportunity of being of service to the English Consul as he had always been their friend, and had often protected them from the unjust exactions & acts of oppression of the Turkish Pachas.

They gave us letters to the Sheikhs of the tribes whose districts we should pass through, and also sent a man to remain with us at Cyrene for the purpose of getting everything we required which the country afforded. [8]

Everything being at last ready we left Benghazi on the 12th December, [9] *our small caravan consisting altogether of seventeen men, seven horses & ten camels. We were accompanied by Mr G. Cesareo, the Cancellier of the consulate, who has remained with us ever since. From his knowledge of the language & the people his presence has been of the greatest service to us.*

As the Firman gave us authority to excavate and remove Antiquities, we got four blacks at Benghazi and brought them with us to be employed digging. [10] *A few days ago we got a fifth. I brought a few tools from Malta which, with the tents, H.E. the Governor was kind enough to allow me to draw from the Military Stores.*

The journey from Benghazi occupied twelve days, but we could not proceed very rapidly on account of the rain which made the ground slippery for the soft feet of the Camels. The Country is remarkably fine the whole way, & the scenery generally of a very pleasing description. It not unfrequently resembles an extensive park in England. The population must be very small in proportion to the extent of country as we did not see more than three or four Bedowin Encampments the whole way, which, by the somewhat circuitous route we followed could not be less than 180 miles. Almost all the soil seems well adapted for cultivation, although only a very small portion is ploughed by the Arabs. When there is the usual amount of rain in Winter, this portion yields a plentiful harvest of corn. No means whatever are taken by the Arabs for storing the winter rains. In Summer they are consequently obliged to drive their flocks long distances to obtain water, and many extensive and beautiful plains are then absolutely deserted. After a dry Winter the people are reduced almost to starvation by the failure of the crops and the death of their cattle which form their sole property.

[8] S & P (1864) Chap. IV, 14-15.
[9] S & P (1864) Chap. V, 18.
[10] S & P (1864) Chap. V, 23.

About half way from Benghazi we halted for two days at Merdj,[11] *one of the two Turkish military posts in the Cyrenaica-. The other, Gaigeb, is about four hours distance from Cyrene. At these two places there are small Castles with garrisons of about 100 men. They are the residences of the Mudirs whose only duty seems to be to extort as much money as possible from the Arabs, first for themselves, Secondly, for the Caimacam, & lastly for the Hasneh or Public chest. The Mudirs of Merdj and Gaigeb are always Arabs. They are changed very frequently as the sale of the Office is a profitable source of revenue to the Caimacams.*

At Merdj the site of the ancient Barca, we were received most hospitably by the Mudir, Il Hadj Bin 'l Aghar. Beside supplying all our wants during our stay, he gave us as much barley for the horses & Camels as we could carry besides a Sheep, dates, figs bread etc for ourselves.

We reached Cyrene on the 23rd December[12] *in the midst of a storm of wind and rain, from which we sought shelter in some tombs near the Fountain of Apollo. Finding them very convenient from their vicinity to the fountain we fixed our residence in them.*

Cyrene stands on the northern or seaward edge of an extensive plateau whose elevation is about 2,000 feet above the sea. The ground descends abruptly to another plateau about 1000 feet below. The latter extends nearly to the sea, where there is a rapid descent similar to the upper one. The face of the upper slope presents a succession of rounded hills separated by deep ravines or Wadys as they are termed by the Arabs.[13]

The City of Cyrene occupies two of those hills so that it is naturally defended on three sides by steep declivities, and is divided by the Wady into two nearly equal portions. Most of the buildings, however, are on the Western one.

The principal Cemeteries are on the face of the slope overlooking the lower plateau, East[14] *and West*[15] *of the city itself. All round the city, however in a southern direction, there are innumerable tombs.*

From the position thus occupied by the city Your Lordship will be able to imagine the magnificence of the view which it commands. There is an unbroken prospect, East & West of a plateau beautifully diversified by Woods and Wadys as far as the eye can reach, while to the north, the sea itself is seen beyond at a distance of seven or eight miles.

[11] 16th December 1860 S & P (1864) Chap. V, 19.

[12] S & P (1864) Chap. V, 22.

[13] S & P (1864) Chap. VI, 25.

[14] This was defined as the *'Northern Necropolis'* by Porcher when naming his watercolours **[Pls. 57-89]**. The area was called *'Eastern Necropolis'* by the Italian Antiquities Department, but since 1955 it has again been known as *'Northern Necropolis'* (Cassels (1955) Figs. 1-5 Pl. I).

[15] *'Western Necropolis'* probably refers to the tombs in Wadi bel Ghadir **[Pls. 13-16]**.

Having only four men we thought the cemeteries would afford the best field for excavation as the objects to be found there would probably be more portable than those in the city itself. We accordingly commenced work in the Western cemetery. A short experience, however, convinced us that very little was to be found among the tombs. Being for the most part excavated in the rock they could be easily rifled by the successive inhabitants of the country.

One tomb in particular [16] showed me how little was to be expected by further excavation. The door was buried four or five feet underground, and when I entered I found the tomb almost filled with long thin stalactites reaching nearly to the floor. I had in fact to break them off to get in at all. I found, nevertheless, that the tomb had been entered and completely robbed of its contents. The depth of the door below the surface and the great length of the stalactites, which must have formed since the tomb was entered would seem to show that it had been pillaged very many years ago, probably in the time of the early Christians under the Byzantine Empire.

We accordingly gave up the cemeteries at the end of a fortnight, & turned our attention to the city itself. [17] We chose a prominent central position [18] which seemed to be a small temple with a large peribolus enclosed with a wall and portico.

We began digging all round the walls of the temple which I found had no peristyle. The front had a pronaos with four columns, the outer ones of which were engaged in the lateral walls. It seemed to have been originally of the Doric order, but restored in later times in Corinthian. Its size [19] was only 47 by 26 feet, while the colonnade of the portico enclosing the peribolus [20] was nearly 300 by 200 feet. The colonnade could be easily traced on three sides consisting altogether of 87 columns, viz: – 33 on each side and 21 in the end. [21] I could not make out exactly how the opposite end which was the front had been arranged. [22] A gateway [23] and part of the peribolus wall on the S.W.side is still standing nearly perfect. The rest is a heap of ruins, while the position of the temple itself was only shown by a swelling of the ground in the middle.

---

[16] 1st January 1861; S & P (1864) Chap. VII, 39 gives more detail.

[17] Edin.draft: *'to the remains of buildings within the walls.'*.

[18] Edin.draft: *'prominent site near the centre of the city'*.

[19] S & P (1864), 43 original plan lost. At the eastern end five steps lead up to the level of the pronaos floor, with the stumps of four columns. The front and sides of the statue base core at the far end show the remains of a revetment of white marble, while across its front and extending partially along its sides are the imprints of rectangular marble slabs, bedded in opus signinum. This bears out Smith's description of the Bacchus statue lying on the floor *'paved with marble slabs.'* Outside the temple lie the fragments of the Doric entablature.

[20] Internal measurements of Caesareum (WARD PERKINS (1958), 140).

[21] Describes north, south and west sides of Caesareum.

[22] East side of Caesareum.

[23] South-east portico.

After clearing out the [24] *outside of the temple we commenced digging inside the Cella and were soon rewarded by finding a beautiful statue of Bacchus, which of course, identified the whole building. It was about four or five feet underground lying on the floor which was paved with thin marble slabs. The whole of the interior, besides bore evidence of having been veneered with marble.* [25]

The statue is as nearly as possible life size. As found it was perfect with the exception of the head, the right forearm, and the left hand. The head and left hand, however, were discovered afterwards. The whole statue, the head included is in an excellent state of preservation, and the head and hand can be replaced without leaving any very perceptible trace of the fracture [**Pls.2-5**].

No 1 of
Enclosure

No 3 + 4
of
enclosures

The style, in my opinion, is very good indeed, but Your Lordship will be better enabled to judge of that by the enclosed photograph of the head [**Pl. 2**], *than by any description of it I can give. I also enclose a photograph of the statue which will serve to give Your Lordship an idea of its appearance. It is very imperfect however, as I could not get either distance for focusing or sufficient light in our Tomb, where it had been placed for safety. The lower part of the statue, not shewn in the photograph is quite perfect. The drapery over the feet, as also on the rest of the body, is exceedingly graceful. It is all very much undercut & highly finished* [**Pls.4-5**].

We had considerable difficulty in removing it to our tomb without injury, owing to the total want of any means of raising and transporting weights. While making preparations we had a tent pitched close to it in which the blacks lived to protect it from the Arabs whose fanaticism leads them to destroy every statue and inscription which they see. We then made a sort of sledge of the trunk & lower branches of a tree. On this we got the statue placed by means of poles used as levers with slings attached. After packing and lashing it securely to the sledge, a camel was yoked in, which, with our assistance, got it down in safety. It is now in the tomb covered with a tent & walled up. [26]

---

[24] Edin.draft: *'space outside the temple'*.

[25] S & P (1864) Chap. VII, 40, 106 no. 118 Pl. 61.

[26] S & P (1864) Chap. VII, 40. The wood on a hill beyond the *'north-eastern cemetery'* where Smith and Porcher felled a large cedar *'with three prongs'* no longer exists. In the publication a more detailed account of this operation is given. The felling, an operation which took an entire day, had to be carried out using just two small hatchets, as their large axe had been either lost or stolen between Benghazi and Cyrene. Two sides of the trunk were stripped of bark and trimmed to make flat upper and lower surfaces, the lower one as smooth as possible, with a series of deep grooves cut across it to take the ropes which passed round the statue. Several long, straight spars were also cut from the cedar branches for using as levers. The following day, with the newly-formed sledge now at the site of the excavations, the statue of Bacchus was raised upright by means of slings under its shoulders and much heaving with the spars. The

Before leaving the temple we found three nondescript animals sculptured in sandstone. One somewhat resembled a dog,[27] *another a serpent,*[28] *and the third a walrus.*[29] *The two former had collars of vine leaves.*[30]

After finishing the temple we made some excavations immediately above one of the theatres on the side of the street which leads up the central valley of the city. Here we found a number of marble bases of columns[31] *in situ. As the ground was ploughed and sown we were prevented following out the line*[32] *of the building – In the course of the excavations we uncovered two draped statues*[33] *about life size. They were without heads, and one of them was broken below the knee. Otherwise they were in a pretty good state of preservation. From the appearance of the marble I imagine that they were originally placed in the open air in the spaces between the columns. They are of later style than the Bacchus, and seem to belong rather to the Roman than the Greek period. They are not destitute of merit however, and would repay, in my opinion, the*

sledge, covered with the Benghazi mats, was also raised and then lashed to the back of the statue, with the ropes passing round Bacchus being well padded with more mats. The whole contrivance was then lowered carefully and, by means of a drag rope round the *'prongs'* and *'much hauling and shouting'*, the Bacchus covered half the distance to the Tomb of Residence before being left under guard for the night. Nursing their *'torn and blistered'* hands that night, Smith and Porcher had the idea of attaching the drag rope to a camel, a method which worked wonderfully well, as before the next morning was over the statue was safe in one of the chambers of the upper terrace, where it was later walled up for security.

[27] Porcher's list of antiquities sent in June 1861 gives Case 20; B.M.Reg. 61, 11-27, 156; S & P (1864) Chap.VII, 40, 106 no. 119; Smith *Cat*.ii, 255 no. 1477; Huskinson no. 35. By the time this *'dog'* was shipped it had been re-identified as the panther of Bacchus.

[28] and [29] These two pieces in local limestone remain elusive. Some confusion probably arose between entries in the original excavation records and the version which appeared in despatches and lists of cases. In the first letter to Newton this group is described as: an animal *'not in marble.. resembling a goat'* with a *'collar of vine leaves'*; the head of another animal *'half dog, half serpent also with a collar of vine leaves'*; and a *'small head of an animal exactly like a Walrus'*. Smith's *'goat'* is interpreted by Huskinson as a bull in limestone, although no collar is evident. I suggest that the second animal may have been listed as *'dog/serpent – collar of vine leaves'* which, when Smith wrote his despatch, became separated into two animals. The walrus seems to have disappeared, but its identification could stem from the fact that Smith and Porcher were faced with a number of fragments which they had not the facilities to match properly. Indeed, the limestone panther itself bears some resemblance to a walrus.

[30] Edin.draft lacks this entire paragraph.

[31] From its position, this may possibly represent the 'Forehall', just south of the 'Market Theatre', where Ward-Perkins noticed a marble base with its fallen column and capital, also traces of another - and internal recesses for statuary (WARD-PERKINS 1987).

[32] Edin.draft: *'and getting a plan'*.

[33] These figures do not appear in Porcher's list, contained in his Despatch of June 7th 1861, of statues shipped on board 'Assurance'. However, Case 60 taken by 'Melpomene' held a small female statue from the colonnade above the theatre, with its feet in Case 61, as if one of the pair had been retrieved.

trouble of removal. To protect them from injury we reburied them where they were found.

For the last two or three weeks we have employed the blacks at the ruins of a Temple near the Fountain of Apollo. It is the one mentioned by Captain Beechey as the Temple of Diana, but, from the inscriptions which I have found on the site I am rather inclined to call it the Temple of Apollo. [34] *It stands in the middle of the platform in front of the Fountain in one of the finest positions in the City.*

The Fountain issues into the middle ravine from a channel about a quarter of a mile long cut into the heart of the Western hill of the City. Below the fountain this ravine is bridged across by a lofty and massive [35] *wall still standing as the revetment of the platform thus formed behind it. The water of the fountain, after traversing the platform, falls over the wall,* [36] *and finds its way down the Wady to the plains below.*

The Temple of Apollo stands on this platform about half way between the Fountain and this Wall. It is of the prevailing order of architecture viz. the Doric. It is of considerable size the columns being 4' 2" in diameter.

One of the inscriptions which we found is interesting as it contains the well known name of Mark Antony. In cursive Greek I make it out as follows: – [37]

Υπερ τ – – – – –
Καισαρος νικης και σωτηριας
Και του οικου αυτου παντος
Απολλωνι Μυρτοω. Μ. Αντωνιος
Γεμελλος εκτων του Απολλωνος

No 5 & 6 of enclosure *Two days ago* [38] *while digging inside the walls of the Cella, we found a small female draped statue* [39] *in marble. Instead of describing it, I refer Your Lordship to the enclosed photographs. It is about 3' 6" high. The surface is in perfect condition, and as we found it nine feet below the surface I hope to find the head* [40] *also. Your*

[34] S & P inscriptions no. 5, no.15 Pl. 82 and no. 24 Pl. 84.

[35] Edin.draft: *'retaining'*.

[36] Sanctuary wall overlooking Wadi bu Turchia.

[37] S & P inscription no. 13 Pl. 81 **Note**: this inscription was most likely the original no.2 as referred to in Smith's Despatch 6 of Aug 11th 1861, the original no.1 being probably S & P inscription no. 3 Pl. 77 found as a surface find on the site of the Temple of Apollo, *C.I.G.* 5133, but not mentioned in Smith's Despatch 1 of Feb 23rd 1861. In 1911 Richard Norton found S & P inscription no.13 left near their Tomb of Residence in October 1861 (ROBINSON (1913), 199).

[38] Feb 21st 1861.

[39] S & P no.11, Mendel 628.

[40] The sought-for head of this statuette seems to have remained missing, although the Athena head, Huskinson 25, found later was at first thought to belong to it (Smith's Despatch 3 March 21st 1861).

Lordship will see from the photograph that the head was not originally in one piece with the [41] *statue. We have not yet reached the pavement at one corner at a depth of nine feet or ten feet so that there is a probability of our finding some valuable sculptures or inscriptions before finishing the excavation.*

The above gives your Lordship a short account of what has been done in the way of excavations hitherto. The [42] *means being limited to five men, a crowbar, and half a dozen pickaxes & spades,* [43] *we could not undertake anything of a more extensive nature.*

As we are convinced that the statues particularly the one of Bacchus, would form a very valuable addition to the Collection of Greek Sculptures in the British Museum, [44] *we have the honour to place them at the disposal of Her Majesty's Government, and to request Your Lordship to take into consideration the propriety or otherwise of furnishing us in Summer with the means of removing them. The means I would suggest as best adapted to the purpose I have detailed to Your Lordship in a separate Despatch No 2.* [45]

With reference to the question of transport Lieut. Porcher and myself went lately to Marsa Souza, the ancient Apollonia, for the purpose of examining the road and the anchorage. [46] *There is no harbour for a vessel in Winter, but in Summer a steamer might remain with safety long enough to embark everything. The road for the greater part of the way follows the track of the ancient one. Although by no means good, and in some places, as in the descent of the lower plateau, difficult, there is no insuperable obstacle. Such a Carriage as an Artillery drag could, with a little trouble, be taken over any part of it. The distance is three* [47] *hours, about 14 miles.*

Before removal, the statues would require to be placed [48] *in strong cases, for which purpose a ship's carpenter supplied with the proper material would be sufficient.*

Since our arrival Lieut Porcher has made a large number of drawings of the different objects of interest here particularly the tombs. I have also made plans of some of the more Characteristic of them, so that we hope before leaving to be able to furnish such detail as will give a pretty accurate idea of this remarkable Necropolis. [49]

Our operations have been somewhat delayed during the two months we

[41] Edin.draft: 'body of the'.
[42] Edin.draft: 'Our'.
[43] Edin.draft: 'shovels'.
[44] Edin.draft: 'addition to the Department of Antiquities of the British Museum'.
[45] Original Letters and Papers Vol. LXIX Jan-May 1861 fol. 378.
[46] 14/15th January S & P (1864) Chap. X, 57.
[47] Edin.draft: 'four'; S & P (1864) Chap. X, 57 'four hours'.
[48] Edin.draft: 'packed'.
[49] Porcher watercolours; S & P (1864) Frontispiece and Plates 11-38.

have been here by the uncertainty and sometimes by the inclemency [50] *of the weather. We intend commencing now a series of tours in the surrounding country.*

Ten days ago we went to a place the Arabs told us of, called by them Imgernis. It contained a number of buildings still standing to a considerable height, besides tombs and cisterns cut in the rock. Not having any books of reference I cannot identify the place, but we will shortly return to make a plan and take a few photographs of the ruins. Next week we propose going to Derna, [51] *visiting any remarkable places there may be on the road.*

Our intercourse with the Arabs has generally been of the most friendly nature. We have had only one serious question with them, when one man threw stones at us, and another threatened to shoot us. After a month's delay on the part of the Mudir the two men were at last apprehended, by the orders of the Caimacam, and sent to Benghazi. This morning however, I heard that the Mudir, having received a bribe of 200 dollars allowed them to escape. The result, I have little doubt, will now be his own deprivation of office.

The Arabs are not controlled in any way by the Turkish Government, except in the matter of Taxes which are levied by the Pachas and Mudirs through their own Sheikhs. They are almost always in a state of war among themselves. Murder is thought no crime and is taken no notice of by the government. If a man of one tribe kills a man of another, the friend of the deceased shoots, not the murderer, but the first man of his tribe whom he sees. This is considered a point of honour by them. The men, even when ploughing, always go armed with one or two pistols, a knife and a long gun which is generally fitted with a bayonet. This is the case throughout the country, although the importation & sale of gunpowder are strictly prohibited.

The following is a list of the photographs in the enclosure. They are numbered on the back.

No 1 Head of the Statue of Bacchus, front view. [**Pl. 2**]

> *2 The same, profile.* [**Pl. 3**]
>
> *3 Statue of Bacchus, front view.* [**Pl. 4**]
>
> *4 The same, profile.* [**Pl. 5**]
>
> *5 & 6 Small female statue from the Temple of Apollo.* [**Pls. 6-7**]
>
> *7, 8, 9 + 10 Consecutive views of the face of one of the hills in the Eastern Cemetery.* [**Pls. 8-11**]
>
> *11 Excavated tombs in the Eastern Cemetery.* [**Pl. 12**]
>
> *12 View in the Wady Bil Ghadir of the* [52] *road along the face of the cliff leading to the Western Cemetery.* [**Pl. 13**]

[50] Edin.draft: *'severity'*.

[51] 26th February 1861, presented by Mudir – a silver sphinx and Roman silver coin, S & P (1864) Chap. X, 59, also Porcher's Despatch 7th June 1861 Case 21.

[52] Edin.draft: *'retaining wall and of the'*.

13, 14 & 15 Excavated tombs in the Western Cemetery. [**Pls. 14-16**]
16 Group of three young Arabs. [**Pl. 17**]
17 -"- -"- of our [53] *blacks.* [**Pl. 18**]
With this Despatch I send the other referred to above, concerning the removal of the statues.

I have the honour to be My Lord,
Your Lordship's most obedient humble Servant, R.M. Smith
Lieut Rl. Engrs

Source: [Original Letters and Papers Vol. LXIX Jan – May 1861 fols. 374-377 (no B.M. stamp)]. A published copy of this Despatch is in (DICKSON (1901), 150-162) from drafts in Edinburgh, NLS ACC 9569 fol. 82-2.

Lieut. Smith's Despatch 2 – February 23rd 1861

My Lord,

With reference to the question of removing the statues referred to in my despatch No 1 of this date, [54] *I have the honour to suggest the following as the best means of transport, should Your Lordship deem it advisable to have a vessel belonging to the Fleet sent here in summer. The vessel ought, I think, to come to Marsa Souza about the month of May when the summer weather has fairly commenced. She should* [55] *be landed for a short time to make packing cases.*

The following articles are also necessary. All of them could be obtained from the military stores at Malta, with the exception perhaps of the rope, planks, and old hammocks, which might be supplied by the Dockyard.

Artillery four wheeled drags – 2 or 3 (2) | _ [56]
Spare wheels for -do- 6 (4) |
$2^{1}/_{2}$ inch deal for packing Cases.
               feet. 250 to 300 [57]
3/8 inch rod iron for bolts [58] *for do- feet 100*
Two dozen old hammocks for packing
An Artillery Gyn with a 4" fall.

---

[53] Edin.draft: *'four'*.
[54] Original Letters and Papers Vol. LXIX Jan-May 1861 fol. 374-377.
[55] Edin.draft: *'have one or two Carpenters on board who could be landed for a short time to make packing cases.'*
[56] '2', '4' marked in pencil – see Captain Ewart's despatch 24th October 1861.
[57] See Smith's Despatch 3 of 21st March 1861.
[58] Ship's log 'Assurance' PRO ADM 53/7011 May 21st-June 5th 1861. Blacksmith making washers and spiked nails.

One coil of 3 inch rope with half a dozen blocks [59] *to match.*
Half a dozen handspikes

> *I have the honour to be, My Lord,*
> *Your Lordships most obedient Humble Servant*
> *R.M. Smith, Lieut Rl. Engineers*

Source: [Original Letters and Papers Vol. LXIX Jan – May 1861 fol.378 (no B.M.stamp); NLS ACC 9569 fol. 83]

SMITH to NEWTON – February 25th 1861

My dear Newton,

    I have barely time to write you a hurried note to go with the courier I am sending to Benghazi. He goes with a long despatch to the Foreign Office detailing our proceedings here. I think I told you most of what it contains in my last letter, but should you be at the Foreign Office at any time you might look at it as it contains an enclosure of 16 photographs which I have taken here. [60] *I inclose you a photograph I took of the head of the Bacchus [**Pl. 2**]. I also send you one of the statue itself but it is so imperfect that it can only serve to give you an idea of the arrangement of the drapery [**Pl. 4**]. Being inside our tomb I could not get distance for focusing nor light enough to make any thing like a photograph. Since I wrote last we have found a small female draped statue about 3'6" high in the cella of what I take to be the Temple of Apollo. I enclose a photograph of it [**Pl. 6**]. It is much inferior to the Bacchus, but from its perfect state of preservation is a nice little thing in its way. I have not reached the pavement at one Corner at a depth of 9 or 10 feet so there is every probability of finding the head & some more sculpture as it is a large temple. The columns are 4'2" in diameter. In my letter to the Foreign Office I have asked for a ship about the month of May to remove the things, also for some tackle for the land transport of about 12 miles. I suppose they will give it as the expense will be trifling*

    I am a long way behind in the way of news as I have had no letters or papers since leaving Malta more than three months ago. I expect a budget by the Courier when he returns from Benghazi.

    I address this as formerly to the care of Mr. Panizzi.

    Believe me, Yours mo: sincerely
    R.M. Smith

Source: [Brit.Mus.Dept. of G & R Antiquities, Orig.Lett. 1861 fol. 708]

[59] Edin.draft: *'(stopped)'*.
[60] According to the despatch, 17 photographs were sent with it.

Smith's comment on the limited supply of men and equipment which governed the scope of their exploration cannot fail to have been taken on board by the authorities. In his publication he describes the difficulties of teaching the use of tools to workmen who had never held such things as a shovel or pickaxe before. They had no knowledge of leverage, and if confronted by a heavy, immovable stone their instinct was to break it, instead of using a crowbar.[61] The lieutenants very quickly abandoned their attempts to find a tomb which had not been disturbed. It is doubtful whether their first excavation really involved a tomb, being described as *'a heap of stones lying against an artificial escarp'* near an enormous tomb past Wadi bel Ghadir opened by Bourville. Although this heap could represent a fallen built façade, they reached rock bottom with the cut rock face yielding no sign of an entrance of any kind. Their second attempt was in Wadi bel Ghadir itself, where the tomb they eventually found, a *'plain square chamber with recesses'*, was filled with stalactites that had formed where lime-saturated moisture had seeped through the roof. Smith deduced that the tomb had been emptied of its contents long ago, and that there was no point in opening any further tombs, as the same fate had probably befallen all of them. He therefore turned away from the necropolis and sank all his efforts into the city and the Apollo Sanctuary.

These substantial letters landed on the leather-topped mahogany desks of London in early April, creating another small flurry of correspondence among the British Museum, the Admiralty and the Foreign Office. The Duke of Somerset wrote to Vice-Admiral William Fanshawe Martin on April 8th regarding *'the removal of some antiquities from the Cyrenaica for the British Museum. I hope you will be able to make arrangements for their safe shipment as they are monuments in which the authorities of the Museum take a great interest'* [62] and the Foreign Office on April 9th sent Smith an extract of a letter received from the British Museum: *"The Trustees have made application to the Secretary of State for War to sanction an extension of Lieut. Smith's leave, and to direct that he may be supplied with the necessary stores to enable him to continue the research which he has so successfully begun. His Grace the First Lord of the Admiralty has kindly issued instructions to Vice Admiral Martin to render Lieutenants Smith and Porcher assistance, to facilitate the removal of the Antiquities discovered."* [63]

At the end of February, Smith and Porcher set out to visit Derna, taking Cesareo and Abderrahim, the brother of Amor. They passed Labrak, which

[61] S & P Chap.VII, 39.

[62] His Grace the Duke of Somerset K.G., First Lord of the Admiralty; British Museum MSS Dept. 41411 fols. 95-96.

[63] NLS ACC 9569 fols. 86-87; S & P Chap. X, 59-61.

Smith noted as being the scene, *'some thirty years'* before, of a battle between the Birasa and Haasa tribes. The Birasa, who were the victors, were led by Sheikh Hadood, a formidable character mentioned by the Warrington family in the 1820s. About 700 of the Haasa, Smith states, *'are said to have been buried on the battle-field'* – an immense number by tribal standards. The group rode past Gabiout Younes and through Tirt, and then the rough road ran through woodland of arbutus and juniper to Lamloudeh, where they saw extensive ruins and filled their water-skins from some reservoirs. At Gubbah with its fountains of pure water they made camp, and early next morning rode on over a rolling treeless plain, passing ruins and rock-cut tombs at Beit Thamer. After about ten miles they came upon another area of woodland which stretched to the edge of the escarpment of the lower plateau. From here they could see right along the coast to where the whitewashed houses of Derna nestled at the foot of the high, bare hills, in a green oasis made fertile by the water which flowed down the great wadi dividing the town. They descended the escarpment with difficulty, as the horses' feet tended to slip on the rock where it had been worn smooth, [64] and rode along the beach over loose stones for another two hours, feasting their eyes, as they approached the town, on the fresh green of its gardens and the tall palm and banana trees. The party was welcomed by Vice-Consul de Fremeaux, who had already been instrumental in sending supplies to Cyrene, and now took them to stay at his house. There, during the evening, they met the Mudir of Derna, who had been a fellow passenger aboard 'Boxer' from Tripoli to Benghazi. He later sent them the Roman silver coin and small silver sphinx which went to England with other small objects in June. The lieutenants stayed in Derna for three days, visiting the shops in the bazaar and riding with de Fremeaux up the reed-filled Wadi Derna, among the oleanders. The next day they returned to Cyrene, to find that their workmen had made the first discoveries of sculptures in the excavations which had been begun at the Temple of Apollo.

---

[64] Paolo Della Cella recorded experiencing the same difficulty in 1817: *'Upon quitting these perilous defiles, we found ourselves within sight of the sea and near Derna, to which we descended on the sloping face of a naked and slippery rock, with the loss of several of our horses.'* Similarly, five years later the Beechey brothers regarded the descent as *'scarcely practicable'*, and described the face of the mountain as *'devoid of vegetation, occasionally polished like glass.'* In 1848, travelling in the opposite direction, Bourville wrote: *'je franchis la montée escarpée et difficile d'El-Eukba et je passai ma première nuit dans une grotte sépulchrale, au milieu d'une forêt vierge, où l'olivier sauvage dominait.'* (DELLA CELLA (1822); BEECHEY (1828); BOURVILLE (1850), 580).

Photographs:

1-2. S & P no.118 head Reg. 61 7-25, 2, Album photo 19-1 Edinburgh album 1-2 Pl. 61 [**Pls. 2-3**].

3-4. S & P no.118 torso Reg. 61 7-25, 2, Album photo 19-2 Edinburgh album 3-19 Pl. 61 [**Pls. 4-5**].

5-6. S & P no.11 torso Reg. 61 7-25, 6, Album photo 19-3 Edinburgh album 14-22 Pl. 64 [**Pls. 6-7**].

7-10. Eastern slope of Wadi Haleg Shaloof, N. Necropolis [**Pls. 8-11**].

11. Archaic Tombs, N. Necropolis. Cassels Tombs N. 6-N. 9 [**Pl. 12**].

12. Wadi bel Ghadir Ancient Road [**Pl. 13**].

13. Wadi bel Ghadir W. Necropolis. S & P (1864) Pl. 18, Cassels Tombs W. 27-30 [**Pl. 14**].

14. Wadi bel Ghadir W. Necropolis. S & P (1864) Pl. 38, Cassels Tomb W. 33 [**Pl. 15**].

15. Wadi bel Ghadir W. Necropolis. S & P (1864) Pl. 38, Cassels Tombs W.48-49 [**Pl. 16**].

16. Group of three young Arabs [**Pl. 17**].

17. Missing S & P (1864) Pl. 10 [**Pl. 18**].

Plates:

2-5 Huskinson pp. 17-18, no. 32, Pl. 13.
6-7 Mendel 628 torso.

Fig. 3 – Castle and Village of Merdj (Barca).

Fig. 4 – Mudir's Room in the Castle of Merdj.

60

Fig. 5 – Wadi Muchgun, two miles to the Westward of Cyrene.

Fig. 6 – Amor Bon Abdi Seyat and Sheikh Bochlega.

61

IV. A REGULAR NEST OF STATUES ...

Despatches 3 and 4 for March and April seem to have travelled together to England, arriving towards the end of May. Smith had dated the original draft of the first despatch *'March 14th'*, altering this when he wrote the fair copy a week later to *'March 21st'*. Similarly, in the draft version Mr. Cesareo is leaving *'tomorrow'*, while in the second version he left *'last week'*. On May 22nd the Foreign Office sent to Panizzi the *'Despatches with their Inclosures.. reporting the discovery of further antiquities at Cyrene'* and requested the return of the papers *'when done with'*. The Trustees were to *'make such arrangements they may deem requisite for the conveyance of these Antiquities to England'*. [1]

Lieut. Smith's Despatch 3 – March 21st 1861 [2]

My Lord

On the 23rd February last I sent two despatches addressed to Your Lordship to Benghazi for transmission to England. They gave Your Lordship an account of our proceedings up till that date.

*We have since made a great addition to our collection of Sculptures. I informed Your Lordship that we were engaged in excavating a Temple near the Fountain of Apollo. This, instead of being as I supposed the Temple of Apollo, is no doubt the Temple of Asculapius as we have discovered a colossal statue of the latter divinity within the walls of the cella. There is no inscription but the statue is shown to be one of Asculapius [3] by the presence of a serpent wound round the trunk of a tree and entwining a rod [**Pl. 21**].*

The height of the statue is eight feet. Fortunately for the means of transport

---

[1] Original Letters and Papers Vol. LXIX Jan-May 1861 fol. 639 (B.M. stamp P. 4937 23 May 1861).

[2] Edin.draft: *'14th'*.

[3] Their first identification of the temple was correct, as the statue was of Apollo; S & P (1864) Chap. VII, 40.

we found it broken in three nearly equal parts besides the head. – The body is nude, but there is some very graceful drapery deeply undercut hanging from the left shoulder [4] *over the knees. The right arm is extended upwards. The style is remarkably fine, and although broken, the statue is in an excellent state of preservation. I enclose photographs of the lower part of the statue and of the head* [**Pl. 22**]. *I did not photograph the two other parts, because I was afraid that their edges would be damaged if placed upright. –*

Your Lordship will observe that the right foot and part of the leg are broken off. We found them however, near the statue. We have also two large fragments of the tree and serpent in addition to the part shown in the photograph attached to the base. – We have I believe, almost every fragment necessary for the complete reconstruction of the statue except part of the right arm, and the left hand. – The right hand [5] *was found a few days ago, and we hope soon to find the other also.* [6] *Close by the statue we found the ornamented marble casket* [7] *shown in the Photograph No. 1.* [**Pl. 21**]

We have also discovered five marble statuettes [8] *not including the one of which I enclosed a photograph in my despatch No. 1. They are all perfect. Their style and condition Your Lordship will be able to judge of by the enclosed photographs No. 3 & 4. No. 3 represents a female perhaps Diana strangling a lion. I could not place the head properly,* [9] *as part of the neck is broken away: – We have the lower part of this statue* [10] *and also the part broken off the left knee, so that it can easily be restored* [**Pl. 23**]. *No. 4 shows two of the statuettes and the head of the small statue referred to above of which Your Lordship has already received a photograph.* [**Pl. 24**]

Our five workmen suddenly left us the other day, but fortunately four others sent by Mr Crowe arrived the following day from Benghazi. Their arrival was particularly opportune as the statue of Asculapius had not yet been removed to a place of safety. It and also the statuettes are now in our tomb. We got up the several parts in the same way as we did the Bacchus. –

On account of this addition to the number of the sculptures we will require more timber for packing cases than I mentioned in my despatch No. 2. Should Your Lordship sanction the grant of the means of transport detailed in the

---

[4] Edin.draft: 'which forms itself into large deeply undercut folds *over* the lower part of the legs *the knees.'*

[5] Edin.draft: 'has just been brought in, *was only found this morning and so we* will probably *hope to find the other also.'*

[6] S & P no. 1 The right hand was not listed as being shipped in June; Huskinson no. 12.

[7] The *'ornamented marble casket'* refers to the sound box of Apollo's lyre.

[8] *'Diana'* (Cyrene) and the lion, Huskinson no.61 [**Pl. 23**]; a male statuette Huskinson no. 98 and a Diana, Mendel 621 [**Pl.24**]; also two further unidentified figures.

[9] Edin.draft: *'on the shoulders'*.

[10] Edin.draft: *'statuette'*.

despatch I would suggest that 600 feet of 2½ inch deal be substituted for the 250 or 300.

We are very sorry to have lost the company of Mr Cesareo, who [11] left for Bengazi last week, his presence being required there for the settlement of business affairs. He has been of the greatest service to us ever since our arrival at Bengazi and I take this opportunity of letting Your Lordship know how much we are indebted to him for the manner in which he has always cooperated with us in attaining the objects of the expedition. –

I have the honour to be, My Lord,
Your Lordship's most obedient humble Servt.
R.M.Smith Lᵗ Royal Engineers

Source: [Original Letters and Papers Vol. LXIX Jan-May 1861 fol.640 (copied 25/5/61); NLS ACC 9569 fol. 84]

Very few of Porcher's letters survive, but he wrote to Newton giving a very similar description of the statue of *'Aesculapius'*, later found to be an Apollo. This statue was later painstakingly reconstructed from a total of 123 pieces by J. Sumsion, who was foreman of the masons at the British Museum. [12]

In the Ruins of Cyrene
23rd March /61

My dear Newton

*Although Smith wrote to you very lately, I will give you a few lines to tell you how we have been getting on since that time as you must take a great interest in the exploration which we have lately undertaken. We have been lately excavating at the Temple in front of the Fountain of Apollo and first commenced round the Colonnade where we found only a Cippus, we then went to the Cella, and after a few days came upon a regular nest of statues, above 9 feet underground. The principal one was Aesculapius of a colossal size, and gave the name at once to the Temple. It was broken into three mostly equal pieces which enabled us to remove it all, or else with our slender means I doubt if we could have managed it. It is a beautiful piece of sculpture and you will have an idea of what it is like by the Head, and the lower part of the body, which shows also part of the snake & Medicine chest [**Pls. 21-22**]. You will see that the nose is broken but the remainder is perfect. We have collected all the pieces together, and the only thing that is now wanting is the arm. It measures 8 feet in height. Amongst the others were 3 female statues of a smaller size. One was strangling a lion, which I send you a Photograph of, [**Pl. 23**] the face & lower part of the*

---

[11] Edin.draft: 'le⁽ᵗ⁾aves for Benghazi ~~tomorrow~~ last week'.
[12] JENKINS (1992), 192.

body we have, part of the neck was broken, which prevents the Head appearing natural, but we have every thing of consequence. I send you also a Photograph of another, and the Head of the third one larger. Altogether we found within a few feet of each other 8 statues and 10 heads, so that before we have done with it we expect to find some others, as the remaining arm of Aesculapius. Before this we considered it to be the Temple of Apollo, as we found the word Απολλονος *on nearly all the inscriptions about the place, but on one was* ασχλαπος, *which with the statue that we have found, must give the Temple for the future the name of Aesculapius. We have not found any Vases or pottery with the exception of one lamp. Smith has written to the Foreign Office enclosing the same Photographs, so we hope that the Government will think it worth while sending a steamer down here during the summer to embark them. After that we shall probably return to Benghazi, having a look at Ptolemata and Teuchira on the way. We shall not have time or means to excavate at either of these places, as we think it better making a good trial at the capital & leaving the latter to some future explorers. Smith will be much obliged to you, if you will look over the best authorities about Cyrene, and see if the Temples of Bacchus & Aesculapius are mentioned, and if so the particulars about them, as well as any other information about the names or positions of the buildings – We found yesterday in digging at the same place the following inscription* [13]

].[ΑΙΟΝΚΟΡΝΗΛΙΟΝΛΕΝΤΟΛΟΝ
ΠΟΠΛΙΩΥΙΟΝΜΑΡΚΕΛΛΙΝΟΝΠΡΕΣ
ΒΕΥΤΑΝΑΝΤΙΣΤΡΑΤΑΓΟΝΤΟΝ
ΠΑΤΡΩΝΑΚΑΙΣΩΤΗΡΑΚΥΡΑΝΑΙΟΙ

on a piece of marble above 10 feet under the ground, and a long block of marble close by as if it stood over the inscription with a socket in the end, as if for the reception of a head. This latter was also found. –

We were glad to see in the papers that you are again installed in the Antiquarian department of the Museum, where I shall come and see you on my return to England which I hope will be in the autumn. –

Smith begs to be remembered to you,
Believe me, Yours sincerely
E A Porcher

Source: [Original Letters and Papers Vol. LXIX Jan – May 1861 fol. 310 (B.M.stamp P. 4938 23 May 1861)]

[13] S & P inscription no. 1 Pl. 77, B.M. inscription 1054, see Smith's Despatch 4 of April 8th 1861.

List of ~~articles~~ stores requested by Lieutenant Smith for the packing and Transport of Sculptures from Cyrene.

Artillery four wheeled drags	*3*
N.B. the wheels if possible to be cast iron with wrought iron bands, like those supplied	
~~to Mr Newton~~ from the consul at Malta to Mr Newton for the Bodrum expedition	
Spare wheels for do ----------------	*10*
3/8 inch rod iron for bolts for packing cases	*feet 300*
2½ inch deal for packing cases	*feet 600*
3 inch do -------------------------------	*feet 200*
~~Six dozen~~ old hammocks for packing	*dozens six*
Gyn Artillery with 4 inch fall ------------------	*1*
Rope (three inch) coils ----------------------------	*2*
Blocks for three inch rope -----------------------	*12*
Handspikes -------------------------------------	*12*
Smith's forge ----------------------------------	*1*

Source: [Original Letters and Papers Vol. LXIX Jan-May 1861 fol. 655 (B.M.stamp P.5076 27 May 1861)].

Photographs:
1. S & P no.1 Reg. 61 7-25, 1 Album photo 20-1 Edinburgh album 14-38 Pl. 62 [**Pl. 21**]
2. S & P no. 1 Reg. 61 7-25, 1 Album photo 20-2 Edinburgh album 1-1 Pl. 62 [**Pl. 22**]
3. S & P no. 6 Reg. 61 7-25, 3 Album photo 20-3 Edinburgh album 5-26 [**Pl. 23**]
4. S & P no. 9 Reg. 61 7-25, 4 Album photo 20-6 [**Pl. 24**]
   S & P no.13 Reg. 61 7-25, 8 Album photo 20-6 [**Pl. 24**]
   S & P no.11 Reg. 61 7-25, 6 Album photo 20-6 [**Pl. 24**]

Plates:
19 Sanctuary of Apollo
20 Fountain of Apollo
21 Huskinson pp. 6-7, no. 12, Pl. 5
22 Huskinson pp. 6-7, no. 12 head, Pl. 5
23 Huskinson p. 32, no. 61, Pl. 25
24 Huskinson pp. 55-56, no. 98, Pl. 38
   Mendel 621
   Mendel 628 head

E. A. P. del.

Fig. 7 – Interior of Mohammed el Adouly's Tent.

V. THE RIGHT HAND HOLDS A SNAKE ...

The April despatch, dated only eighteen days after that of March, was an interim affair, as explained by Smith in his first paragraph. In his letter to Newton of April 28th he gave a relaxed account of their journey to visit Tolmeita and Tocra – and the staff problems they encountered on their return. It was a good decision to make this excursion in the spring, when the Jebel Akhdar is truly the 'Green Mountain'. At that time the harvest was nearly full-grown, the shepherds and goatherds, wrapped in burnouses, were guarding the new lambs and kids from ravening wolves or hyenas, and in the remaining damp areas the bullfrogs were croaking fit to burst. After the cold and rain of a Cyrene winter, Smith and Porcher enjoyed the lush new grass and vibrant colours of the spring flowers, making alpine meadows on the hillsides which, only a few weeks later, would be parched and brown.

The publication tells [1] how they set off with Amor, his three friends and a camel from Cyrene on April 13th and headed in the direction of Benghazi, skirting Beida and travelling along the spectacular, deep Wadi Il Aggur in the Wadi Kuf area, its steep sides of honey-coloured limestone gouged with caves. [2] Smith, in holiday mood, rapturously describes the wadi as being full of sweet-scented flowers, *'roses, honeysuckle, myrtle and oleander'*. The two lieutenants had ridden along this road in the winter, two days before their arrival at Cyrene, when they merely noted that the wadi was *'a deep narrow ravine with rocky sides'*, filled with immense pines and *'a perfect thicket of smaller trees and shrubs'*. They camped on high ground at the Roman fort of Gasr Biligadem, and the next day passed through a countryside of rolling, wooded hills. In the evening they were joined by a large group of Arabs, who invited them to share their supper of bazeen and plied them with water – a valuable gift – and the delicious buttermilk, laban. In turn, Smith and

---

[1] S & P (1864) Chap. X, 62-68

[2] This wadi was described by Hamilton, who referred to it as *'Aggher bi Haroubeli'* (HAMILTON (1856), 127).

Porcher contributed some partridges they had shot, which the Arabs cooked by throwing them into the fire *'as they were, feathers and all'*. They also gave the Arabs something very English – a cup of tea. They had never seen tea before, which is difficult to imagine, given the enormous quantity consumed in Libya today. Smith describes how their Arab companions solved the problem of eating with a clear conscience the game shot by himself and Porcher, which had not been slaughtered in the way prescribed by the Koran. Their method was to pursue each bird as it fell, and cut its throat in the Muslim way *'before it had given its final kick.'*

The next day they reached the edge of the upper plateau and saw at their feet the great expanse of the plain of Merdj. At the castle they stayed again with the Mudir, where they met Suliman Captan, an ex-Mudir of Ghegheb, bearing the scars of his time in office. He was the grandson of Peter Lyell, a Scots captain who had taken the Islamic faith and served under the Pacha of Tripoli, where in 1821 the Beechey brothers made his acquaintance. From Merdj their way led over the grassy plain to the edge of this lower plateau, from which a better road than that at Apollonia descended through the now familiar red and green hilly country to Tocra by the sea, where they camped in a flea-ridden quarry. Smith and Porcher were not very impressed by the ruins of the city, but rather more so by the city walls and towers. They noticed the traces of *'temples and churches'* and rock-cut tombs in the quarries, many of them with inscriptions cut by the entrances. The weather was bad, with the sudden squalls common around those shores, together with heavy bouts of rain like thick curtains drawn along the coastline, and after little more than a day at Tocra they continued along the coast road eastward to Tolmeita. The large mausoleum tomb outside Tolmeita (Fig. 9) could be seen for miles before they reached it, and they camped in a quarry between it and the city, to escape the wind. Some Arab neighbours *'were anxious to sell us part of a dead camel'* and were puzzled when their offer was declined, as they said the flesh was good for food because after the animal had broken down they *'had cut its throat to "save its life"'*.

The lieutenants had narrowly missed a visit to Tolmeita by Captain Spratt's 'Medina', which had anchored offshore, three of the officers landing with an interpreter. Smith and Porcher spent two days studying the remains of the ancient city, describing particularly the vast subterranean reservoir and mausoleum tomb, and noting the tombs with inscriptions in the neighbouring quarries, similar to those at Tocra. On the night of 20th April the wind must have swung round to the south, as they suffered the effects of a ghibli *'which nearly choked us with clouds of dust and sand, and necessitated our turning out every half-hour to hammer in the pegs of the tent.'* They left the next day with the ghibli still blowing and the sun a silver disk, and in the bad conditions their guide took the wrong path, leading them up a wadi from which there was no visible exit, but Smith and Porcher, grit in their mouths and stinging their faces, stubbornly refused to go back, and with their horses climbed the steep hill in front of them. Their companions were unable to persuade the equally stubborn camel to go this way, and retraced their steps to find the right route, while Smith and Porcher rode resolutely on across country, through a maze of hills and wadis, until they again reached the plain of Merdj.

This journey in the suffocating heat of the ghibli gave them a raging thirst, and they were blissfully appreciative of the laban given them by the Arab women when, limp and dehydrated, they entered their encampment in search of something to drink. By early evening they reached the castle, and were treated by their garrulous friend the Mudir, to a *'really sumptuous dinner of bread, rice, mutton, and eggs'* which they heartily enjoyed, followed by a good night's sleep. The following day, however, the ghibli was hotter than ever, and the sand-laden air blotted out the sun altogether. Starting in the afternoon, they reached the Libiar Il Gharib, where there were ancient wells, and spent the night under a rocky crag wrapped in their burnouses. After this the ghibli died out and the air was again fresh and cool, but the travellers were glad to be *'home'* at Cyrene again on April 24th. Shortly afterwards they paid a visit to the Mudir of Ghegheb at his castle, which they found to be identical to that of Merdj. On the way they passed the large cisterns at Safsaf, resembling others seen by Smith at Tolmeita but larger, covered by arched stone roofs springing from ground level.

Lieut. Smith's Despatch 4 – April 8th 1861

My Lord

Lieutenant Porcher and myself being about to start for the ruins of Ptolemeta and Teuchira passing on the way the military post of Merdj from which letters can be sent to Bengazi I take the opportunity of reporting to Your Lordship our further discoveries here since the 21st of March the date of my last despatch. –

We have continued the excavation of the Temple of Aesculapius where we have found several statues and inscriptions in addition to those already reported to Your Lordship. – I enclose photographs of some of them.

Near the west end of the Temple we found a head rather larger than life size [**Pl. 25**] *and near it the following inscription:* [3]

---

[3] S & P inscription no. 1, Pl.77, B.M. inscription 1054, see Porcher Despatch June 7th 1861.

ΑΙΟΝΚΟΡΝΗΛΙΟΝΛΕΝΤΟΛΟΝ
ΠΟΠΛΙΩΥΙΟΝΜΑΡΚΕΛΛΙΝΟΝΠΡΕΣ
ΒΕΥΤΑΝΑΝΤΙΣΤΡΑΤΑΓΟΝΤΟΝ
ΠΑΤΡΩΝΑΚΑΙΣΩΤΗΡΑΚΥΡΑΝΑΙΟΙ

The head does not belong to the[4] statue but was placed on an oblong marble pedestal[5] which stood on the block bearing the above inscription. –

The next object found was a colossal statue 7 feet in height – From its appearance there is little doubt of its being a portrait[6] – We found parts of the pedestal which is inscribed, but owing to its damaged condition, no entire words can be made out.[7] In one of the lines the letters ΒΑΣ occur, which[8] may probably have been part of the word Βασιλευς[9] – We found the statue apparently just as it fell, broken in two.[10] – The fracture however is clean so that the parts may be easily rejoined. – It is draped – The style is inferior to the Aesculapius and is evidently of late[11] date – It is in good condition, and no part necessary to its restoration is wanting. –[12]

Immediately under this statue we found a very beautiful female head unbroken. – It wears a helmet, on the peak of which are the eyes of an owl,[13] so that there is little doubt of its belonging to a statue of Minerva. – It is rather smaller than life [**Pl. 26**].

At the South West angle of the Temple we found a small female statue somewhat similar to the first one we discovered. The right hand holds a snake by the head, the body of which encircles the arm [**Pl. 29**].

In the same part of the Temple we found two small male statues partially draped.[14] I enclose a photograph of one of them, which, in respect of style, may be taken as a type of all three [**Pl. 27**].

Near the statuettes we discovered two colossal female heads. One of them much resembles the head of Aesculapius[15] in style, but unfortunately is not in so good a state of preservation [**Pl. 26**]. *– The other[16] is rather larger and is in much better condition, being perfect with the exception of part of the nose,*

[4] Edin.draft: *'a'*.

[5] Left near Tomb of Residence October 1861.

[6] S & P no.2 Reg. 61 7-25, 10, see Porcher's Despatch June 7th 1861, Case 19.

[7] Porcher's Despatch June 7th 1861.

[8] Edin.draft: ~~lead me to think that the statue is one of a King~~.

[9] Inscription transcript S & P (1864), 42; see Smith's Despatch 6 of Aug 11th 1861, item 5.

[10] S & P no. 2 Reg. 61 7-25, 10.

[11] Edin.draft: *'considerably later'*.

[12] Edin.draft: Photo No. 1.

[13] Edin.draft: Photo No. 2.

[14] Edin.draft: Photo No. 3.

[15] Edin.draft: Photo No. 2.

[16] Edin.draft: Photo No. 4.

which is broken off. – The Photograph No 4 will enable Your Lordship to judge of the style [**Pl. 28**]. *The other head is photographed with the Minerva in No 2* [**Pl. 26**].

Besides the above there is a colossal male portrait head found yesterday. The features are peculiar and very marked. I hope to send Your Lordship a photograph of it in my next despatch.

We have also discovered a ram life size [17] *and some fragments including two right hands of colossal size one of which holds what seems to be a horn.* [18]

All the above, besides the statues formerly discovered, were found in the western half of the Cella at an average depth of 10 or 11 feet below the surface. We have just finished the excavation of this half, which is separated by a wall from the Eastern or Front one.

I am at a loss to understand how so many statues of different varieties and ages came to be found in a Temple of Aesculapius. Mr Hamilton in writing of another building in Cyrene says that he considers it the Temple of Aesculapius and Treasury of the State. [19] *I do not know on what authority he connects the two, but if it be the case that the Temple of Aesculapius was the Treasury of the State, we might expect to find in the building monuments of distinguished individuals, who had done the State good service. –*

The temple is not in its original state but has evidently been used in later times for other purposes. It is intersected by numerous walls and arches of concrete which probably belong to the Byzantine times. –

The following is a list of the objects discovered since our arrival in Cyrene:

Three large statues viz. Bacchus, Aesculapius, and the one mentioned above; [**Pls. 2-5, 21-22, 25**]

Nine small statues from the Temple of Aesculapius; [20, 21]

Eighteen heads including those belonging to the above statues [22] *and various fragments* [23] *lamps etc.* [24] *from the Temples of Bacchus and Aesculapius.*

The following is a list of the enclosed photographs which are numbered as formerly on the back.

No 1 Two heads viz Cornelius Lentulus and the head of the colossal statue mentioned above. [**Pl. 25**]

No 2 Head of Minerva and colossal female head. [**Pl. 26**]

---

[17] Untraced.

[18] Untraced.

[19] Hamilton (1856), 47-48.

[20] Edin.draft: ~~'and two Statuettes from the Temple of Bacchus'.~~

[21] S & P nos. 11, –, 6, 9, 13, 12.

[22] S & P nos.118, 11, –, 1, 6, 9, 13, 5, 2, 4.

[23] S & P no.118 fragments and others.

[24] Porcher's Despatch of June 7th 1861, Case 21; Smith's Despatch 6 of Aug 11th 1861 item 6.

No 3 Small half draped statue. [**Pl. 27**]
No 4 Colossal female head. [**Pl. 28**]

> *I have the honour to be, My Lord,*
> *Your Lordship's most obedient, humble Servant,*
> *R.M. Smith Lt R.E.*

Source: [Original Letters and Papers Vol. LXIX Jan – May 1861 fols. 640-642 (copied 25/5/61); NLS ACC 9569 fol. 85]

Smith's puzzle as to why so many varied pieces of sculpture should be found together is reminiscent of Donald White's discoveries in the Sanctuary of Demeter which, with the rest of Cyrene, had suffered in the two recorded earthquakes of A.D.262 and 365. Here, large quantities of intact, broken or fragmentary statuary were brought to light, and the excavation team came to the conclusion that although some pieces had been thrown down by either of the earthquakes, others had been broken previously and discarded in buried dumps.[25]

SMITH to NEWTON – April 28th 1861

My dear Newton

Many thanks for your kind letter of Mar 14 which on account of the 'Immediate' on the address was forwarded by an Express and reached me today. I have especially to thank you for the excellent means you have taken for setting the affairs of the expedition so fairly on their legs. You have exactly anticipated everything I applied for to Lord John Russell with the important addition of the money which will greatly relieve the state of the Exchequer. I see from the date of your letter that there is not yet time for an answer from the F.O. but your letter makes me quite easy as to what will be its purport when it comes. I wrote you about three weeks ago, giving an account of our proceedings. Since then our time has been taken up in a journey to Ptolemeta & Teuchira from which places we arrived here only two days ago.[26] From what I have seen of them and Apollonia I am glad that we did not waste any time in doing anything among their ruins before coming here. At Ptolemeta there are some very interesting remains but good results from digging I should consider more than questionable. Everything wears a Roman look. I should have been sorry however to leave the country without visiting them. The journey of itself was delightful. The scenery is exceedingly beautiful, and the season of the year allowed us to see it to great advantage. While we were away our blacks left

---

[25] White (1984), 105-106 Figs. 106-112.
[26] S & P (1864) Chap. X, 64-67.

74

after a grand battle with our servants Maltese and Arabs in which one had his teeth knocked down his throat with the butt end of a gun. We have got a few Arabs however to work with the prospect of increasing their number. Since I wrote nothing has turned up at the Temple of Aesculapius which however is now nearly finished. When it is finished we will I think commence at a large Temple in the Eastern part of the city the structure of which is quite colossal.[27] The columns are some 7 or 8 feet in diameter as far as I can judge at present. The style is the all but universal one here, Doric. If you have Beechey's plan you will recognise it as the one near the Stadium. Our affairs with the Arabs are in a good state now. The old Mudir was turned out on our representation and another has arrived from Tripoli with strict orders regarding us from the Governor General. The courier with your letter informs me notwithstanding that he was laid hold of on the road, a pistol presented at his head, and ordered to give up the letters which they said he was carrying to the Nazarene dogs. Fortunately he had letters for the Mudir at Ghegeb which he showed telling them they were all he had. But one must put up with their fanaticism & the weakness of the Government. They are afraid I think of actually attacking us although not long ago they made a great demonstration. We have now however a large party in our favour which makes a wonderful difference. If we had given in in the least at our first collision it would have been all up with us long ago. I saw in the papers that you had accepted office at the Museum. Is it the case? If so I hope you got such arrangements made as suited you. I fear I will not have time to write by this opportunity to Panizzi as the Courier is fretting to be off again. Is the Campana Museum to come to London after all?

    Porcher joins me in best regards
      Believe me, Yours most sincerely
        R.M. Smith   *over*

    I hear today that there will probably be some Engineer Officers employed in the Exhibition of '62. Should you come across any one that has a voice in the matter you may tell him I would like very much to be one of them. The work would be interesting and as my Foreign Service time will be up and I must go home I should prefer a year in London to any other place. <u>*RMS*</u>

Source: [Brit.Mus.Dept. of G & R Antiquities, Orig.Lett. 1861 fol. 709]

On May 28th Panizzi wrote to the Admiralty regarding an extension of leave for Porcher, and the reply three days later stated that the Lords Commissioners of the Admiralty *'have granted Lieutenant Porcher twelve months ad-*

---

[27] The Temple of Zeus.

ditional leave, and have directed Vice Admiral Martin to communicate with these Officers, and consider by what means he can best arrange to afford them all necessary assistance, and he is to supply them as far as may be in his power with the Stores and Implements which may be required'. They cautiously added *'but a separate and particular account as of such supplies is to be kept with a view to a reimbursement of expenses by the proper Department.'* In addition, *'should Captain Spratt of H.M.S. Medina be enabled to afford assistance without materially interfering with the duties on which he is employed he is to do so as the opinion of that officer may be useful in suggesting the means of embarkation with reference to the nature of the Coast and the facilities for anchoring'.* [28]

A telegram which eventually reached Cyrene was forwarded by Rear Admiral W.J. Codrington on June 6th and addressed solely 'Lieut. Porcher R.N., Cyrenaica'. It had been transmitted to Codrington by the Admiralty and sent from Gibraltar on the P & O steamer 'Sultan'. In Spanish and inaccurate English it reads:

Rec^d 6 June 1861 at Malta by P & O Steamer from Gibraltar

W.J. Codrington
    Londres 27 de Mayo de 1861
Depositado con el num 4522 en Londres el 27 à las 11 horas 5 minutos
Recibido en S. Roque 27 à las 4 horas 20 minutos
                Admiral Superintend at Malta
                  Port S. Roque
            "By first opportunity inform
        "Lieuts Smith and percher now escavating
        "at Malta that they may expected
        "assistance shortly and that they are
        "to remain at Cyrene until they hear
        "further
                  Admirally Whitehall
El Director   *London*
(S^d) Franc: Cuartero

Source: [NLS ACC 9569 fols. 88-89]

Vice-Consul Frederick Crowe at Benghazi had suffered much ill-health during his life. Even as a young man he had to travel from Tripoli to Eng-

---

[28] Original Letters and Papers Vol. LXIX Jan-May 1861 fol. 668 (B.M.stamp P. 5263, 3 Jun 1861).

land for treatment for the ophthalmia which dogged him. When Smith learned of his imminent departure from his post he wrote about him to Lord Herbert:

HERBERT, War Office to RUSSELL – June 5th 1861

Dear Lord John

I think you ought to see the testimony borne by L! Smith R.E. who is digging for antiquities at Cyrene, to the merit of Mr Crowe your consul in those parts. As his letters are long .... and refer to antiquities found under ground I have had the extract referring to Mr Crowe copied and send it to you.

'.... I have heard from Mr Frederick Crowe HM's Vice Consul at Benghazi that he is about to start for England on six months leave.

In all probability we will not see him again at Benghazi and we will have left before the expiry of his leave – I therefore take the occasion of his leaving to let you know how much we are indebted to him for the very efficient and even indispensable aid he has given us ever since our arrival in the Country.

It must be but seldom that a Consul at Benghazi has an opportunity of shewing the value of his services beyond the routine of his daily duties. Our testimony therefore may be considered of greater weight than might otherwise be the case.

His kind hospitality I have already told you of – on this occasion therefore I will only mention the assistance he has given us in the exercise of his official duties –

Before we left Benghazi he not only obtained everything we required from the Government authorities but used his influence in our behalf with Sheikhs of different Bedoin Tribes –

The longer we have been in the Country the more have we felt and valued all this – and it is not to be supposed that such influence is owing merely to his official position. On the contrary I am convinced from what I now know of the Arabs that it is dependent almost entirely on personal grounds. The people do not call Mr Crowe the English Consul but 'par excellence' <u>The Consul</u>.

In proof of the great value of his protection I have only to state that we have lived here nearly four months in the immediate vicinity of a Zauyah one of the hotbeds of Mussulman fanaticism where we do as we please without molestation.

The Chief of this Zauiyah I may add was one of the Emissaries of a sect who some time ago tried to stir up an insurrection against the Christians.

Shortly after our first Collision with the Zauyah he took his departure on hearing that we had written to the Consul.

The Mudir or Governor of the district not being particularly well affected towards us has been removed and another appointed conditionally on his do-ing everything he can for our benefit.

For this we are indebted to Mr Crowe.

The fame thus spread of our power at Benghazi stood us in good stead only last week when at Imgernis the Arabs of the place came in a body to attack us.

Resistance against such a number would have been of little use but they shortly went away without interfering with us on being told that we were the Christians who had defeated the Zauyah and turned out the Mudir and conse-quently that the slightest injury received by us would they might rest assured be amply avenged by the Consul. In order not to enter into further particulars I can most safely say that it is entirely owing to the excellent measures taken by Mr. Crowe that we have hitherto been allowed by the arabs to remain in the country at all.

I am afraid Lord John Russell might consider it presumptive on my part thus to enter into particulars in a formal despatch. I have therefore addressed myself to you in the hope that you will do me the kindness of bringing under the immediate notice of his Lordship in whatever way you consider best our deep sense of gratitude to Mr Crowe.

It will not be ungrateful to his Lordship to hear of our testimony to the worthy manner in which H.M.'s Government is represented in this compara-tively unknown country.

Owing so much to Mr Crowe we feel it our duty to express to the proper au-thorities our appreciation of his services but I considered I was best fulfilling that duty by writing to you.'

Source: [Public Record Office FO 101/48]

An interesting facet of the story of the Smith and Porcher expedition is the part played in it by Mr William Dennison, the British Museum carpenter who lived with his wife Rebecca in Clerkenwell and rose from relative obscurity when, because of his reputation as an excellent supervisor, he was selected by the Trustees to travel to Cyrene, where he assisted by making packing cases and packing statuary ready for transportation, as well as acting as foreman of the labourers. To him, the Tomb of Residence must have appeared very much like parts of the Museum basement. Between June 5th-7th Panizzi, Newton and Dennison himself wrote a series of official letters to cover the financial and travelling aspects of his journey. Dennison wrote a letter to Panizzi, wit-nessed by John Chave: *'During my absence from England, under the arrange-ments made with you to go to the Cyrenaica to assist Lieutenants Smith and Porcher in the excavations now being carried on there, I authorise and empower you to pay to my wife, Rebecca Dennison, the sum of 8s/4d for each working day, – this amount to be deducted from the 17s/6d per day, which you have agreed to*

pay me for my services as above.' [29] The Foreign Office prepared letters of introduction for him to show to Consul Herman and Vice-Consul Crowe, while
Newton wrote to another Consul who was to act as a stepping stone, E.W.
Mark at Marseilles: *'The bearer William Dennison a carpenter by trade is sent
out by the British Museum to join Lieut. Smith R.E. now excavating at Cyrene
near Benghazi. I am requested by Mr Panizzi to ask you to be so good as to give
Dennison any assistance of which he may stand in need on his way via Marseilles to Malta. His passage is paid from London to Marseilles and Mr Panizzi
will be much obliged to you to be good enough to advance to him on the production of his account such a further sum as he may require for his passage from
Marseilles to Malta 2nd class and for his maintenance till he leave Marseilles and
on the voyage.'* [30] Finally, Panizzi addressed himself to Crowe at Benghazi, the
final fixed point on Dennison's journey, beyond which he would be on his
own.

Panizzi to Crowe – June 7th 1861

Sir,

  This letter will be delivered to you by William Dennison, who is sent out by
the Trustees of the British Museum to act as foreman of the labourers and
others employed in the important excavations now being carried on in the
Cyrenaica, under the directions of Lieutenants Smith and Porcher.

  I have desired Dennison to ask you for any advice that may be of use to
him in his progress. – Will you be good enough to put him in the best way for
reaching Lieutenants Smith and Porcher, wherever they may be; and advance
him what money you think will be actually necessary for his journey and
expenses to them, taking from him, in exchange, his draft drawn upon me at
ten days' sight for the amount, which upon its presentation here, I will duly
honor.

  Dennison will have delivered a similar letter of introduction to Colonel
Herman, Consul General at Tripoli.

  Requesting you to accept my apologies for thus troubling you,

I remain, Sir,
Your obedient servant,
A. Panizzi

Source: [NLS ACC 9569 fol. –]   *Principal Librarian*

[29] Original Letters and Papers Vol. LXX June-Aug 1861 fol. 24 (B.M.stamp P. 5302, 5 June 1861).

[30] Original Letters and Papers Vol. LXX June-Aug 1861 fol. 28 (B.M.stamp P. 5467, 8 Jun 1861).

One has to admire William Dennison. Sent from his native London to a distant and very strange country where he knew not a word of the language and nothing of the customs, armed only with a letter asking a remote Vice-Consul to point him in the direction of Smith and Porcher *'wherever they may be'* – it must have seemed a daunting prospect, and he probably clung to that letter like a talisman. On May 28th Panizzi had also written to the Secretary of State for War *'suggesting that Lieut. Smith R.E. might have his leave extended to 12 months for the purpose of completing his research in the site of the Ancient Cyrene'*. The War Office replied on June 13th, transmitting from Lord Herbert *'the enclosed copy of a communication received from the Military Secretary to the General Commanding in Chief on the subject'*.[31] This *'communication'* is given below:

Horse Guards
5ᵗʰ June 1861

Sir,

    Having had the honor to submit to the General Commanding in Chief your letter of the 31ˢᵗ Ultº with its enclosures stating that it would appear that the services of Lieut. Smith R.E. in connection with the discoveries, now being made on the site of the ancient Cyrene, will be required for 12 months; I am directed to acqᵗ you for the information of Lord Herbert that Lieutᵗ Smith's present leave of absence extends to the 18ᵗʰ Novʳ next, which will complete his leave to 12 months & which HRH presumes is the period for which that Officer's services will be required.

I have &c
(signed) W.F. Forster

Source: [Original Letters and Papers Vol. LXX June-Aug 1861 fol. 79 (B.M.stamp P. 5689 14 Jun 1861)]

BURGOYNE to NEWTON – June 8th 1861

My dear Sir

    I quite forgot to ask for your address yesterday but I hope this will reach you.

    By forgetfulness I have I believe omitted to show you a letter from Lieut.

---

[31] Original Letters and Papers Vol.LXX June-Aug 1861 fol. 79 (B.M.stamp P. 5689, 14 Jun 1861; copied 22 June 1861).

Smith of 2nd May, but which I will send you as soon as I know the proper direction for you. [32]

I find that Mr Smith's leave has been sanctioned by all the authorities up to the completion of a twelvemonth, which will be on 18 Nov[r] & as the reason for asking for it was, that he might complete <u>before winter set in</u>, it was considered that would be sufficient, but if not a further extension may be asked for, <u>when this period approaches</u> –

My dear Sir
Yours faithfully
J. F. Burgoyne

Source: [Original Letters and Papers Vol. LXX June-Aug 1861 fol. 51 (B.M.stamp P. 5538 10 Jun 1861)]

WATKISS LLOYD, 77 Snow Hill, E.C. to PANIZZI – June 8th 1861

My dear Sir,

At the meeting of the committee of the Dilettanti Society at which you were present I became cognizant as you are aware of some of the proceedings at Cyrene.

In common with other members of that Committee I rejoice to hear that private enterprise was obtaining very valuable results, – so valuable as to merit a public subsidy. Other circumstances casually alluded to were by no means so satisfactory.

The search, – praiseworthy & enterprising in itself, appears directed exclusively with a view to the discovery of sculpture, – especially such as may be desirable acquisitions for a Museum. So far as I gather architectural records & antiquities are quite unprovided for in respect of accurate measurement and drawing.

If this be the case not only will a valuable opportunity be lost, – but it will be destroyed. The mischief to be apprehended is that remains which have continued as they fell undisturbed, will be rifled and disarranged & no advantage taken of the hints that can only be gained from original collocation.

Structural members that are only significant to the eye of an architect will be reburied & when once the ruins have been deprived of the sculpture which is the great inducement of excavators we may wait long before another expedition combining mechanical & intellectual force is brought again upon the same ground.

Irregular & uncalled for as it may appear, & with the fear before my eyes of becoming or seemingly intrusive or a bore, – I must though only as an

---

[32] Letter untraced.

*individual, represent how much damage may be done in this way & must urge
the desirableness of so directing any public assistance that may be given, as to
preclude or qualify the mischief.*

*That after excavations at Budrum we are left with the architectural enigma
of the Mausoleum still unsolved, must I fear be ascribed to the late period at
which architectural aid was associated with the explorers – & at least such a
question should not be open.*

*I write this note less with a view [to] urge any measures respecting what is
doing at Cyrene – for which it is probably too late, – than to place on record in
a certain way an opinion that I would hope may not be without influence
hereafter. Still I should be glad indeed if anything could be done to save a record in sufficiently accurate drawings of the details of Doric Temples that
must be coeval with the temple at Aegina & the colossal structures of Sicily –
& would probably illustrate the relation of the two schools in an age when Pindar & Pindar's friends were equally familiar with both.*

*The passion for collection may become so reckless that a little guidance is
very desirable. A one sided discoverer easily becomes a depredator –*

Very faithfully yours –
W. Watkiss Lloyd [33]

Source: [Original Letters and Papers Vol. LXX June-Aug 1861 fol. 52 (B.M.stamp P.
5521 10 Jun 1861; copied 22 June 1861)]

---

[33] William Watkiss Lloyd, a classical scholar instrumental in the layout of the British
Museum's Elgin Room. His views expressed here are surprisingly modern and, as it happens,
well-founded and intuitive.

Photographs:
1. S & P nos.5 and 2 Reg. 61 7-25, 11, 10, Album photo 20-4; [**Pl. 25**]
2. S & P nos. – and 4 Reg. 61 7-25, 13 Reg. 61 7-25, 12, Album photo 20-5; [**Pl. 26**]
3. S & P no.8 Reg. 61 11-27, 26; [**Pl. 27**]
4. S & P no. – Reg. 61 7-25, 14, Album photo 21-4; [**Pl. 28**]
The female holding a snake [**Pl. 29**] was not photographed until ca. August, and no print was sent to London.

Plates:
25 (left) Rosenbaum pp. 40-41, no. 11, Pl. XI, 3-4; Huskinson pp. 33-34, no. 63, Pl. 26.
25 (right) Rosenbaum pp. 51-52, no. 34 head, Pl. XXVII,1; no. 34 statue, Pl. XXVI, 1-2; Huskinson pp. 38-39, no. 69, Pl. 28
26 (left) Rosenbaum p. 46, no. 21 Pl. XVI,3-4; Huskinson p. 35, no. 65, Pl. 26
26 (right) Huskinson p. 14, no. 25 Pl. 10
27 Huskinson p. 56, no. 99, Pl. 39
28 Huskinson p. 70, no. 133, Pl. 51

FIG. 8 – Arab Camp near Teuchira.

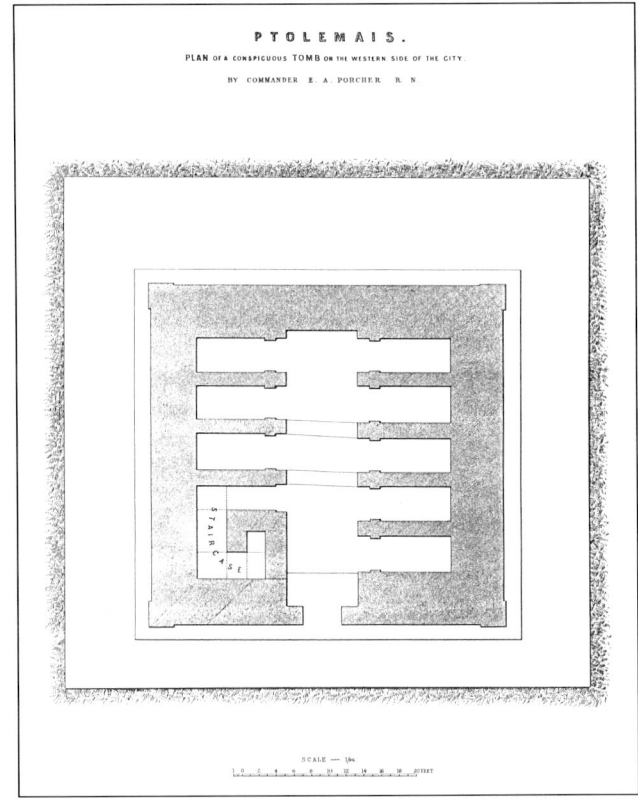

FIG. 9 – Plan of a Conspicuous Built Tomb to the West-ward of Ptolemais.

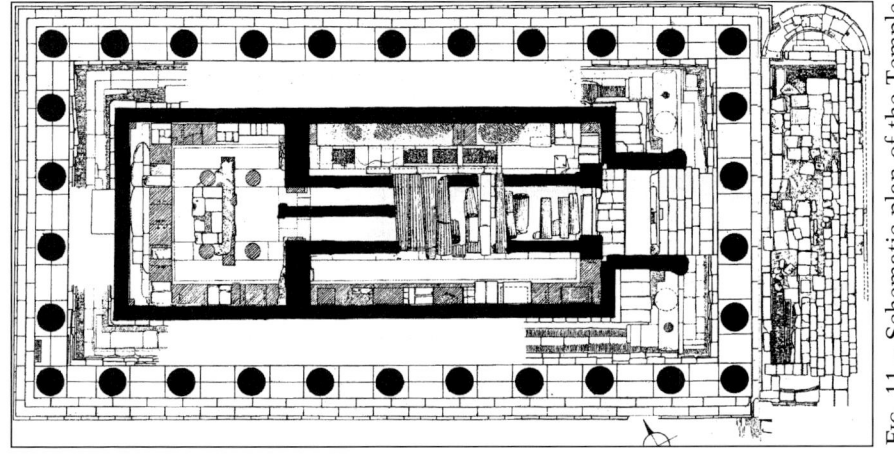

FIG. 11 – Schematic plan of the Temple of Apollo (after Stucchi).

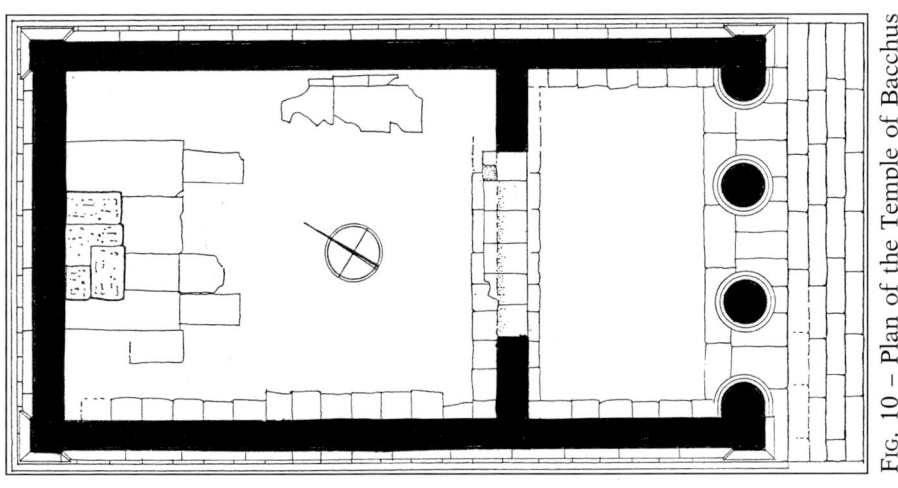

FIG. 10 – Plan of the Temple of Bacchus (after Ward-Perkins).

85

VI. ARRIVAL OF H.M.S. 'ASSURANCE'

Under instructions from the Admiralty in London, the Navy was preparing to deliver to Cyrenaica the stores needed by the expedition and to collect the antiquities as a return cargo, and the orders for this operation were sent to the Commander of the screw sloop H.M.S. 'Assurance' on 3rd May. The granting of Porcher's additional leave at the end of this month, after requests made by Panizzi, illustrates the impact of the news of the discoveries in Cyrene.

ADMIRAL WM F. MARTIN to CAPTAIN C. AYNSLEY,
H.M.S. 'Assurance' – May 3rd 1861

Enclosed are two letters from the Sec^t. of the Adm^{ty} with ref to the discovery of Antiquities by Messrs. Smith & Porcher employed in exploring the district of Cyrenaica.

And after you have rec^d. on b^d. H.M.'s Ship under your command the Stores enumerated in the enclosure to the letter of the 13th April & are in all respects ready you are to put to sea & proceed in the first instance to Suda Bay Candia ^{1} where you will probably find the Agamemnon. Having delivered to Captn. Hope or the Senior Offr. the accompanying Despatch you will proceed to Marsa Sousah provided the weather be fine & the Barometer not low but as nothing could be done there during Easterly winds or when the weather is not fine you will be governed by this in leaving Candia.

There appears to be no shelter at Marsa Sousah but 10 miles to the Eastward is Ras-el-hilal a Bay with good Shelter from Southerly or Westerly winds. The Exploring party is at Cyrene about 2 hrs distance from Marsa Sousah & you will be governed by circumstances as to whether your Vessel should beat

---

^{1} Candia: Irakleion, Crete; 'Agamemnon': pioneer screw-steam battleship built at Woolwich, launched 1852.

Ras el Hilal or Marsa Sousah while you are upon the Coast – you will give all the assistance in your power to Messrs Smith & Porcher respecting the removal of the Antiquities from Cyrenaica but you are to be careful not to expose your crew to the Sun while assisting in the transport of the Statues which is a service that could probably be better performed by the Arabs of the District. – Having rec^d. on board the Statues for the Brit Museum you will return to regain my Flag at this Port. –

Dated 3rd May/61.

C. Aynsley Esqre   *(sd) W^m F Martin*

H.M.S. Sloop

Assurance   *By command &c*

(sd) G. C Martin

Source: [Original Letters and Papers Vol. LXX June – August 1861 fol. 159 (B.M.stamp P. 6205 1 Jul 1861)]

'Assurance' arrived off Marsa Sousa on 10th May, but because of a strong onshore wind she continued on to shelter at Ras el Hilal, 'Cape of the New Moon', 15 miles away to the east. [2] Her officers sent a letter to the lieutenants, who by now were famous in the country, and this was delivered to them by an Arab who had walked all night and earned himself a very considerable bakshish, as Smith and Porcher were overjoyed to receive the first news to reach them from the outside world. They set out at once with the footsore Arab for Ras el Hilal, together with Amor and his brother. The journey on horseback along the rugged coastal plain, cut by dry wadis, took eight hours. As they approached the place where the 'Assurance' was anchored several officers from the vessel were to be seen on shore shooting the wildlife – one of an English officer's favourite leisure activities – and they went on board for the night, no doubt to catch up on the news of the past six months or more.

By the next day the wind had dropped and Captain Aynsley took the 'Assurance' back to Marsa Sousa where she moored, and the ship's boats took thirty bluejackets and marines ashore under Lieutenant Luard to make an encampment on the beach, provisioned by the ship. Next, the artillery wagons and all the other items which had been requested and drawn from stores were landed, along with two ship's carpenters, borrowed from H.M.S. 'St Jean d'Acre', who were sent at once to Cyrene, to begin making the necessary packing cases so that the statuary would be ready for moving once the wagons arrived. The ship's log describes the 'Assurance'

[2] S & P (1864) Chap.VIII, 44

88

carpenters being busy, and the blacksmith making washers and spike nails *'for the Scientific Expedition'*.[3]

The faithful Amor and his friends had the thankless task of searching for enough camels to transport everything to Cyrene, but it was harvest-time, and all the camel owners were occupied in this vital work. After two days a dozen camels had been found, and Smith and Porcher explained that some were needed to take stores to Cyrene, for which their owners would be paid for each trip, while other camels were required to accompany the working party of sailors pulling the artillery wagons, to carry their baggage and essential water, and their owners would be paid per day. The owners then argued among themselves for a full day over the distribution of the loads, and when finally the camels were ready to start, the owners of the working party camels decided that if they were not going up to Cyrene, they were not going anywhere. The camels were unloaded again. To the rescue next day came Mohammed el Adouli, who materialized at Marsa Sousa and agreed to supply all the camels that were needed.

The working party set off on 14th May across the narrow red coastal plain, following the ancient road, and dragged the wagons as far as humanly possible up the scrubby, boulder-strewn hillsides, where the stunted olive and carob trees themselves fought for a footing, and the remaining traces of road became fragmentary and overgrown. Progress in these conditions was not at all easy. The men had to force their aching and increasingly battered legs up and over the thick patches of knee-high vegetation, or else plough through it and be tripped by the woody roots and stems. When the going grew too tough and the gradient too steep for even these determined sailors, the bolts of the wagons were undone and the vehicles were taken apart and carried up piece by piece. It must have been utterly exhausting work, made even more so by the terrain, with its loose scree of rough boulders to turn ankles and cut boot leather, scratchy clumps of *'shebrik'* bushes with a network of spines which tore at legs, and sudden drops into dry gullies which had been carved out by innumerable winter rains. It took three days just to reach the top of the *'Augubah'* in this way. The wagons were then reassembled and the party began the rest of the journey across the plateau, clearing and making a road as they went.

Work began in the misty chill before sunrise and continued until 8 or 9 o'clock, by which time the heat of the sun had grown in ferocity. The men rested until mid-afternoon, when a light breeze would begin to blow from the sea, and then worked until sunset. In the evenings, anyone looking out from the heights of Cyrene would have seen on the dark plateau a cluster of pinpricks of light, which grew nearer each night. These were the huge fires

---

[3] PRO ADM 53/7011.

built by the sailors after supper, round which they sat talking and singing, enjoying the cool air and relaxing after the day's labour. Cyrene was reached on 24th May, where the carpenters, probably under Porcher's supervision, had been packing the statues in their wooden cases. According to Smith, the cases were ready to go, but Captain Aynsley reported later that the carpenters' work was unfinished, which made an excellent opportunity for the working party to have a well-earned break, and take a leisurely look at their surroundings under the lonely cry of the hawk and the chirring of rock doves, and to soothe their scratched and bruised legs in the cold water of the Apollo Fountain. During the three or four days which the sailors spent actually at Cyrene, some of them explored its subterranean channel and inscribed their names, together with that of their ship, in the wet clay on the wall, amongst the ancient graffiti. [4]

Early on 29th May the wagon party left Cyrene and reached the foot of the upper plateau by nightfall. The long-neglected ancient road towards Marsa Sousa, its white limestone surface worn into deep ruts by long-ago chariot wheels, was followed for five days over the lower plateau, and when the line of the road could no longer be traced, the wagons were lowered by means of tackle and anchors down the last perilous hurdle, the scrub-dotted, corrugated face of the descent from the Jebel Akhdar. From here many miles of coastline were visible, and the wagon parties saw their ship riding at anchor half a mile out from the shore on the Mediterranean, an incredible kingfisher-blue streaked with jade, and the tiny, milling figures of bluejackets and marines at the beach encampment far below. At this point a wagon carrying the statue of Apollo was nearly lost when an anchor gave way, and it went bounding away with its precious cargo down the precipitous limestone mountainside, an echo of the disaster which almost befell the Cnidus lion. [5] One can only guess at the horror which Smith must have experienced, and the thoughts which flew through his mind while his prize was in jeopardy. This incident was not retailed in any of the letters, except

---

[4] The local Arabs would not enter the subterranean channel – they considered it to be the home of demons – but such beliefs had not concerned the ancient Greeks, who left their names for posterity in the clay coating the walls. The name of Porcher also occurred, in very small letters, resembling the somewhat upright painted name on his watercolours, although his signature using a pen was more fluid. Other European names could also be seen, as well as the name of 'HMS Assurance' (Ghislanzoni (1927) Tav. II Fig. 6 no. 13). During the winter of 1954 torrential rains pouring down the hillside caused a landslide and flooding to attack the Antiquities Department buildings which stood in the natural line of flow for water trying to descend by way of Wadi Haleg Shaloof. In a letter of 10th November from the Controller of Antiquities, Richard Goodchild, to Sheppard Frere, he states 'the Fountain of Apollo flowed like Niagara'. Unfortunately, this spectacular natural event scoured the channel and obliterated every ancient inscription.

[5] S & P (1864) Chap.VIII, 46.

for a meaningful hint in Smith's letter to Newton shortly after the incident. He recorded that, not surprisingly, three cheers went up from the party when both wagons safely reached the bottom, 2,000 feet below the level of Cyrene.

The 'Assurance' log recorded that *'Six cases containing Marbles'* were taken aboard at 5pm on 31st May[6] – this must have been the first load of small articles, such as heads, that could be carried by the camels, which left Cyrene a day after the wagons. The ship, it was recorded, received a consignment of 66 lbs of fresh beef on 2nd June, which three days later was condemned as being *'unfit for human food'*, thrown overboard and replaced the next day. Meanwhile, on 4th June there were received on board *'4 Cases, 2 Casks containing Marbles'*.[7] Two days later the vessel shifted her position so that she lay directly opposite the place where Smith had descended, and the next day the large cases which had been carried on the jolting wagons were loaded into the ship's boats by means of a gyn set up in the shallows. The last camel-load came down too, and everything was stowed by the evening of 7th June.

Vice-Admiral W. Martin, from 'Supply' at Malta, reported to Lord Paget on June 20th that he had sent the 'Assurance' with the two carpenters from the St. Jean d'Acre and stores for Smith and Porcher, and *'that all the Antiquities yet discovered having been brought here by the Assurance are now on board the Supply for conveyance to England'*.[8] Porcher's June despatch was sent to Panizzi by the Foreign Office on July 5th, together with his *'List of Antiquities sent to Malta in Her Majesty's Ship "Assurance".'* These were copied on 13th July.[9] The letter below, addressed to Panizzi, was most likely a near duplicate.

Cyrene – June 7th 1861

Sir,

I beg to enclose a list of the Antiquities sent from here a few days ago, and which will be forwarded from Marsa Sousah to Malta in H.M.S. Assurance. This vessel was sent down by the Commander in Chief to render us assistance in embarking the statues, and arrived off Cape Helal on the 10th May. After our Communicating with her she steamed round to Marsa Sousah, where she

[6] PRO ADM 53/7011 – the last entry in that volume of the log.

[7] PRO ADM 53/7012 – the word *'Casks'* is puzzling, but quite clear in the manuscript. Casks were used on board ship for the stowage of either liquids or of solid material, so were quite likely employed for transporting the smaller pieces of marble.

[8] Original Letters and Papers Vol. LXX June-Aug 1861 fol. 155 (B.M.stamp P. 6205 1 Jul 1861).

[9] Original Letters and Papers Vol. LXX June-Aug 1861 fol. 206 (B.M.stamp P. 6409 8 Jul 1861; copied 13 July 1861).

landed all the stores for our use, consisting of Gun waggons, planks, rope etc. without delay. Two Carpenters were sent off at once to Cyrene with the plank, and commenced making the packing cases. All the other stores that could be carried on Camels, were also sent on as soon as possible.

The distance from here to Marsa Sousah is about 11 miles, and the road which follows the course of the ancient one is now very indifferent. On leaving the latter place it runs in a Westerly direction for 3 miles through a rough and stony plain to the foot of the Achbar, or first range of hills that extends along the East of the Cyrenaica nearly parallel with the shore from which it is here about 1½ miles distant, and 1000 feet in height – The ascent is so tricky, narrow and bad, that the two waggons were obliged to be taken to pieces, and carried up by a party of men that were landed from the vessel. On reaching the summit the waggons were put together and dragged slowly along the road, which leads up a varied incline towards Cyrene, most of the way through a wood composed of Juniper, Arbutus and Olive trees.

This journey took a week as the number of men that could be spared from the vessel only amounted to 32 assisted by 7 Blacks (whom we had engaged from Benghasi for the purpose of excavating), hardly sufficient for the work, as the road had to be made in several places in order to let the waggons pass.

The heavy Cases Nos. 1, 2, 3, 4 & 10 being ready by the 30th May were placed on the waggons, and taken down in 8 days by the same party, being eased down the steep part of the Achbar by tackles secured to anchors, All the other cases were taken down by Camels – Three of the Statuettes being too heavy for these animals were obliged to be left behind as well as a large statue of a King (of a late period and inferior workmanship), measuring 7 feet in height.

The statue of Bacchus with an animal like a Panther and 2 very small marble statuettes in Nos 1 & 20 were found in a temple about the middle of the city, the whole of the others were obtained from a building in front of the Fountain of Apollo marked by Beechey in his plan of Cyrene as the site of a temple – Most of the statues we now send are nearly complete that of Bacchus and some of the statuettes being the most perfect. We also hope that you will find very little wanting in the fine statue of Aesculapius, as all the parts we could discover have been collected together and packed in 6 different Cases, [10] as well as a few fragments in some of the others – All the Heads of the Statues have been found, and although they are broken off will join on without the fracture being very perceptible – In Nos. 17 & 18 are three large Heads, one Male and two Female, the Statues of which have not been found [11] – In No 19

[10] Cases 2, 3, 4, 9, 11, 12; Ship's Log 'Assurance': 6 cases 5 pm 31st May 1861, ref. PRO ADM 53/7011.

[11] Reg. 61 7-25, 13; Huskinson no. 65 [**Pl. 26** left]; Reg. 61 7-25, 14; Huskinson no. 133 [**Pl. 28**]; S & P no. 128, Reg. 61 7-25, 9; Huskinson no. 80.

are two Heads the larger being to the Statue which we suppose to be a King,[12]
and portions of a marble pedestal were found lying by it with the following
fragments of an inscription,[13]

ΟΚΡΑΤΟΡΜ   ΑΡ
ΑΙΑΝΟΝ ∴Μ   ΟΝ
. . . . . ΒΑΣ

The other[14] *in the same case is the Head of* Κορνηλιος Λεντολος *who seems
by another inscription to have been a Leader of the Cyrenaica Army.*[15]

ΙΑΙΟΝ ΚΟΡΝΗΛΙΟΝ ΛΕΝΤΟΛΟΝ
ΠΟΠΛΙΩ ΥΙΟΝ ΜΑΡΚΕΛΛΙΝΟΝ ΠΡΕΣ
ΒΕΥΤΑΝ ΑΝΤΙΣΤΡΑΤΑΓΟΝ ΤΟΝ
ΠΑΤΡΩΝΑ ΚΑΙ ΣΩΤΗΡΑ ΚΥΡΑΝΑΙΟΙ

*The above was cut on a block of marble having a squared block a few in-
ches in the top for the reception of a marble pedestal 5 feet long that was lying
close by,*[16] *this again had a socket on the top for the Head, which seems by its
form to have rested against the wall.*

*As the Assurance has brought us down a few additional tools of which we
were in want, and workmen can now be procured with less trouble than in the
Winter, L!. Smith and myself have thought it better to continue the excavations till the end of the summer, by which time we have great hopes in making
further discoveries of sufficient importance for another vessel to be sent here,
provided you consider the specimens we now send to be Valuable – The road
having been much improved, the Communication with the coast has become
more easy.*

I have the honour to be

> *Sir*
> *Your obedient Servant*
> *E A Porcher [Lieut R N.*

---

[12] [**Pl. 25**]: S & P no. 2, Reg. 61 7-25, 10; Huskinson no. 69; S & P no. 5, Reg. 61 7-25, 11; Huskinson no. 63.

[13] Transcript S & P (1864), 42; Smith's Despatch 6 of August 11th 1861 item 5.

[14] S & P no.5; Reg. 61 7-25, 11; Smith's Despatch 4 of April 8th 1861.

[15] S & P no. 5; inscription no. 1, Pl. 77. B.M. inscription 1054; Smith's Despatch 4 of April 8 1861. Another example found in 1927 (OLIVERIO (1929), 141 Fig. 39).

[16] Left near Tomb of Residence, October 1861; S & P (1864) Appendix II, 93, 'head' S & P no. 5.

List of Antiquities sent from Cyrene in June 1861

1. *Statue of Bacchus with head & 7 fragments of the drapery.*
2. *Lower part of the statue of Esculapius with the right foot parts of the pedestal and snake 3 pieces of the arm and 2 fragments of the drapery.*
3. *Middle part of – do –*
4. *Upper – do – do with 5 fragments of the drapery.*
5. *Statuette of a Female strangling a Lion –*
6. *Lower part of – do – in 5 pieces –*
7. *Head of Bacchus –*
8. *– " – Minerva –*
9. *– " – Aesculapius –*
10. *Large female statuette with the head.*
11. *Esculapius – Part of the snake & numerous small fragments*
12. *– do – Medicine chest & fragments.*
13. *Female statuette with the head and feet in separate case.*
14. *Statuette with rams horns with the head, parts of the right arm & head.*
15. *Male statuette with the head & some fragments –*
16. *– do – – do – – do –*
17. *Large female head. –*
18. *Two large heads male and female.*
19. *Heads of a King and a General.*
20. *An animal made of stone and 2 small marble statuettes found in the Temple of Bacchus.*
21. *Four terracotta lamps with a small gold winged figure 1 Silver and 12 Copper Coins from Cyrene and a Silver Sphinx and Coin from Derna.*
22. *Part of a large marble leg.*

E A Porcher [Lieut. R.N.

Source: [Original Letters and Papers Vol. LXX June-Aug 1861 fol.30 (B.M.stamp P.6328 5 July 1861; copied 27 July 1861)]

Porcher prepared this despatch and list of antiquities at Cyrene, probably post-dating it, but the following two letters to Panizzi and Newton were written in haste by Smith aboard the 'Assurance' – using the Captain's own cream writing paper, embossed with 'CMA' for Charles Murray Aynsley – as the last cases were being stowed on the evening of June 7th. The vessel did not leave until nearly noon the next day, but no doubt Smith, thinking of the dark and weary journey back to Cyrene, did not wish to delay his own departure.

94

My dear Sir,

I have only a few minutes left me to write, while the cases that came by the Wagons from Cyrene are being embarked.

I received your kind letter containing the form of a bill of exchange for £100 which I have filled up according to the letter of instructions. It will be presented by the Accountant General of the Navy. Will you please give my thanks to the Trustees for voting the Grant.

Ever since the arrival of the "Assurance" I have been with the party that landed. The difficulty of getting the empty wagons up & the loaded ones down was very great, and could only be overcome by the perseverance & determination of the men. They exerted themselves from first to last in the most praiseworthy manner. My time being thus occupied with the Wagons I could not write until now, but Lt. Porcher has written to you enclosing a list of the 22 cases containing the Antiquities.

As the "Assurance" has brought us a number of tools &c which will be very useful in digging, and as the harvest is over and workmen can be got more easily than before we have decided to go on with the excavations during the remaining summer months. I hope that with the means now at our disposal we shall be able to do a good deal before the weather breaks up in October. If a ship comes down again in September she could take away any thing we may find, bringing with her the Wagons & some plank & iron for packing cases. Even should we find nothing we might take the three large statuettes still at Cyrene and the stores of different descriptions we have there. I am afraid that there would not be time to report any discoveries in time to have the vessel sent on this account, before the bad weather, the communication with England by Benghazi or Tripoli being so very slow and uncertain.

I cannot express too strongly my admiration of the manner in which all the work connected with the transport of the heavy statues was done by the party landed by Capt. Aynsley for the purpose.

With best thanks to you for your kind attention to our wants and for the manner in which you procured us such efficient aid, Believe me in haste

Yours most truly
R.M. Smith

Source: [Original Letters and Papers Vol. LXX June-Aug 1861 fol. 35 (B.M.stamp P. 6923, 23 July 1861; copied 27 July 1861)]

My dear Newton,

I am very much pressed for time as I have been with the wagons ever since the ship came here. The difficulty was very great in fact another case of the big lion. The distance is some 12 miles "across country" over rocks, hills, woods and all sorts of obstacles, with a descent from Cyrene to the sea of 2000 ft. This descent is chiefly in two places viz Cyrene & near the sea, the hill near the sea being over 1000 ft. high & very steep & rocky very much like Cnidus in fact. Our means of transport were platform wagons great carriages for heavy guns with four high wheels. On the whole I think they are the best things we could have had as anything smaller must have given way. We were 10 days going up and 9 coming down, the party consisting of a Lieut (Luard) & 30 men landed by Capt. Aynsley and 8 niggers of ours. Lowering the wagons over the hill near the sea was rather nervous work and forcibly reminded me of the lion. However we happily got the wagons down to the beach this forenoon, & just as I write they are getting the last case on board. The ship being all but out of provisions besides being expected at Malta a fortnight ago, Capt. Aynsley is naturally eager to be off. I have therefore no time for writing but Porcher has written to Mr Panizzi & the F.O. enclosing a list of the 22 Cases. The Aesculapius I am sure will please you and also the Bacchus. The other things are not of so much account.

The Assurance has brought us a number of tools &c & two stone trucks. With these and now that the harvest is over & workmen may be obtained I hope we shall do a good deal before September. Being in such favourable circumstances for going on I thought it would be a pity to stop now & go to Malta in the Assurance especially as she brought me no orders to do so. We will therefore go on till the beginning of September. At that time I should like to get another ship to embark anything we may find. Even should we find nothing one would require a ship for the different stores &c now at Cyrene, & some things which for want of time and means we cd not send in the "Assurance". Capt. Aynsley is of opinion that in any future operations a vessel capable of landing 90 men shd be sent with three platform Wagons and abundance of plank 2½ inch and 1 inch (say 500 f¹ of each) with rod iron in proportion and plenty of spike nails. I quite agree with him. Each wagon takes 30 men. Should we find nothing no harm will be done as the stores would not be landed and would return with the ship. All this looks like counting ones Chickens before they are hatched but the fact is that communication with England is so slow and uncertain that after the Assurance goes I shd not have time to report any discoveries and get an answer before the bad weather begins. I shall be eager to hear from you as soon as possible. If you can get it arranged about a ship in the beginning of September I will of course be very glad. With regard to

*funds the £100 was a great help but of course the expedition has cost consider-
ably more. But I should think the expense will be paid some way or other. It
wont be ruinous however if they do not pay us.*

*I have written I fear a very confused scrawl but I am so hurried you must
excuse it. I have written a short note to Panizzi. I am sorry I have no time to
write him more fully.*

We will continue digging at the large Temple near the stadium.

*Believe me
Yours very truly
R.M. Smith*

Source: [Original Letters and Papers Vol. LXX June-Aug 1861 fols. 37-39
(B.M.stamp P. 7071 26 July 1861; copied 27 July 1861)]

AYNSLEY to VICE ADMIRAL MARTIN – June 11th 1861

Sir,

*I have the honor to report that in pursuance of your orders of the 3rd Ult I
left Malta at 3.30 P.M. on that day & proceeded direct to Suda Bay arriving
there at 9 A.M. on the 7th. I found lying there H.M.S. James Watt & I transferred to her the mails &c for the Agamemnon.*

*The Barometer being low I remained at Suda Bay till 10 A.M. on the 9th
when I proceeded in the direction of Marsa Sousah in the neighbourhood of
which place I arrived a little before noon on the following day but the wind being from the N.N. westward caused such a heavy swell on the Coast that it was
necessary to proceed to Raz el Hilal for better shelter.*

*During the course of the same afternoon I was able to send a letter to
Lieuts Smith & Porcher at Cyrene a distance of 25 Miles which occupies about
8 hrs & the following afternoon they came down to meet me but the swell still
continuing I could not go round to Marsa Sousah till the morning of the 12th
landing the Stores and a party of 30 men under Lieut P.S. Luard intended for
the expedition to Cyrene during the afternoon of that day.*

*The Arabs being occupied in getting in the harvest great difficulty was expe-
rienced in obtaining Camels but the two Carpenters lent to me from H.M.S. St.
Jean D'Acre & some plank were sent up at once, the lighter portions of the
stores following as soon as means of transport could be obtained. The Arty Gin
& spare waggon wheels were obliged to be sent on board again The Arabs refusing to put them on their Camels on account of their size & weight.*

*The party finally left the beach on the 16th dragging the two waggons the
first three miles of the road over a rough stony plain intersected by deep water*

courses, as far as the foot of the Okber a range of hills very nearly parallel to the Shore –

These hills rise to the height of 1000 ft above the plain & some idea of the steepness & difficulty of the ascent may be found from the fact that altho the path runs diagonally along its face it is impossible to ride either up or down. – It was therefore necessary to take the Waggons to pieces & carry them up by main strength. On arriving at the top of the Okber they were put together again & altho the road was still very rough & uneven not much further difficulty was experienced till reaching the foot of the hill on which Cyrene was built when another ascent of 800 ft takes place. In many places the remains of the ancient road were available but in others it had to be remade from the accumulation of earth. – The party arrived at Cyrene on the Cyrene [sic] & the cases for the Statues being incomplete they were enabled to rest until the morning of the 30th May when they started on their return to the Ship the waggons being loaded with the heaviest portions of the Statues &c & the descent being accomplished in 8 days & a half.

The waggons being loaded were this time lowered bodily down the face of the Okber & instead of being taken to Marsa Sousah were embarked from the nearest part of the Beach there only distant about $\frac{1}{2}$ a mile from the hills the Ship having been shifted round for the purpose. The smaller portions of the discoveries such as heads Statuettes &c having been brought down by Camels everything was on bd. by the Evening of the 7th Inst. and I was enabled to leave for Malta a little before noon on the 8th reaching this place at 6 A.M. today.

During the absence of the party the Ship was obliged on the 15th May to take shelter from a strong N.Westerly Breeze at Raz el Hilal returning to Marsa Sousah on 18th.

Messrs. Smith & Porcher being still engaged in carrying on their excavations with good prospect of success in making further discoveries I wd. beg to suggest that should any Ship be sent to assist them at the end of the Summer that she should be prepared to land at least 30 men for each waggon as we experienced much delay from only being able to drag one waggon at a time.

With regard to any assistance to be obtained in the Country It appears impossible to get an Arab to join in any real labour the only workmen that had been procured were Blacks from Benghazi & there with some difficulty. 7 only assisted in the transit of the waggons.–

Bull beef & goats appears to be the only sort of supplies to be obtained in the Country. Vegetables & fowls are unprocurable whilst Sheep are very rare & expensive. – With the exception of one nearly inaccessible & little known spot water is not met with till arriving at the foot of the Cyrene Hills a distance of about 10 miles from the Coast & all supplies of that necessary article have to be conveyed either from the Ship or Cyrene & as the Cattle will not allow them-

98

selves to be driven when separated from the herd they have to be killed inland & the meat carried wherever it may be wanted.

Lieut Smith before leaving the Ship spoke highly of the hard working & cheerful manner in which the men performed their very heavy duty & I am glad to say that no accident occurred to the landing party with the exception of two slight bruises & one man stung by a centipede. The two Carpenters lent from the St. Jean D'Acre deserve great praise for their steady conduct & hard work during the whole time they were landed. – Enclosed are the two letters dated 18 March & 13 April/61 which you ordered me to return. –

I have &c
(sd) C Murray Aynsley,
Commander

Source: [Original Letters and Papers Vol. LXX June-Aug 1861 fol. 159 (B.M.stamp P. 6205, 1 Jul 1861)]

To be worthy of mention in the captain's report, the *'two slight bruises'* must have been rather spectacular. One wonders if the *'centipede'* was in fact a scorpion, until reading that the Beechey brothers encountered very few scorpions, but were bothered by large numbers of dark-coloured centipedes with red feelers and legs which inhabited areas of grassland. These were always to be found under the mats in their tents, hiding like earwigs, and if chopped into pieces each portion would still run around as if nothing had happened. The only way to exterminate them was by crushing the heads. [17]

Less than two months later in Benghazi, Smith heard how, by word of mouth, the visit of the 'Assurance' had been magnified by the Arabs. The ship had turned into a fleet, the sailors who had landed had become several thousand soldiers occupying the country, and even the current Malta-Alexandria telegraph cable-laying was considered to be part of this general plan. A chatty letter from a friend in Malta dealing mainly with domestic matters reflects the notoriety which Smith and Porcher's exploits were attracting, and although not quoted in full due to its rambling nature, gives information on the date of the arrival of the statuary at that port, and the despatch via the ubiquitous Hopwood, seemingly a naval doctor, of more drawing paper, which must have been needed for Porcher's watercolour work.

---

[17] BEECHEY (1828), 519. A Libyan friend, Abdul Rheem Saleh, recognised these characteristics and told me that these creatures are known in Arabic as *'Umm arba wa arba'in'* – the *'mother of 44 (legs)'*.

My dear Smith

Thanks for your letter which was very welcome. It was very satisfactory to hear of your great success which you deserve well for risking an expedition which was sure to be attended with difficulty and danger. I send you an "Official" from Chapman about your extra pay. –

I find that Mrs. Rich who has not yet left Malta, has paid your servants' wages up to the end of April and I will therefore continue to pay them at the rate of £2.10 a month from that date; under the circumstances I suppose Rich will not place any money to my credit at Cox's so that the £5 you have placed to my credit will pay the Wages up to the end of June. Hopwood did not give me the message that you sent and I don't know what it is to this day – I only know that you had sent a message, through Brine, who you told so in your letter to him; Brine is very seedy with Rheumatism and in all probability will have to go home on sick leave. ....

Hopwood arrived this morning in the "Assurance" and your Statues I believe are quite safe on board.. ....[the letter continues]

Remember me to Porcher
and believe me
Yrs. very truly
H.H. Lewin

Malta
June 11th/61

I send herewith a letter from the Col. and the Dress Regulations which, I should think, would be very useful in Cyrene – I have given Hopwood 6 sheets of Royal 6 of Imperial and 12 of Cartridge Drawing Paper to send to you which I believe will go by the "Scourge" by which this letter leaves on the 17th Instant – H.H.L

Source: [NLS ACC 9569 fol. 90]

Lewin's facetious reference to the new set of 'Dress Regulations' issued from Horse Guards on 1st April 1861 raises the question of Smith and Porcher's appearance while the expedition was in progress. They each possessed a woollen burnous, the practical waterproof garments bought in Benghazi.[18] In the publication Smith describes them as being ideal for riding as they protected the horse as well as the horseman. These were probably reserved for cold, wet weather or for extra coverings at night when even in summer the temperature dropped rapidly, as the lieutenants do not seem to have tried to disguise themselves, unlike the Beechey brothers, who

---

[18] S & P (1864) Chap.V, 18.

adopted Turkish dress when travelling across Libya. Smith, in the list of equipment at the end of his second chapter, places clothes right at the end and states that they took *'as little as possible.'* In the engraving of the interior of the Tomb of Residence, Smith sports a pillbox type of headgear resembling a smoking cap, with a dark jacket, white shirt with tucks and light-coloured trousers, probably of Russia drill, a coarse linen. With imagination, the cap could be a forage cap, part of the Royal Engineers undress uniform, with the peak omitted by the engraver. Porcher is wearing what appears to be a foreign service helmet, coupled with a light-coloured long jacket and trousers, possibly those which unwittingly feature in some of the original photographs, a buttoned waistcoat with lapels and a white shirt. He appears in some of his own watercolours wearing these or similar clothes, with a gun on his shoulder and his dog running beside him, going out to shoot game for the pot, which was probably the mainstay of their diet, and certainly must have kept the lieutenants' expenditure to a minimum. Onions they had brought from Benghazi, eggs and a certain amount of dairy produce were available locally – also rice, when the bag they took with them ran out. They bought the occasional sheep or bullock from the nomads, also barley and wheat, which an old woman called Fatima ground to make their bread. Their emergency supply of tinned meat might have been used on those days when they were too occupied, on site or elsewhere, to spare time for hunting. The other provisions which they took with them were two bags of ship's biscuit, sugar, salt and spices, two small cheeses, a large quantity of tea and coffee – and what seems like an inordinately large supply of brandy.

Sent out on the 'Assurance' were extra tools and equipment from the stores at Malta, which must have been a welcome addition to the small collection of implements which the team at Cyrene was using. Included in this shipment were more picks, shovels, spades and crowbars, handspikes, two wheelbarrows and two very useful stone trucks, which the inventive lieutenants employed in more ways than one, as can be seen from the photographic plates.

One of the ships engaged in telegraph cable-laying was H.M.S. 'Scourge', a paddle sloop built at Portsmouth in 1844. This vessel called at Marsa Sousa on 18th June [19] while en route to Alexandria, and Captain Jones with several of the officers disembarked, carrying mail for Smith and Porcher, and made their way up to Cyrene, following directions given them by officers of the 'Assurance', newly arrived back at Malta, where the happenings at Cyrene were probably the prime topic of conversation. However, they lost their way among the woods and wadis, and it was early evening before

---

[19] PRO ADM 53/7122.

they arrived unexpectedly at the Tomb of Residence, red with dust and exhausted from their day's journey across the plateau in the summer heat. They brought with them William Dennison, who had survived his journey across Europe and had fortuitously been able to get a passage on 'Scourge',[20] which sailed on the morning of 15th June, after his arrival in Malta the previous night, giving him just enough time to purchase a few necessary articles. Although he arrived after the first consignment of statuary had been taken, he was nevertheless of considerable help; he probably shared the living quarters in the Tomb of Residence. All the naval officers were accommodated somehow for the night, and the following day the whole party was invited to a large Arab celebration. It was the feast of Melood, the anniversary of the birth of the Prophet, and a tremendous display of horsemanship took place, all at great speed and with much enthusiastic firing of guns and raising of dust.

Smith and Porcher took the opportunity to hitch a lift on 'Scourge' to Derna for a shopping spree in the bazaar, and stayed again with Vice-Consul de Fremeaux for a few days before returning overland to Cyrene on horseback. The Vice-Consul most likely accompanied them, as he is known to have visited Cyrene soon after the 'Assurance' left. A quantity of *'deals'* were bought in Derna, from which they made for the Tomb of Residence a table and some shelving. The shelves were probably put up in the recesses, which appear large enough to contain a great deal of equipment and small items of statuary, or fragments. They would also be advantageous in keeping their meagre amount of clothing and other personal belongings away from the cold, damp limestone of the walls and floor. As Dennison was a carpenter by trade, it is more than likely that it was he who carried out this work, rather than the two officers. The following letter was probably written in the house of the Vice-Consul, and in this case the paper was folded in on all four sides to form a rectangle, bearing the address.

SMITH from Derna to PANIZZI – June 23rd 1861

Dear Sir

I take the opportunity of the arrival here of H.M.S. "Mohawk" to acknowledge the receipt of your letter of 7th Inst. brought by William Dennison. Most fortunately he reached Malta just in time to get a passage to Marsa Souza in H.M.S. "Scourge" which communicated with us on her way to Alexandria. Although too late for the work of moving the statues, I have no doubt Dennison will be useful in many ways.

[20] [British Museum Greek & Roman Dept. Original Letters 1861-1868 A-K fol. 15].

Lieut. Porcher and myself are much gratified by the manner in which you mention our work in your letter of the 31st May. Will you be pleased to convey to the Trustees our best thanks for the aid they have given us.

We came here a few days ago in the "Scourge" and return to Cyrene by land tomorrow.

We are digging a large temple near the Stadium in the Eastern part of the city. One or two small fragments of sculpture in good style turned up before we left. We write to Malta by the "Mohawk" for a few more pickaxes & wheelbarrows, as we hope to get more workmen now that the harvest is nearly over. I suppose there will be no difficulty about their issue.

I will write to you again from Cyrene when our Excavations are a little more advanced.

I am, Dear Sir
Yours very truly
R.M. Smith

Source: [Original Letters and Papers Vol. LXX June-Aug 1861 fol. 139 (B.M.stamp P. 6438 9 Jul 1861; copied 27 July 1861)]

As a result of the interest generated by Smith and Porcher's excavations, a letter was written to Lord Russell by an ambitious gentleman who saw possible advantage to himself by joining them. This copy of his letter was passed to Panizzi by Lord Wodehouse of the Foreign Office on July 11th, who wished to know *'whether Mr Robinson's offer of assistance should be accepted or not'.*[21] Even had his request been granted, he could not have reached Cyrene before the departure of the expedition.

JOHN ROBINSON, London to LORD RUSSELL – July 5th 1861

My Lord

Having observed in the Public Journals notices of explorations at Cyrene which are now being carried on under the direction of the F.O., I beg to inform Y. L that having within the last 3 weeks gained in competition the appointment of Travelling Student of Architecture to the Royal Academy of Arts, London I am about forthwith to proceed to Italy and the East and as it becomes my duty while holding that appointment to direct my attention to subjects of Architectural, Antiquarian or Archaeological interest, I take the liberty to enquire whether the Experience I possess, of which the appointment I hold

---

[21] Original Letters and Papers Vol. LXX June-Aug 1861 fol. 234 (B.M.stamp P. 6602 12 July 1861; copied 13 July 1861).

may be considered by Your Lordship to be a sufficient guarantee, may not be rendered available in the service of the Gov[t]. in assisting on those explorations on the shores of the Mediterranean which are now being conducted under your auspices – As regards further qualifications I may add that in 1845 I became the pupil of Mr. Pennethorne the Architect to the Comm[rs] of H. Majesty's Works &c & have remained in this office until the present time. In 1850 I gained the Silver Medal & in 1851 the Gold Medal in Architecture of the Royal Academy & I have been engaged on all the large public works in London that have been executed by Mr. Pennethorne within the last 15 years.

I have &c
(signed) John Robinson

Source: [Original Letters and Papers Vol. LXX June-Aug 1861 fol. 205 (B.M.stamp P.6602 12 Jul 1861; copied 13 July 1861)]

On July 8th the Admiralty advised Panizzi *'that the "Supply" with Antiquities from Cyrenaica has arrived at Portsmouth and will proceed this day to Woolwich'*.[22] Immediately upon receipt of this the next day, Panizzi requested to be informed of her arrival at Woolwich *'in order that an officer from the Museum may be sent there to take charge of some Antiquities from the Cyrenaica'*, and the Admiralty responded that same day (the postal system was excellent in the nineteenth century) with the news that the ship was now at Woolwich.[23] This was confirmed on July 11th by H.M. Dockyard.[24] The Treasury Chambers, in reply to a letter from Panizzi, informed him on July 10th that *'directions have been issued to the Commissioners of Customs for the delivery unopened of the cases of antiquities expected from the Cyrenaica'*.[25] Meanwhile, Panizzi was still trying to ensure that the officers were granted enough time for the expedition to continue, and his efforts were repaid when the War Office informed him that Smith had been granted an extension of leave of absence to 28th May 1862.[26] He also made a request to the Admiralty in connection with the collection of the next consignment of statuary, and his

---

[22] Original Letters and Papers Vol.LXX June-Aug 1861 fol. 216 (B.M.stamp P. 6404 8 Jul 1861; copied 13 July 1861).

[23] Original Letters and Papers Vol. LXX June-Aug 1861 fol. 226 (B.M.stamp P. 6525 10 Jul 1861; copied 13 July 1861).

[24] Original Letters and Papers Vol. LXX June-Aug 1861 fol. 235 (B.M.stamp P. 6617 11 Jul 1861; copied 13 July 1861).

[25] Original Letters and Papers Vol. LXX June-Aug 1861 fol. 230 (B.M.stamp P. 6554 11 Jul 1861).

[26] PRO WO 55/1056 fol. 110; Original Letters and Papers Vol. LXX June-Aug 1861 fol. 339 (B.M.Stamp P. 7172 30 Jul 1861; copied 12 Oct. 1861).

letter was answered the same day, to the effect that *'Vice Admiral Sir W.F. Martin has been desired to send a Ship of War about the 1st September to remove such further specimens of Sculpture &c as may have been discovered by Lieutenants Smith and Porcher in the Cyrenaica, provided the distribution of the Force under his command will admit of his doing so.'* [27]

---

[27] Original Letters and Papers Vol. LXX June-Aug 1861 fol. 348 (B.M.stamp P. 7297, 2 Aug 1861; copied 12 Oct. 1861).

VII. NEAR THE CENTRE OF THE CITY...

As their workforce had been strengthened by the addition of the *'seven blacks'* sent from Benghazi in mid May, Smith and Porcher felt able to begin work on the large temple near the stadium – now known as the Temple of Zeus. Because of the great extent of the ruins, which seemed not to have been disturbed, they were confident that the site would produce the statuary for which they yearned. It had indeed been a massive structure, the diameter of the fluted columns of the colonnade being about six feet and that of their capitals an impressive nine feet, but Smith found that the building had suffered extensive deliberate damage. All the columns were seen to have fallen outwards, and the statuary which was discovered consisted of cracked and broken fragments. Because of this, the excavation was halted after seven weeks. Investigation of the smaller temple nearby showed that this, too, had been purposely destroyed, like its neighbour, and it seems to have been rendered even more fragmentary, making Smith's plan *'partly conjectural'*. Parallel work being carried out in the city produced two female statues, one of which was of Minerva, and to convey these down to the Tomb of Residence the stone-trucks sent on 'Assurance' were brought out for the first time.

Smith's fifth despatch of July 3rd from *'Cyrene by Benghazi, Barbary'* and its enclosures *'containing further information respecting his explorations'* were passed to Panizzi by the Foreign Office on August 5th, but for some reason were not copied until October 12th. [1] A subsequent note is written on the Foreign Office letter: *'Inclosing letter dated 3 July, similar to that add^d to Mr Panizzi of that date T.B.'* The official despatch addressed to the Foreign Office has not been found, and the text given below is that of Smith's letter to Panizzi, of which he says the *'greater part'* was duplicated for Lord Russell.

---

[1] Original Letters and Papers Vol. LXX June-Aug 1861 fol. 377 (B.M.stamp P. 7414, 6 Aug 1861; copied 12 Oct 1861).

Lieut. Smith's Despatch 5 – July 3 1861

Dear Sir

I sent you a short note about ten days ago by H.M.S. "Mohawk" from Derna. As she called there only for a few hours on her way to Alexandria I had barely time to acknowledge the receipt of your letter of the 7ᵗʰ June brought by William Dennison. [2]

Since the departure of the "Assurance" we have gone on with the excavation of the large Temple near the Stadium. We continue to find fragments of statues there but as yet nothing more perfect. Some of the fragments evidently belong to statues of great size. They are in good style.

The arrangement of the interior of the cella is peculiar. The entrance is in the East end. Towards the West end there is a sort of pedestal, some 15 feet square, built of massive blocks of stone. On this probably stood the statue of the Divinity to whom the Temple was dedicated. As far as we have excavated we have found an interior colonnade parallel to the walls of the Cella, the space between the walls and the faces of the columns being about six feet. This colonnade is of marble and I imagine of the Corinthian order, while the building itself is Doric. [3]

Last week our work at the Temple was interrupted to bring down two statues we had discovered in another part of the city. Near the centre of the City there are the remains of a building supposed by Beechey to have been a palace. [4] *Immediately above this palace a number of <u>frusta</u> of fluted marble columns are lying above ground. While examining this site a short time ago our attention was attracted by a small piece of marble cropping out above the surface. Clearing away the earth a little we found that it was a statue.* [5] *We accordingly set some men at work to get it out when it proved to be a large draped female statue* [**Pl. 30**] *about 6'9" in height including the head, which however we have not found. In digging round it we came upon another somewhat smaller, being about 6'6" in height.* [6] *This is also a female statue*

---

[2] Letter untraced.

[3] The massive Temple of Zeus.

[4] The 'palace' is a complex of rooms and corridors within the city of Cyrene, referred to to-day as the House of Jason Magnus, a prominent Cyrenean citizen and priest of Apollo under Commodus. A variety of statuary was found here, with a wide date range, as if it were the collection of a connoisseur.

[5] Scholars cannot agree on the identification of this figure, some regarding it as a classical goddess, while others consider it to be an imperial portrait statue.

[6] The smaller Hellenistic statue was that of Athena. A head of Athena was discovered by Norton in 1911, supposedly from the Necropolis, but was claimed by Paribeni in 1956 to have come from the Agora. It is suspected that this head, now in Cyrene Museum, may belong to the statue found by the lieutenants, and Neil Adams of the British Museum agreed with this supposi-

draped. The style seems to me much superior to that of the larger one, but of this and also of their condition you will be better able to judge by the inclosed photographs than by any description I could give. The smaller statue you will observe has a small head in relief sculptured on the girdle between the breasts. I send two photographs of this statue, one of the whole, and one at a larger scale of the upper part [**Pls. 31-32**].

We have kept four men digging where the statues were found, but nothing has been discovered to show what they are, or the nature of the building in which they were placed.

We have only eight workmen altogether, but write by the bearer of this letter to Benghazi to see if the Consul can send us more. We are unwilling to employ Arabs if it can be avoided, as they are but indifferent workmen and are besides very proud, quarrelsome and unmanageable. Should we fail however in getting more blacks from Benghazi we must have recourse to the Arabs.

I inclose a Statement of all our expenses from November last when we left Malta up till the 30th ult°. Many of the items will be explained by the fact of our being obliged to feed the workmen and otherwise provide for their wants generally. We have now a fixed rate of pay viz. 5 piastres (10^d) a day and food for each workman. Formerly we provided everything for the men we had with us, the only money payments being in the form of "Bakshish". The whole amount of expenses from Nov. 1860 till June 30. 1861 is £253 – I inclose also a statement of Dennison's expenses on the journey out as given me by him. [7]

The third inclosure contains four photographs which are numbered on the back and are as follows: –

No.1   *Larger of the two female statues. The workman is holding on the right arm which is broken off at the shoulder & wrist. He also serves as a scale for measurement.* [**Pl. 30**]

No.2   *Smaller of the two statues. Full length* [**Pl. 31**]

No.3   *The same on a larger scale. Upper part* [**Pl. 32**]

No.4   *Portrait of Mohammed el Adouly* [8] *an influential Arab of the Cyrenaica who has always been a particular friend of ours, & who has often been of considerable service to us.* [**Pl. 33**]

Regarding our future operations we think it desirable to have a ship here if possible before the weather breaks up, say about September. From what I saw

---

tion on stylistic grounds, considering also the nature of the break and the matching of the hair at the back with that of the statue. He declared the head to have been found in a pit in the Agora.

[7] Dennison's expenses have not been traced.

[8] See Dramatis Personae.

of the means of transport when the "Assurance" was here, I do not think we could have anything better adapted to the work than the "Platform Waggons" we then used. They require at least 30 men each, I should think three waggons and consequently a working party of 90 or 100 men about the means required. It would be difficult to supply a larger party with water, camp equipage &c. And unless before Septr. we find some more heavy objects, one trip of the three waggons would be sufficient. Should it not be so, they might come up for a second load without occupying more time in the two trips than we did formerly in one, as then we had two waggons but only strength to man one at a time. The ship should therefore be such as could land a party of 90 or 100 men. She would have to bring tents for the party on shore. We should require two or three Carpenters with their tools as formerly.

The only stores we should require are timber, iron &c for packing. The following list which I have gone over with Dennison is as nearly complete as I can make it here.

Platform Waggons	*No. 3*
Spare Wheels for Do.	*Sets 1.*
2¹/₂ Inch Deal for cases	*feet 600*
1¹/₂ Inch Deal for cases	*feet 300*
Rod Iron 3/8 inch [9]	*feet 200*
Washers for Do. for bolts	*No. 150*
Hoop Iron 1 inch [10]	*bundles 1*
Nails 5 Inch	*No. 200*
Nails 3¹/₂ Inch	*lbs 15*
Nails 20ᵈ.	*lbs 15*
Nails 10ᵈ.	*lbs 10*
Nails Clout 1 Inch	*lbs 6*
Old Hammocks	*No. 50.*
Rope. 3 Inch	*Coils 1*
Rope 4 Inch	*Coils 2*
Stone saws [11] *for cutting off Inscriptions on heavy blocks of Marble*	*No. 2*
Grit sand for Do.	*bags. 1.*

[9] See Glossary.

[10] Was this for the 'casks' mentioned in Chapter 6?

[11] Fortunately for the monuments, there is no record of the stone saws being supplied. Only five inscriptions appear in the list of cases shipped, and the others which were recorded were all done by 'squeezes'. Those inscriptions which could not be physically shipped were concealed in an underground chamber – possibly once a cistern – below the Tomb of Residence.

I send a duplicate of the greater part of this letter to Lord John Russell.

It would be well if the ship brought say £100 in English Sovereigns and Silver Five franc pieces, for which I would give the Paymaster a bill on you, as money cannot be obtained nearer than Malta.

I am, Dear Sir
Yours most faithfully
R.M. Smith

Source: [Original Letters and Papers Vol. LXX June-Aug 1861 fol. 196 (B.M.stamp P. 7337 3 Aug 1861; copied 12 Oct. 1861)]

Panizzi evidently acted upon this letter immediately, as he wrote to the Admiralty on the day it was received, asking for the assistance which the expedition needed. On their part, the Admiralty replied that this request had been passed to Vice Admiral Martin. [12]

SMITH to NEWTON – July 5th 1861

My dear Newton

I sent you a short note by the 'Scourge'. I now write to Panizzi and send a duplicate of the letter to the Foreign Office. In this letter I have expressed my views regarding our Future operations. From former experience I daresay you are well aware how difficult it is to predict or to look far beyond the present in digging. I have therefore confined my observations to the present Summer and its wind up by a ship coming about September before the weather breaks up. What may have turned up by that time or whether it may be desirable to remain here during the Winter I cannot yet say.

I must refer you to Panizzi's letter for an account of what we have been about. It contains photographs of two statues we discovered the other day [**Pls. 30-32**]. *I should have sent you copies of them but unfortunately I am nearly out of printing materials. It does not much matter now however as I have just received a good stock of glasses from Malta so that I can keep all the negatives. One of the statues, the smaller one, I like very much. I shall be anxious to hear your opinion of it and also of all the things that are already gone home. There are not very many inscriptions here, but I will send all I can get that are portable and take impressions of the rest. I have now impressions of all I know of.* [13] *In the requisition for stores in Panizzi's letter I have put*

---

[12] Original Letters and Papers Vol. LXX June-Aug 1861 fol. 380 (B.M.stamp P. 7554, 9 Aug 1861; copied 12 Oct. 1861).

[13] A total of thirty-three inscriptions was eventually published.

down two stone saws to cut the inscriptions off the faces of the heavy blocks. I do not know that one will have time to cut them while a ship is here but we may as well try one or two.

Sir John Burgoyne writes me that you have been indefatigable in making appeals to the authorities all round for our support. [14] The liberal way in which they have given it shows that your applications have not been in vain. We are of course infinitely indebted to you. I think it would not be impolite if you were to get the Trustees to send a letter of thanks to Captn. Aynsley, the officers & crew of the 'Assurance' for their assistance. It would please them and the Admiral too I should think, and they are certainly deserving of it. The work was very hard and they stuck to it well without a grumble. The operation was in fact _barely_ practicable. Former travellers & excavators thought it impossible. Bourville had to leave behind everything he found that would not go on a camel.

I have also sent to Panizzi the account of expenses up to June 30th. They amount altogether to £253 which sum includes our personal expenses here for housekeeping. I cannot tell how much is due to this item as I kept only our account. It would in fact be almost impossible to say how much is personal & how much not as we have to feed all the workmen, besides Arabs &c after the manner of the country. I have not much compunction however in putting all down, first as the whole sum is small and secondly because I received the other day a letter from the Horse Guards informing me that being 'On leave' I could draw nothing beyond my subsistence pay of 6/10 a day since I left Malta. This is something of the nature of hairsplitting. I am technically 'on leave' certainly, inasmuch as I was not _ordered_ here by H.R.H., still I did not think their practice would be so sharp.

Dennison arrived in the 'Scourge' as I told you before. I daresay he will be very useful as a Carpenter when the ship comes. As a foreman I fear he will not be so useful as of course he knows nothing of the ways of the people or the language.

The large Temple near the Stadium has hitherto yielded nothing but fragments and I begin to despair of getting anything else there. We will go on however and clear it out. I am afraid that the marble of the temple has been _purposely_ smashed at some former period. [15]

---

[14] Letter untraced.

[15] Smith was right that the temple had been _'purposely smashed'_ – it was a victim of the Jewish Revolt in A.D. 115, when the enterprising rebels undermined the columns of the peristyle, shored them up with baulks of timber and filled the gaps with dry vegetation and probably oils, fats and other combustible substances. This was then torched, the fierce fires resulting in a collapse of the fabric which must have fallen with a protracted thunderous crash that could have been heard for miles. One can see how the base of each great column subsided crookedly into

I write to Benghazi by the present courier for all the workmen that can be got. For the reasons given in my letter to Panizzi we are unwilling to employ the Arabs. I hope the Consul will find us a number of blacks. Our present force is only seven one having gone away yesterday. They get through a good deal of work however somewhat after the style of our old friends their fellow country-men Sourour and Merion. [16]

If by any means we could hear beforehand when the ship will be here (exact date) it would be a great convenience as we could make arrangements before her arrival for the supply of camels &c. I fear however it is impossible, there being no regular or frequent communication between Malta and Benghazi. By the bye, letters addressed to the Vice Consul at Benghazi gene-rally reach us in shorter time than those addressed to Tripoli, the overland journey from Tripoli to Benghazi occupying three weeks.

When will the book be out? Are there the requisite number of subscribers yet for the large one? Is there any talk yet of what to do with the Mausoleum sculptures? They surely do not intend the present arrangement to be a perma-nent one.

Any information you can send regarding Cyrene would be very acceptable. Is any mention made by Ancient authors of any of the buildings of the City? Porcher is going to send home to Dr. Hooker whom he knows a little bag of Sylphium seed. [17]

I shall be very glad to hear from you whenever you have a spare moment, and do not forget to let me know your opinion about the statues. I do not much care about any other.

Porcher desires to be kindly remembered –

> *Believe me*
> *Yours most sincerely*
> *R.M. Smith*

P.S. The torso that Beechey mentions and wh. he thinks a Ptolemy [18] *from the*

---

the void beneath it, sending the shaft teetering outwards like a falling tree, dragging apart and taking with it the elements of the entablature and roof, the column drums separating as they hit the ground, and the other massive pieces of masonry falling on and about them. Inside the cella, especially on the north side, the evidence of a fiercely raging fire is unmistakable, with the limestone blocks burnt red and yellow, and no trace remaining of the marble colonnade which Smith declared was in small fragments. (GOODCHILD (1958), 30-62; BONACASA (2000), 139 plan).

[16] Obviously a reference to Newton's workmen.

[17] See Chapter 9 n. 8.

[18] The whiteness of this cuirassed torso can easily be distinguished in [**Pl. 49**], standing towards the northern end of Smith and Porcher's upper terrace. Wroth identified the statue as one of Hadrian (WROTH (1886), 138-142).

devices on the armour is still here [**Pl. 48**]. *It is very heavy but I think it would be a pity to leave it. The seated figure* [19] *he mentions at the Temple of Apollo, Aesculapius, Diana or whichever it is, is also still in existence* [**Pl. 42**]. *R.M.S.*

Source: [Brit.Mus.Dept. of G & R Antiquities, Orig.Lett. 1861 fol. 710]

Silphium, the cure-all and gastronomic delicacy of the classical world, played an important role in the economy of the Cyrenaica, equal to that of oil today from the Libyan Desert, so much so that the plants featured on the coins of the district. It flourished in ancient times in an area mostly around Cyrene, but by the time of Pliny it had become extremely rare. Frederick Crowe claimed to have a plant growing in his garden, and described how *'when the middle stem sprouts and the seeds are formed it is exactly what one sees on the Cyrenaica Coins'.* [20] Although true silphium is now considered to be extinct, sightings of possible surviving examples are still eagerly reported. *'Dr Hooker'* refers to Joseph Dalton Hooker, who followed in his father William's footsteps as director of the Royal Botanic Gardens at Kew. The pair jointly produced a quantity of learned botanical books, and the younger Hooker was also the author of works which were a result of his travels – four exciting years as surgeon-botanist aboard HMS 'Erebus' in the Antarctic, followed by journeys in India, where he spent two years exploring the hitherto unknown flora of the Himalayas, New Zealand, Morocco and finally the American continent. Funded by the British Government, Hooker travelled to India with Lord Dalhousie in 1847, when the latter went out with his wife and entourage to take up his post as Governor General. The journey was evidently by the 'Overland Route', whose only claim to land travel, in spite of the name, was the 220 miles through Egypt between Alexandria and Suez with the mails, a distinctly shorter journey than that round the Cape of Good Hope or through the Ottoman Empire. Porcher seems to have struck up a friendship with Hooker on board ship when en route to Alexandria, and when he went on shore leave he must have joined the party on track-boats towed by horses along the Mahoudiah Canal and thence on a small Nile paddle steamer to Cairo, where the two men walked over the *'petrified forest'* in the Mukattam Hills a few miles outside the city. Some of the tree trunks lying in the desert were forty feet long, with their branches beside them, and Hooker must have

---

[19] This figure can be glimpsed in [**Pl. 49**], but features mainly in [**Pl. 42**]. It was abandoned when Smith and Porcher left, and lost its identity; only recently was it recognised by the author in the position it must have held for the last 70 years, at the foot of the Sacred Way (THORN D (1999), 69-76 Figs. 1-6).

[20] F.H. Crowe, letter dated 8th May 1860 – Department of Greek and Roman Antiquities, British Museum.

compared them with those of the fossil forest he had been fortunate enough to explore five years earlier in Tasmania. [21]

Smith from Benghazi to Panizzi – July 12th 1861

Dear Sir,

I have the honour to advise you that I have this day drawn a bill on you of this day's date payable after ten days' sight to the order of Antonio Aquilina Esqre H.B.M. Vice Consul Benghazi for the sum of Two Hundred Pounds.

I have the honour to be Sir
Your most obedient servant
R.M. Smith
Lt. R.E.

Source: [Original Letter and Papers Vol. LXX June-Aug 1861 fol. 247 (B.M.stamp P. 7338, 3 Aug 1861; copied 12 Oct. 1861)]

Smith postscript from Benghazi to Panizzi – July 12th 1861

Dear Sir,

I came down to Benghazi to look after the means of getting money here if possible and also to get workmen. I have been fortunate enough to find both by the assistance of Mr. Aquilina. I start for Cyrene today with 25 blacks thus making up our force to 32. I came down with only one Arab as guide, and to save time, without a Water Camel. I reached Benghazi in three days & a half, resting only six hours on the way. I was not sorry when the journey was over as the last 20 hours were without water.

I am
Yours very truly
R.M. Smith

Source: [Original Letter and Papers Vol. LXX June-Aug 1861 fol. 246 (B.M.stamp P. 7338, 3 Aug 1861; copied 12 Oct. 1861)]

This headlong dash to Benghazi in the heat of summer, taking only the water which could be carried, was a badly planned move which was

---

[21] Allan (1967), 125, 161; Blackwood's (Feb. 1845), 212; Baedeker (1929), 126-128 and map; Cook (1929), 184-185.

uncharacteristic of Smith, and one for which he paid dearly later. He obviously regarded the acquisition of more workmen and money as imperative for the success of his expedition, and did not wish to waste valuable time in sending letters which possibly might not arrive, or waiting for replies. He probably thought he could rely on encountering an Arab encampment or two on his journey, where he could obtain water. The episode was reminiscent of an occasion when he left Bodrum to visit the Pacha on money matters and was away for eight days, but this ride took place in the cooler days of May, and he had enough leisure to do some drawings en route. The return journey from Benghazi with twenty-five negroes (the publication and the official despatch of August 11th state twenty-eight) was exasperating, to say the least. After combing Benghazi for enough girbehs, Smith had difficulty in preventing his charges from using all their water before the skins could be refilled, and all their food was eaten well before they reached Merdj. For the rest of the journey they had to subsist on dates which he managed to obtain there. The climax came when, as Smith related to Newton and in his despatch to Lord Russell, the caravan was attacked by Arabs in a wood and one of the negroes abducted, presumably never to be heard of again. It was not surprising that, with such hazards attached to going to work out at Cyrene, Smith had to pay good wages in order to induce his men first to go there, and then to stay. The fabulous rate of 5 Turkish piastres was paid per day, equal to 10d in English money at the time, now about 4^1/$_2$p, with food included.

Photographs:
1. S & P no.120; Reg. 61 11-27, 39 Album photo 20-7 [**Pl. 30**]
2-3. S & P no.121; Reg. 61 11-27, 31 Album photo 20-8 [**Pls. 31-32**]
4. Album photo 25-3 [**Pl. 33**]

Plates:
30 Rosenbaum p. 95, no. 167, Pl. LXXV,2; Huskinson p. 61, no. 110, Pl. 43.
31, **32** *JHS* XLI (1921) Pl. XVIII; Smith *Catalogue* ii p. 255 no. 1479; V. Muller 'A Chronology of Greek Sculpture from 400 B.C. to 40 B.C.', *Art Bulletin* XX (1938), 396.
33 Wanis S. and Thorn D. (1995) Fig. 2; see Dramatis Personae.

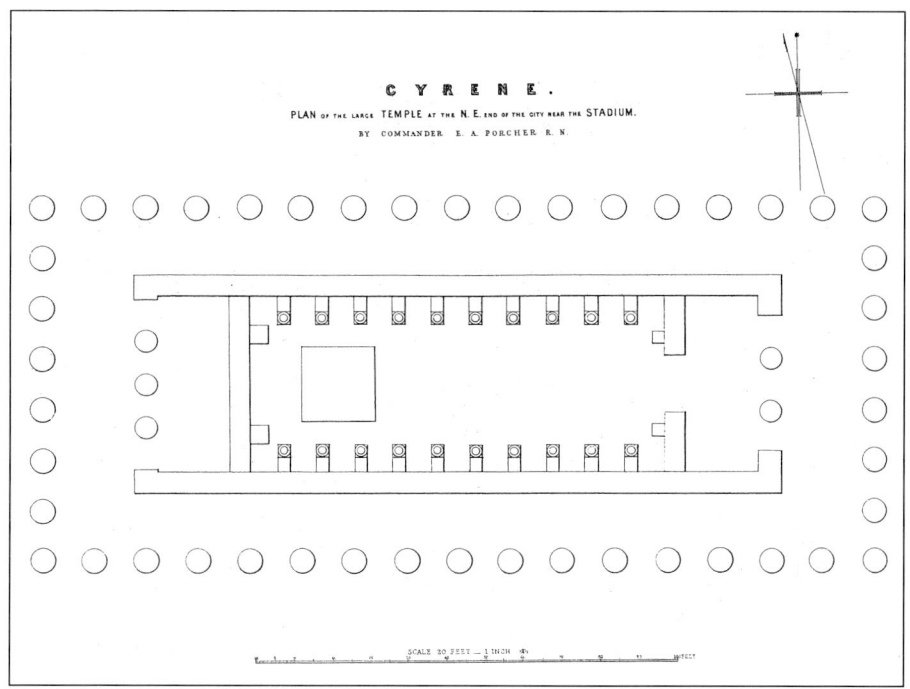

Fig. 12 – Plan of the Large Temple near the Stadium at Cyrene.

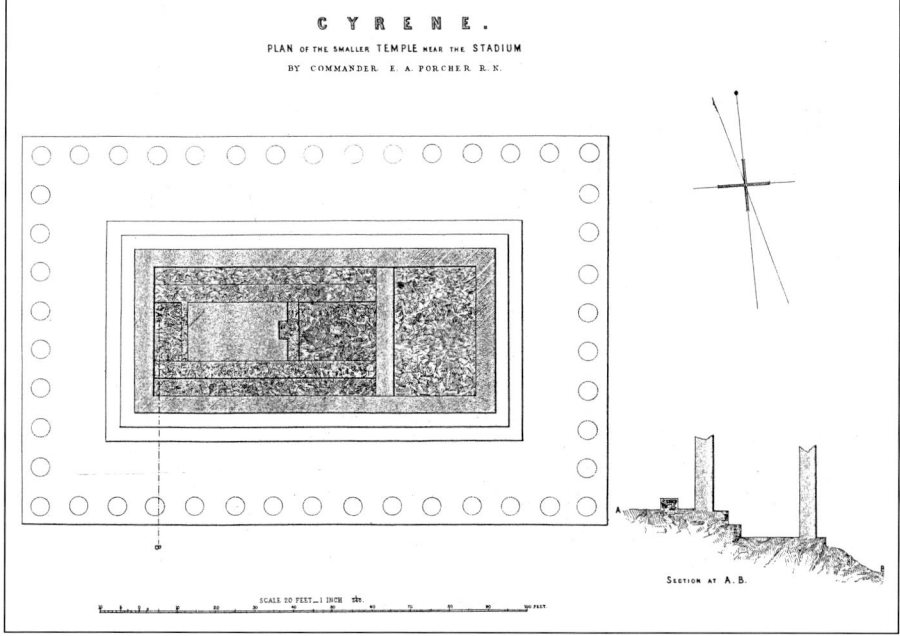

Fig. 13 – Plan of the Smaller Temple near the Stadium at Cyrene.

VIII. THE HEAD WREATHED WITH GRAPES...

After their skirmish around the stadium and in the city the excavators returned in force to the Sanctuary of Apollo and the area surrounding the temple. In the publication Smith noted the discovery in this neighbourhood of four statues, four statuettes, fourteen heads, seven inscriptions, the large seated figure of Archippe, the smaller seated figure, a colossal female statue, a lifesize figure of the elderly Nerva and a small Bacchus. Meanwhile, he was still 'dining out' on the story of the kidnapped negro. Interestingly, he seemed to have completely lost track of how many workmen he had, as the total differs slightly with each telling.

All this time, Porcher with his paintbox under the wide Cyrene skies had been trudging cross-country over the surrounding areas and transforming what he saw on to paper, and in this way he probably gained a better knowledge of the built and rock-cut tombs in the vast necropolis than any other early explorer. He was out and about before dawn, seeing the early mist rolling up the wadis and watching the light creeping over the lower plateau long before the first rays of the sun burst upon Cyrene over the eastern hills. Then the undergrowth dried out, the cold rock grew warm, aromatic herbs released their heady, unfamiliar scents underfoot and he experienced the pure magic of a Cyrene morning. Although he may have gone out on horseback, many of his watercolours show tombs which would be completely inaccessible for any horse, and must have involved the artist in much clambering up and down the treacherous hillsides and in and out of the wadis for many miles in his quest. As the shadows grew shorter the heat increased, until at midday the sun stood overhead, reflected by the white rocks in a merciless glare, and there seemed to be a great breathless silence, broken only by grasshoppers and cicadas.

The routes Porcher took could be worked out from the known locations of the external and internal views of tombs which he painted, and by their measured plans. Featuring in so many of the watercolours he produced were these beautiful weathered remnants of Greek architecture, shown half buried in thick spring vegetation or basking on the shrivelled, sere landscape of faded late summer, the limestone stained a golden honey colour or blindingly white in the sun. He peopled them with passing Arabs and showed in certain interiors transitory inhabitants who may in some cases have been in residence, but were probably imaginary. In the same way he added groups of glossy-haired goats, or wild dogs. He found, and illustrated, tiny painted chambers open at one side, their colours worn and subtly muted by weather and the passing centuries. On the walls of some were counterchanged coloured panels under a frieze of ribbons and garlands. Another, under a frieze of swags, was covered with painted latticework enclosing little red honeysuckle buds, a small fragrant breath of a long-forgotten spring, and a design which was echoed in a great tomb which Porcher painted, where the swallows swooped in and out from their nests by the ceiling in the cool dimness.

Even after the sun had passed its zenith the afternoons were very hot and still, but each day at about four o'clock a small breeze sprang up and revitalized everyone, both man and beast. As the sun slid down the western sky its low rays struck horizontally through the atmosphere over the plateau, creating a haunting quality of amber light, a signal for Porcher to pack up and make his way back before darkness fell, because after this time the sun took on the appearance of an enormous grapefruit and sank rapidly with no nonsense. If he were still out in the necropolis after sunset he could find his way back to the encampment through the chirping crickets by following the pale goat-tracks which seemed to hold the reflected memory of the day's sunlight.

Cyrene Augst 5th 1861

My dear Newton

An Arab has just come in to say that he is on his way to Benghazi, so I take the opportunity of sending you a short note I wrote to you in the beginning of last month, adding a postscript at Benghazi. I left Benghazi with 25 Blacks and after a few days very toilsome march reached Cyrene in safety. On the way my caravan was attacked by a tribe of Arabs, and one of the blacks carried off as a prize. I was ahead of the caravan at the time and noticed a number of Arabs lying under the trees by the side of the road, but thought it nothing remarkable. When the caravan came up, they rushed into the midst of the niggers, and while some were lashing one of them the rest formed a square round with their guns cocked and levelled. On hearing the row I rode back but they had disappeared in the wood.

We have finished the two large temples near the stadium. I am sorry they have been so unproductive, as they looked the most likely places in Cyrene. Everything seems to have been deliberately destroyed, even the internal columns are in small pieces. In each of them we found a head both much the worse for wear. [1] *One is very large, and of excellent style but sadly broken.* [2] *In the larger temple we found in the Pronaos two long inscriptions* [3] *They seem to me to be lists of people who had given things to the temple. The building which is upwards of 200 feet in length consists of a cella with pronaos and porticus 16 Columns on a side & 8 in front.*

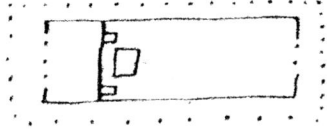

The ends have I think a double row besides the two in pronaos and the 3 of the porticus.

At the west end is one large & two small built platforms [4] *as if for sculpture and down the sides there is a marble colonnade. The diameter of the columns of the peristyle is 6 feet. They are Doric and fluted. It must have been a very magnificent building. The other temple is somewhat similar but much smaller. All the Temples I have examined have built pedestals or rather platforms near the West end of Cella, the fronts are always facing the east.*

We are now at work in the neighbourhood of our old temple that of Aesculapius [5] *or whatever it is We have been four days at work there and have turned up four statuettes, one or two of which are very good. One is nude – I think it is Bacchus, at least his left hand holds a bunch of grapes and his elbow rests on the trunk of a tree on which a vine is trailing. The head also is wreathed with grapes* [**Pl. 37**] *– Another is female, in her right hand she holds a vase* [6] *with a handle* [**Pl. 38**]. *(Just at this moment as I write they say that a large statue or part of one has hove in sight)*

We have also got a number of inscriptions. All the best ones we have brought to our tomb to take away if possible. I have impressions of them all – One begins [7]

---

[1] S & P nos. 112 and 116; Reg. 61 11-27, 162 and 54.

[2] S & P no. 116; Reg. 61 11-27, 54.

[3] S & P inscriptions nos. 6-7 Pls. 78-9; Smith's Despatch 6 of August 11th, letter August 20th.

[4] S & P (1864) Pl. 55. (GOODCHILD (1958), 41-43 Fig. 2). Throne core shown by Porcher, the 'Predella' found by Pesce, but the footstool unrecorded (PESCE (1948), 338-340 Pl. LVI).

[5] Temple of Apollo; Smith's Despatch 1 of 23rd Feb 1861.

[6] S & P no. 37; Reg. 61 11-27, 41.

[7] S & P inscription no. 24 Pl. 84 found *'built into a partition wall in the Temple of Apollo, writing turned inwards'*; Smith's Despatch 6 of August 11th 1861 *'1. An inscription on marble built into a recent wall No. 18 of Inclosure.'* Left by Tomb of Residence October 1861. Found by Richard Norton 1911 (ROBINSON (1913), 199), published by Oliverio, *S.E.Cir.* no. 4.

ΜΑΝΤΩΝΙΟΣ ΚΕΡΕΑΔΙΣ
ΠΤΟΛΕΜΑΙΟΥ //// ΥΙΟΣ
ΑΙΓΛΑΝΩΡ
ΜΗΤΡΟΔΩΡΟΣ / ΤΟΥ
ΜΗΤΡΟΔΩΡΟΥ
etc. etc.
This Ptolemy IV must I suppose be the father of Cleopatra.

I cannot yet say whether where we are digging is a separate building or if it is in the Peribolus of the other temple. We have thirty five men at work every day. Dennison is very useful as an overseer although not knowing a word of the language is a difficulty – Every now and then I have great rows about the diggings to settle with the Arabs. They are an infernal lot altogether and all the romantic talk about Bedouin hospitality, good faith etc is simply bosh. They are frightful thieves liars and murderers. I am a great friend of theirs however, which it is necessary to be.

I write in a great hurry as the fellow is sitting by me yearning to be off. We are sadly off for news so whenever you have time let me hear from you.

Porcher joins in kindest Remembrances

Believe me, Yours most sincerely
R M Smith

Source: [Original Letters and Papers Vol. LXX June-Aug 1861 fol. 378 (B.M.stamp P. 8263, 9 Sept 1861; copied 12 Oct 1861)]

The sixth official despatch, dated only six days after Smith's last letter to Newton, arrived over a month later. It was forwarded to Panizzi by the Foreign Office *'to be laid before the Trustees of the British Museum'* on October 17th.[8] Smith's letter to Panizzi, also dated August 11th, bears a later annotation at the head of the first page: *'Photos Nos.1-9 sent to Mr Newton 19/11/72'.*

Lieut. Smith's Despatch 6 – August 11 1861

My Lord,
I wrote to your Lordship on the 3rd July giving an Account of our proceeding up till that time.
A few days afterwards I went to Benghazi for the purpose of obtaining

---

[8] Original Letters and Papers Vol. LXXI Sept-Dec 1861 fol. 141 (B.M.stamp P.9594 18 Oct 1861; copied 9th November 1861).

more workmen, and also to make arrangements for receiving supplies of money from time to time as we should require it. Through the kind assistance of Mr Aquilina H B M Vice Consul, I succeeded in both the objects of my journey. I brought back to Cyrene 28 blacks thus making up our number to 36. On the way the Caravan was attacked by one of the tribes whose district we were passing, and one of the blacks carried off. I found out who they were, and that the Sheikh of the tribe was himself one of the party. I have written to Aquilina about it, although I fear his representations will not make the authorities take any measures bone fide for the apprehension of the offenders.

I left Cyrene on the 6th and got back with the blacks on the 18th the journey taking altogether nine days.

We commenced work the following day with the whole party. Until the end of the month we employed the workmen in digging where we found the two female statues of which your Lordship has received photographs [**Pls. 30-32**] *and in finishing the excavation of the two large temples* [9] *near the Stadium. We did not succeed in finding either of the heads of the statues.*

At the large temple [10] *we continued to find fragments of Sculpture as before, but nothing in a more perfect state. We got one large head* [11] *of good style but very much damaged. In the Pronaos, however we found two long inscriptions* [12] *on marble, one consisting of 58 and the other in double columns of 23 lines. They seem to record the names of Contributors to the building and furnishing of the Temple. We brought both the inscriptions down to our tomb.*

In the smaller temple we also found a number of fragments including a Colossal head of excellent style but very much broken. [13] *It must have belonged to a statue at least 10 or 11 feet in height. Both temples seem to have been wilfully destroyed, the interior marble columns, even, being broken in small pieces. Plans of both have been made by Lieut Porcher. Inclosure No 1 is a tracing of the Plan of the Larger and more perfect of the Temples.* [14]

On the 31st we removed the whole party to the neighbourhood of our former excavations at the Temple of Aesculapius. [15]

The Eastern half of the cella of this Temple paved with mosaic, was formerly cleared out by us only to the level of the pavement. We therefore employed one party in digging under this, and the remainder in excavating a mass

---

[9] S & P (1864) Pls. 54-55.

[10] S & P (1864) Pl. 55; Temple of Zeus.

[11] S & P no. 112; Reg. 61 11-27, 162.

[12] S & P inscriptions nos 6-7 Pls. 78-79; B.M. inscription 1053.

[13] S & P no. 116; Reg. 61 11-27, 54.

[14] S & P (1864) Pl. 55; Temple of Zeus. **Note:** S & P no. 113; Reg. 61 11-27, 98 small seated enthroned figure from Temple of Zeus – Pesce found a similar figure (PESCE (1949) Fig. 11a).

[15] Temple of Apollo.

of ruins around the north east angle of the Temple and a small temple-like building about 50 yards to the Westwards. [16]

In the Cella of the Temple, under the mosaic pavement, we found the following objects.

1. *An inscription on marble built into a recent wall No 18 of Inclosure No 2*
2. *A small female head of good style and perfect preservation.*
3. *A bronze head life size (Photograph No 1 Inclosure No 3) This head which is perfect was found at a depth of 11 feet beneath the pavement among a number of fragments of bronze work, including small horses heads a man on horseback etc. all of which are very much injured as if by fire.* [17] *The head however, as Your Lordship will see by the photograph, is in very good condition* [**Pl. 34**].
4. *A female head life size in marble (Photograph No 2). This was found about two or three feet under the pavement.*
5. *Inscriptions nos. 20 and 21 of Inclosure No 2, the former on a piece of Architrave of sandstone the latter on the face of a marble pedestal.*
6. *A few plain terra cotta lamps and some gold leaf.*

This half of the Cella seems to have been converted for the purposes in Byzantine times, judging by the quality of the mosaic. The space between the pavement and the rock, a depth of about 12 feet, has been built up of parts of the original temple such as the interior columns etc. into small passages and chambers like cellars. In some places these were in two storeys. We shall finish this part of the excavations today.

Among the ruins around the N.E. angle of the peristyle, we have found at various depths the following objects.

1. *A number of small heads some of which are photographed in No 3-.*[**Pl. 36**]
2. *Inscriptions Nos 2, 15, 16, 17, & 19 of Inclosure No 2.*
3. *A small nude statue of Bacchus (Photograph No 4.)* [**Pl. 37**]
4. *Two draped statuettes male and female (Photograph No 5).* [**Pl. 38**]
5. *A colossal draped statue (female) of excellent style and in a good state of preservation. It is broken in two, but the parts will, I believe, be found to fit almost exactly. We got first the upper, then the lower part & lastly the head. The statue altogether is 8 feet in height. The inclosed photographs Nos.6, 7*

[16] S & P no. 41; Reg. 61 11-27, 93 found in this building.

[17] The small horses' heads could possibly have come from the helmet of a statue of Athena. It seems likely that the fragments Smith describes could represent a hidden cache of pilfered bronze.

& 8 will give Your Lordship a good idea of its present appearance. [**Pls. 39-41**]

6. *A statue rather larger than life of an old man, the head of which I inclose a photograph, was found two days ago. We found the body of the statue only this morning, so that I am unable to send a photograph of it by this opportunity. Your Lordship will however, be able to judge of the whole by the inclosed photograph of the head (Photograph No 9). For distinctions sake we will call it the Statue of a Philosopher.* [**Pl. 43**]

7. *A female draped statue of a huntress, perhaps Diana or Cyrene. It is rather smaller than life. The style is good but peculiar being quite different from that of any of the other statues. It is all but perfect, the right fore-arm being the only part wanting. The surface is in very good condition, and the head is without a scratch. The drapery is gathered up by a double girdle so as to fall only to the knee. On the pedestal to the right of the figure a hound is sitting on his haunches.* [18] *I shall not have time to photograph it so as to send your Lordship a copy by this opportunity.* [**Pl. 45**]

8. *A female seated figure rather smaller than life.* [**Pl. 44**] *It is nearly perfect, wanting only the hands and one of the feet. It is very interesting on account of its style, which seems to be a mixture of Greek and Egyptian, the face having the beauty and expression of the Greek, while the body has the mathematical and precise stiffness of the Egyptian. It is almost a copy of a Colossal seated figure which was lying near it above ground but which we have also removed to our tomb. It is the statue mentioned by Beechey as probably Diana. We have found, however, an inscription on the base, the first line of which is as follows: –* [19]

[upper half of first 6 characters broken away] ΑΡΧΙΠΠΑΝΠΤΟΛΕΜΑΙΟΥ

This I read Αρχιππαν Πτολεμαιου, *and conclude accordingly that the statue is that of a female named Archippa or Archippe of the family of the Ptolemies. It is very much broken, the upper part being altogether wanting* [**Pl. 42**].

The girdle which encircles the waist of the smaller one is coloured on both edges with a narrow stripe of bright vermilion. The statue is in two parts and has been so originally [**Pl. 44**] *Close by it we found a square marble pedestal bearing on one face the inscription* ΤΕΙΣΩΝΙΑΣΟΝΟΣ [20] *Another pedestal also very near it has the following inscription:* [21] *(Not quite cleared out when I was*

---

[18] An identical figure, found near the Odeon at Tolmeta, is now in Tolmeta Museum, Reg.no. 27/35/M/T.

[19] Transcript S & P (1864), 75. Seated statue left by Tomb of Residence October 1861; (Vaux (1862), 416). See Chapter 7 n. 19.

[20] S & P inscription no. 4 Pl. 77; *S.E.Cir* no. 61.

[21] S & P inscription no. 12 Pl. 81; B.M. inscription 1056.

obliged to close this letter). I hope to send Your Lordship photographs of this statue the large seated one (Archippe), the Philosopher and the huntress, by next opportunity [**Pls. 42-43, 45**].

In the small temple like building to the Westward we have found

1. *A small seated statuette* [22]
2. *A head about life-size somewhat broken. It seems to be a portrait* [**Pl. 35**].
3. *Two small heads, one of which is peculiar, the eyes being separate and made to fit into the sockets.* [23] *It is the one on the right of the group of small heads in Photograph No 3* [**Pl. 36**].

Inclosure No 1 [24] *contains a tracing of Lieut. Porcher's plan of the large Temple near the Stadium –*

Inclosure No 2 contains copies of the inscriptions we have discovered hitherto, and of which we have impressions on paper.

Inclosure No 3 contains nine photographs numbered on the back the subjects being as follows: –

No.1 Bronze head from Temple of Aesculapius [**Pl. 34**].
No. 2 Female head, life-size, from the same [**Pl. 35**].
No. 3 Group of small heads from the Temple of Aesculapius and the vicinity [**Pl. 36**].
No. 4 Small statue of Bacchus [**Pl. 37**]
No. 5 Two statuettes [**Pl. 38**].
No. 6 Upper part of Colossal female statue from near the Temple of Aesculapius [**Pl. 39**].
No. 7 Lower part of Do. – [**Pl. 40**]
No. 8 Head of Do. separate on a larger scale [**Pl. 41**].
No. 9 Head of the statue of a Philosopher [**Pl. 43**].

I have the honour to be my Lord,
Your Lordships most obedient humble Servant,
R.M. Smith, Lt. R.E.

Source: [Original Letters and Papers Vol. LXXI Sept-Dec 1861 fols.142-145 (B.M.stamp P.9594 18 Oct 1861; copied 9th November 1861)]

[22] Reg. 61 11-27, 93; Huskinson no. 118.
[23] S & P no. 23; Reg. 61 11-27, 128.
[24] S & P (1864) Pl. 55; Temple of Zeus.

My dear Sir,

I wrote to you on the 3rd ult. giving an account of our proceedings up till that time. I added a postscript at Benghazi before I left to return to Cyrene. I hope my letter reached you in safety. On the way back to Cyrene I lost one of the blacks in an attack on the caravan by one of the Bedouin tribes whose district we were passing through at the time. Their object I suppose was to sell him as a slave. I reached Cyrene with 28, however, so that we have had a working force of 36.

For an account of our operations I am obliged to refer you to my report to Lord John Russell of this date. While in the act of writing today a Courier arrived from Benghazi with letters. He returns at once and I cannot prevail on him to remain here a day to give me time to finish my letters. As another opportunity may not occur for some time I have thought it better to send off my report to Lord John Russell at once especially as I have no doubt His Lordship will send you a copy. I inclose, however, duplicates of the photographs as you may have to refer to them and therefore wish to retain them. Just as I finished the report I was told that another large statue had made its appearance. It is not yet cleared out and I have not had time to visit the excavations so that I have no idea what it may turn out to be. I hope it will prove to be something good.

*We have now in our tomb four large statues, viz the one of the King [**Pl. 25**] left behind by the "Assurance", the two female ones of which I sent you photographs, [**Pls. 30-32**] and the last large female one. I think you will be much pleased with it. The photographs will give you a pretty good idea of what it is like. [**Pls. 39-41**] We have also the other smaller statues mentioned in my report, and Beecheys large seated statue. [**Pl. 42**] We have besides a number of inscriptions, and the three small statues left by the "Assurance". I am afraid that even with two trips of three waggons we shall not be able to take everything away when the ship comes. If obliged to leave anything we will leave the inscriptions and Beechey's statue inasmuch as we have impressions of all the inscriptions and a smaller perfect statue nearly a copy of the large one. I have inclosed in the Report to the Foreign Office a rough copy of all the inscriptions we have hitherto found.*

We shall finish our excavations near the Temple of Aesculapius in a few days. I hope our future fields may prove as productive, although that is hardly to be expected.

We get on very well with the Arabs although there are perpetual difficulties and "rows" to settle. Yesterday for instance they said they would shoot the blacks if they continued digging where we had placed them. This of course may mean anything, or more probably nothing, but the blacks, formerly slaves, are very credulous and timid, hence the difficulties. The Arabs have all sorts of rumours about the overthrow of European influence and a return to the "good old times" of fanatical Mussulmanism by the new Sultan.

The inclosed photographs, 9 in number are numbered on the back, and are as follows.

No. 1 Bronze Head from T. of Aesculapius. [**Pl.34**]
No. 2 Female head, life size from Do. [**Pl. 35**]
No. 3 Group of small heads from Do. & vicinity. [**Pl. 36**]
No. 4 Small statue of Bacchus from near T. of Aescul. [**Pl. 37**]
No. 5 Two Statuettes from Do. [**Pl. 38**]
No. 6 Upper part of Colossal female Statue from Do [**Pl. 39**]
No. 7 Lower part of Do. [**Pl. 40**]
No. 8 Head of Do. on a larger scale. [**Pl. 41**]
No. 9 Head of another statue rather larger than life found this morning. [**Pl. 43**]

Now that we have a large number of men Denison is of the greatest use. He is particularly painstaking and attentive. I hope you will excuse the haste with which I have been obliged to write.

I am my dear Sir
Yours Most Sincerely
R.M. Smith

Source: [Original Letters and Papers Vol. LXX June-Aug 1861 fol. 390 (B.M.stamp P. 9424, 12 Oct. 1861; copied 12 Oct. 1861)]

The following letter to General Burgoyne, although similar in content, nevertheless contains some additional information, particularly among the selection of photographs enclosed, as some of these were not sent to Lord Russell or Newton. A later annotation states: *'Photo No 1 Sent to Mr Newton 19/11/72'*.

SMITH to BURGOYNE – August 20th 1861

My dear General
I wrote to you in the beginning of July before starting for Benghazi. After collecting a number of workmen, I returned with them to Cyrene. On the way my caravan was attacked by one of the tribes, and one of the blacks carried off to be sold as a slave. I afterwards found out who they were and reported the affair to the Vice Consul of Benghazi. It is very improbable however that any

thing will be done by the authorities as they want both the will and the power, the latter especially.

The men I brought made our number up to 36 altogether. We have employed them every day in excavating in different parts of the City.

We first finished the large Temple near the Stadium which we were clearing out when I wrote last. At the same time we excavated the other smaller Temple near it. Both of them seem to have been wilfully destroyed before they fell into ruins, as we found even the marble Columns with which the interior was decorated broken in small fragments.

In each Temple we found a large head,[25] *both of which however were much broken. In the Pronaos of the larger Temple we also found two long inscriptions on marble, one consisting of 58 lines,*[26] *and the other in double columns of 23.*[27] *They record the names and donations of contributors to the building of the Temple but afford no clue to the discovery of the Divinity to whom it was consecrated.*

After finishing the Temple we employed the men in turning over the ground where the two female statues were found of which I sent you photographs [**Pls. 30-32**]. *We wished if possible to get the heads, but were unsuccessful in our search.*

We then moved the men to the neighbourhood of the Temple of Aesculapius on the platform in front of the fountain. To the North and East of the Temple and very near it there was a heap of ruins. I am doubtful whether they belonged to the Temple itself, to a building connected with it within the peribolus, or to a separate structure altogether. Most of the men were employed at this place. The remainder we divided between a small Temple-like building at the west end of the platform,[28] *and the Eastern half of the Cella of the Temple of Aesculapius.*[29]

The Cella was divided by a Byzantine wall running nearly across the middle. To the East of this wall when digging there some months ago, we came upon a Mosaic pavement 3 or 4 feet beneath the surface, and went no deeper. We now however thought it desirable to dig beneath this pavement. As it evidently belonged to a Byzantine building into which the original Temple had been converted, we thought it probable that some of the Sculptures of the Temple might exist beneath it, especially as it was considerably above the level of the floor of the Western half of the Cella.

---

[25] S & P no. 116; Reg. 61 11-27, 54; Small temple.
   S & P no. 112; Reg. 61 11-27, 162; Large temple (Temple of Zeus)
[26] S & P inscription no. 6 Pls. 78-79; Large temple.
[27] S & P inscription no. 7; Reg. 61 11-27, 38; B.M. inscription 1053; Large temple.
[28] Possibly Artemisium.
[29] Temple of Apollo, eastern half of cella. Western half, Smith's Despatch 1 of 23rd Feb 1861.

The following is a list of the things we found while digging in the above mentioned places.

In the small Temple-like building at the West end of the platform we found: –

1. *A small seated statuette* [30]
2. *A male head life size evidently a portrait.*
3. *Two small heads one of which is peculiar, the eyes being separate and made to fit into the sockets* [**Pl. 52**]

In the Eastern half of the Cella of the Temple of Aesculapius, under the Mosaic pavement, we found

1. *Three inscriptions of which I have impressions on paper.*
2. *A small female head of good style & perfect preservation.*
3. *A bronze head life size. This head which is perfect was found at a depth of 11 feet beneath the pavement, among a number of fragments of bronze work, including a man on horseback, small horses heads etc. All of which were very much injured, as if by fire. The head however is in good condition.*
4. *A female head life size found two or three feet under the pavement.*
5. *A few plain terra cotta lamps and a little gold leaf.*

Among the ruins to the north & east of the Temple we found:

1. *A number of small heads*
2. *Several inscriptions*
3. *A small nude statue of Bacchus.*
4. *Two draped statuettes male and female.*
5. *A Colossal draped Statue (female) of excellent style, and in good state of preservation. It is 8ft. in height & is perfect with the exception of the fore-arms which are wanting. It is broken in two but the parts will be found, I believe, to fit exactly.*
6. *A Statue of an old man perhaps the portrait of a philosopher.*
7. *A female draped statue of a huntress, somewhat smaller than life and all but perfect.*
8. *A female seated rather smaller than life & also nearly perfect* [**Pl. 44**]. *It seems a mixture of the Egyptian Style & the Greek. It is nearly a Copy of a large seated figure which was lying near it above ground but which we have also removed to our tomb. It is the statue mentioned by Beechey as prob-*

---

[30] S & P no. 41; Reg. 61 11-27, 93; Huskinson no. 118.

ably Diana, but from the remains of an inscription on the base I find it to be a female of the family of the Ptolemies of the name, as far as I can make it out, Archippe. [31] *The girdle of the smaller statue, found underground is coloured on both edges with a narrow stripe of bright vermilion. The end of the Sleeve has a serrated edge of the same colour. The bands of the sandals are also coloured red.*

9. *Two heads male and female, the latter rather larger than life. In both, the back of the head is cut off as if they had been intended to stand out in relief from a plane such as a wall, into which they may have been built.*

After finishing the excavation of the above places, we brought down to our tomb a colossal statue of one of the Ptolemies in armour [32] *of which particular mention is made by Beechey. It was lying above ground near the centre of the city. We dug all round the place, where it lay in the hope of finding the head but without success.*

We have within the last few days tried several sites in different parts of the city but hitherto without finding any thing. I have no letters yet regarding the ship which we expect next month. We now have in our tomb 7 large statues viz. the one left by the "Assurance" the two female [33] *ones of which I sent you photographs, the Colossal female* [34] *one mentioned above, Archippe,* [35] *Ptolemy,* [36] *and the Philosopher.* [37] *There are also the smaller statues in the above list of discoveries and three other left by the "Assurance" besides 12 inscriptions* [38] *and a number of smaller objects. Even with three trips of three Waggons we should not be able to take the inscriptions and as I fear the ship could not remain longer than to give time for two trips we shall be obliged to leave all the inscriptions and some of the least valuable of the Sculptures behind.*

Should nothing occur to alter my present intention, I shall return to Malta

---

[31] Left by Tomb of Residence in October 1861; Smith's Despatch 6 of August 11th 1861 Edinburgh photo NMS ACC 9565 fol. 6-29. See Chapter 7 n. 19.

[32] S & P no.108; Reg. 61 11-27, 35; (BEECHEY (1828), 527, 544; PACHO (1827) Pl. 59). Edinburgh photo NMS ACC 9565 fol. 2-12.

[33] S & P no. 14; Reg. 61 11-27,136 (head), 52 (torso); S & P no. 37; Reg. 61 1-27, 41; Album photo 22/5.

[34] S & P no. 32; Reg. 61 11-27, 32.

[35] Left by Tomb of Residence in October 1861; Smith's Despatch 6 of August 11th 1861 Edinburgh photo NMS ACC 9565 fol. 6-29. See Chapter 7 n. 19.

[36] S & P no. 108; Reg. 61 11-27, 35; (BEECHEY (1828), 527, 544; PACHO (1827) Pl. 59). Edinburgh photo NMS ACC 9565 fol. 2-12.

[37] S & P no. 34; Reg. 61 11-27, 37.

[38] S & P inscriptions nos. 13, 24, left near Tomb of Residence in October 1861. Inscriptions sent to England: Reg. 61 11-27, 38, 46, 49, 47, 48, 30; B.M. inscriptions nos. 1053-1058, 1061. (1054 previously sent to England June 7 1861, Reg. 61 7-25, 11).

in the ship after she has embarked the statues. Several considerations induce me to do so. I believe we have already got the greater part of the valuable sculptures that existed here. Doubtless others might still be discovered, but as we have dug all the prominent sites, and some of them without result, further excavation must be more or less indiscriminate. Again, if we remained at all, it must be for a period of at least 8 or 9 months, as no vessel could come to this coast before May. In Winter, the ground is so covered with the Crops of the Arabs that the space left open for digging is very limited, and the weather is such that work cannot go on without frequent interruption. There would also I believe be considerable difficulty in getting workmen as the blacks, most of whom are fresh from the interior, cannot stand the severe cold of Cyrene. By remaining 8 or 9 months without an adequate return, the cost of the sculptures already discovered would of course be proportionately increased.

I have not attempted to give you any description of the sculptures, as the photographs which I now enclose will give you a more better idea of their style and condition. They are numbered on the back as usual and are as follows: –

1. Bronze Head from Temple of Aesculapius. [**Pl. 34**]
2. Female Head from Do. [**Pl. 35**]
3. Group of small heads from Temple of Aesculapius and vicinity. [**Pl. 36**]
4. Small Statue of Bacchus from the ruins near the same temple. [**Pl. 37**]
5. Two statuettes Do. [**Pl. 38**]
6. Upper part of Colossal female statue Do. [**Pl. 39**]
7. Lower part of Do. [**Pl. 40**]
8. Head of Do. separate on a larger scale. [**Pl. 41**]
9. Statue of the Philosopher, and large seated figure, Archippe. [**Pl. 42**]
10. Head of the Philosopher, separate. [**Pl. 43**]
11. Smaller seated female statue from the ruins near the Temple of Aesculapius. [**Pl. 44**]
12. Statue of a huntress perhaps Diana or Cyrene Do. [**Pl. 45**]
13. Fragment of Statue of a hunter Do. [**Pl. 46**]
14. Female Head Do. [**Pl. 47**]
15. Colossal statue one of the Ptolemies. [**Pl. 48**]

I am,
My dear General
Yours most faithfully
(signed) R.M. Smith

Source: [Original Letters and Papers Vol. LXXI Sept-Dec 1861 fols.410-412 (B.M.stamp P.9287 10 Oct 1861; copied 12 Oct and 14 Dec 1861)]

PROVENANCE OF FINDS

(Numbers on left reflect numbering in the correspondence)

Despatch 6

Cella, 'Temple of Aesculapius':

1. <u>Inclosure No. 2</u> S & P inscription 24 Pl. 84; Smith's letter August 5th
3. S & P no.3; Reg. 61 11-27, 13; B.M. Cat. of Bronzes no. 268
5. S & P (1864), 42 inscriptions; Porcher letter June 7th 1861
6. Lamps B.M. Reg. 1861 11-27, 5-8 (Bailey Q1881, Q1882, Q1878, Q1877); Porcher letter June 7th 1861 Case no.21
   Gold Leaf Reg. 1861 11-27, 12 (missing); Porcher letter June 7th 1861 Case no. 21

'Ruins around N.E. angle of peristyle':

1. S & P no.22; Reg. 61 11-27, 127; S & P no.23; Reg. 61 11-27, 128; S & P no.24; Reg. 61 11-27, 129; S & P no. 25 trans. La Porte 1870, Mendel 388. Album photo 22/2
2. S & P inscriptions nos. 8, 9, 11, 12, 13 *'found in ruins'* Pls. 80-81; inscriptions nos. 2, 4 *'found in some ruins'* Pl. 77. **Note**: S & P inscription no. 13 is described in Smith's Despatch 1 of Feb 23 1861 and most probably represents the original no. 2 in the above list of items in Inclosure No 2
3. S & P no.36; Reg. 61 11-27, 27, trans. Edinburgh Reg.1886.597. Album photo 22/3 with head of S & P no. 45, Reg. 61 11-27, 92
4. S & P nos.14, 37; Album photos 21/5 and 22/5
5. S & P no. 32; Album photos 21/6 & 7 and 22/4
6. S & P no.34; Album photo 21/8
7. S & P no. 33; Reg. 61 11-27, 159 trans. La Porte 1870, Mendel 619
8. S & P no. 35; Reg. 61 11-27, 36; Edin. photo NMS ACC 9565 fol. 5-25

'Small Temple-like building to the Westward':

1. S & P no.41; Reg. 61 11-27, 93
3. S & P no.23; Reg. 61 11-27, 128 Album photo 22/2

Burgoyne letter

'Small Temple-like building at the West end of the platform':

1. S & P no.41; Reg. 61 11-27, 93
3. S & P no. 23; Reg. 61 11-27, 128 Album photo 22/2

Cella, 'Temple of Aesculapius':

1. S & P inscription no. 5 Pl. 77 Reg. 61 11-27, 46; B.M.inscription 1055
   Note: two other inscriptions could be S & P inscriptions no. 10 Pl. 80 and no. 24 Pl. 84
3. S & P no. 3; Reg. 61 11-27, 13; B.M. Cat. of Bronzes no. 268
5. Porcher letter June 7th 1861 Case no. 21

'Ruins to north and east of the Temple':

1. S & P no. 22; Reg. 61 11-27, 127; S & P no. 23; Reg. 61 11-27, 128; S & P no. 24; Reg. 61 11-27, 129; S & P no. 25 trans. La Porte 1870, Mendel 388. Album photo 22/2
2. Probably those mentioned in Smith's Despatch 6 of August 11th 1861 Inclosure 2
3. S & P no. 36 (torso); Reg. 61 11-27, 27; trans. Edinburgh Museum, Reg. 1886.597. Album photo 23/3
   S & P no.45 (head); Reg. 61 11-27, 92
4. S & P nos.14 and 37; Reg. 61 11-27, 136 and 52. Album photo 21/5
5. S & P no. 32; Reg. 61 11-27, 32
6. S & P no. 34; Reg. 61 11-27, 37
7. S & P no. 33; Reg. 61 11-27, 159; trans. La Porte 1870. (Mendel 619)
8. S & P no. 35; Reg. 61 11-27, 36. Album photo missing. Edinburgh photo NMS ACC 9569 fol. 5-25
9. S & P nos. 34, 39; Reg. 61 11-27, 37 and 61

Photographs:
1. S & P no. 3; Bronze 268 Reg. 61 11-27, 13, see note in this Despatch [**Pl. 34**]
2. S & P no.39; Reg. 61 11-27, 61 [**Pl. 35**]
3. S & P no. 22; Reg. 61 11-27, 127
   S & P no.23; Reg. 61 11-27, 128
   S & P no.24; Reg. 61 11-27, 129
   S & P no. 25 trans. La Porte 1870, Mendel 388. Album photo 22/2. [**Pl. 36**]
4. S & P no.36 (torso); Reg. 61 11-27, 27, trans. Edinburgh Mus. Reg. 1886.597. Album photo 23/3. [**Pl. 37**]
   S & P no.45 (head); Reg. 61 11-27, 92
5. S & P nos.14, 37; Reg. 61 11-27, 52, 136 and 41
   S & P nos.14; Reg. 61 11-27, 136 (head), 52 (torso) and
   S & P no.37; Reg. 61 11-27, 41. Album photo 22/5. [**Pl. 38**]
6. S & P no. 32; Reg. 61 11-27, 37. Album photo 22/4. [**Pl. 39**]
7. S & P no. 32; Reg. 61 11-27, Album photo 22/4. [**Pl. 40**]
8. S & P no. 32; Reg. 61 11-27, Album photo 22/4. [**Pl. 41**]
9. S & P no. 34 and Archippe; Reg. 61 11-27, 37. Edinburgh photo NMS ACC 9565 fol. 6-29. Archippe left by Tomb of Residence October 1861; see Smith's Despatch 6 of August 11th 1861 [**Pl. 42**]
10. S & P no. 34; Reg. 61 11-27, 34. Album photo 21/8 [**Pl. 43**]

11. S & P no. 35; Reg. 61 11-27, 36. Album photo missing. Edinburgh photo NMS ACC 9565 fol.5-25. [**Pl. 44**]

12. S & P no.33; Reg. 61 11-27, 159, trans. La Porte 1870. Mendel 619. Album photo missing [**Pl. 45**]

13. S & P no.80; Reg. 61 11-27, 149, trans. La Porte 1870. Mendel 1111. Album photo missing [**Pl. 46**]

14. S & P no.39; Reg. 61 11-27, 61. Album photo 21/2 [**Pl. 47**]

15. S & P no.108; Reg. 61 11-27, 35. Album photo missing [**Pl. 48**]

Note: Photographic record similar to that in Smith's Despatch 6 of August 11th 1861 and Album photos, pp. 21-22.

Plates:

34 Rosenbaum pp. 35-36, no. 1, Pl. V

35 Huskinson p. 71, no. 135, Pl. 51

36 Huskinson pp. 29, 67, 9, nos. 57, 125, 16, Pls. 23, 49, 6; Mendel 388; Huskinson p. 29, no. 56, Pl. 23

37 Huskinson pp. 18-19, no. 34, Pl. 12; Thorn J (1998), 563 Tav. I-II (showing wrong head)

38 Huskinson pp. 60-62, nos. 109, 112, Pls. 42, 44

39-41 Rosenbaum pp.56-57, no. 45, Pl. XXXII,4 (head), Pl. XXXII,2 (statue); Huskinson pp. 41-42, no. 72, Pl. 33

42 (left) Rosenbaum pp .46-48, no. 23, Pl. XXVI,3; Huskinson p. 36, no. 67, Pl. 28; (right) Thorn J (1998), 565 Tav. III,1; Thorn D (1999), 69-76, Figs. 1-6)

43 Rosenbaum pp. 46-48, no. 23, Pl. XIX (head); Huskinson p. 36, no. 67, Pl. 28 (head)

44 Huskinson p. 64, no. 117, Pl. 45

45 Mendel 619

46 Huskinson pp. 13-14, no. 24, Pl. 8

47 Rosenbaum p. 45, no. 19, Pl. XVII; Huskinson p. 67, no. 126, Pl. 49

48 Rosenbaum p. 77, no. 100, Pl. LXIII,1; Huskinson pp. 39-40, no. 70, Pl. 29

49-50 Tomb of Residence area

51 Rosenbaum pp. 95-96, no. 168, Pl. LXXV,3; Huskinson pp. 61-62, no. 111, Pl. 43

52 (centre) Rosenbaum p. 60, no. 54, Pl. XXXVII,1-2; Huskinson p. 66, no. 122, Pl. 47

53 Huskinson pp. 44, 42, 46 nos. 77, 73, 81, Pls. 50, 30, 32

54 Rosenbaum p. 67, no. 76, Pl. XLIX,1-2; Huskinson pp. 46-47, no. 81, Pl. 32

55 Rosenbaum p. 57, no. 46, Pl. XXXIII,1-2; Huskinson p. 42, no. 73, Pl. 30

56 Rosenbaum p. 58, no. 49, Pl. XXXV,1-2; Huskinson p. 44, no. 77, Pl. 50

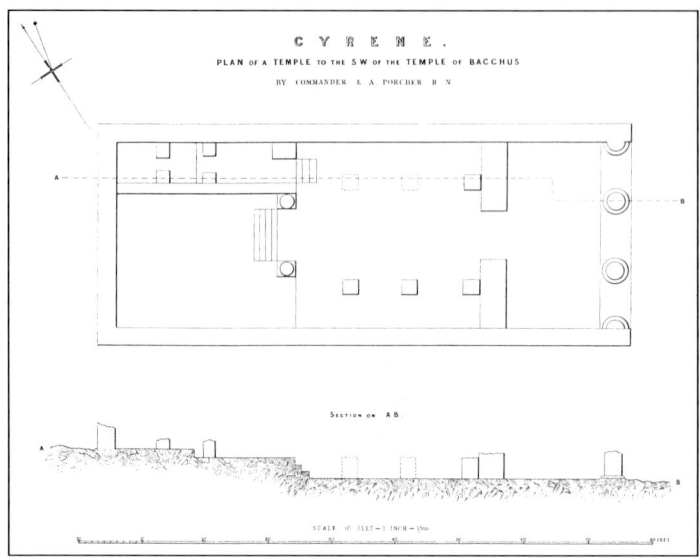

FIG. 14 – Plan of the Temple of Venus situated to the South-West of the Temple of Bacchus.

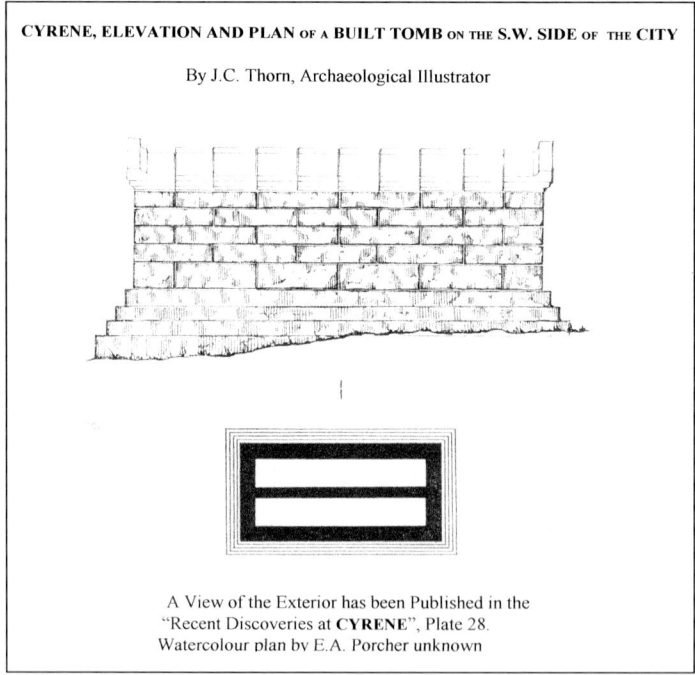

FIG. 15 – Plan of a Built Tomb on the South-West Side of Cyrene.

Fig. 16 – Ruins of the Christian City of Cyrene.

137

IX. WITHOUT A SIGN OF A SHIP...

As the summer's fiercest heat began to diminish, and the margin of time within which the embarkation of the statues could safely be carried out grew shorter, the lieutenants began to map out contingency plans in case they and their party were stranded in the Cyrenaica over the winter. Their Maltese servants, however, from the superior vantage point of the upper terrace *'stood gazing at the sea from morning to night, and raised a shout of joy whenever they detected the slightest speck on the distant horizon.'* Because of Cyrene's altitude, a very great expanse of sea is visible, which appears like a high blue wall beyond the irregular line of the plateau edge. On some days, due no doubt to a trick of light and atmosphere, the sea seems incredibly near, with a sheen like watered silk where the wind has ruffled its surface, while on others it appears more remote. Sometimes it is obscured by a shifting mist, and one has the impression of a line of islands in the distance – like a mirage, but more probably the true horizon seen between low cloud banks. However, under normal conditions any ship on a panorama of at least thirty miles of sea would be seen by the eager eyes of the Maltese, and might remain in their field of vision for the better part of a day, but the vessel promised for September 1st had not made its appearance.

SMITH to NEWTON – September 14th 1861

My dear Newton

Here we are the evening of the 14th of September without a sign of a ship. If she does not make her appearance in a day or two I fear there will not be time to embark the statues before the bad weather sets in when of course, on this open coast, it will be impossible. For the last fortnight we have employed nearly all the blacks in improving the road from this to Marsa Souza. It is now all but finished, so that we are in perfect readiness for the arrival of a ship. We have no news whatever from Europe since the "Scourge" came here with Dennison on the 18th of June, so that we are quite in the dark about every-

thing. I have been laid up with rather a severe attack of fever, and am now picking up my strength again slowly. I had first an attack of continuous fever for three days. This went off, and just as I was beginning to get out again I had a relapse from the effects of which I am now recovering. I hope to be all right again in a few days.

*We have found some things since I wrote last. At the building where the Ptolemy [**Pl. 48**] was found we discovered a colossal draped female statue [**Pl. 51**] of good style and very perfect but without the head. We found also three heads, one colossal male one, another life-size do. with the eyes separate, and made to fit into into the sockets and one smaller one [**Pl. 52**]. We found also three busts one of a girl [**Pl. 54**] and two colossal male ones [**Pls. 55-56**]. All three are perfect or very nearly so. We found also several inscriptions of which I have impressions.* [1] *The building in which all the above were found is I think, a palace. There are a number of rooms or apartments most of which were floored and veneered with marble.*

I do not think it would be advisable to remain here during the winter, for several reasons, the chief of which are two: It would be all but, if not quite impossible to get workmen to remain, in fact, they are all going off even now; secondly, the ground is so thoroughly occupied by the Arabs with their crops, that after the rain begins, when they commence sowing, there are few spots left which are at all likely places, and which we have not already dug. Besides, I think we have already got the marrow of the place. We are therefore beginning to think about our plans for the future, in the event of the ship not coming. Our present idea is to pack up all the heads and small things and take them with us to Benghazi when the rains begin. The statues we will either bury deep in the earth or build up in a chamber of our tomb, getting our man Amor to live here as guard over them, paying him so much a month. The stone trucks we would leave at the Castle of Ghegheb in charge of the Mudir. The winter we would spend in digging for vases, etc in the Cemetery at Benghazi, and if possible, also have a try at Teuchira and Ptolemais. A ship coming in May would pick us up at Benghazi when we would return here via Marsa Souza and remove the statues. All this is, of course, dependent on the ship's non arrival as I do not think the above programme tempting enough to keep us here if the ship does come.

It will take three trips of three waggons to remove all the statues, and even then the inscriptions will have to be left. It is impossible to calculate on less than five weeks for this work even with our new improved road. So even if the

[1] S & P inscription no. 17 Pl. 82.
   S & P inscription no. 18 Pl. 83.
   S & P inscription no. 21 Pl. 83.
   S & P inscription no. 23 Pl. 83.

ship comes to-morrow there will not be a day to spare. I am beginning to get rather anxious on the subject.

The diabolical thing here in making arrangements is the utter want of news. As I told you it is three months since we had a single letter, and then they came by a "fluke". When you write again, address R.E. office Malta. If I am not there my letters will be forwarded.

Dennison has been very useful and I dare say when it comes to packing he will be still more so. I write in a great hurry, as usual, an Arab having come in to say that he is going to Benghazi.

> *Remember me to Mr. Panizzi, and believe me*
> *Ever yours Mo: Sincerely*
> *R.M. Smith.*

Source: [Original Letters and Papers Vol. LXXI Sept-Dec 1861 fols. 40-41 (B.M.stamp none)]

The building in the city which Smith refers to as a palace was a truly magnificent structure, known now as the House of Jason Magnus. Two of its rooms have floors of the best quality opus sectile – coloured marble veneer cut into diverse shapes and laid in intricate patterns, making a harmonious whole. The other rooms and linking passages are paved with mosaic, one floor showing the Four Seasons and another illustrating the story of Theseus, Ariadne and the Minotaur.[2] Besides being a wealthy citizen living in beautiful surroundings, Jason was a man of epicurean tastes: the range of statuary found in his house, probably displayed in the wide corridor outside the triclinium, suggests that he was a collector and a connoisseur. A short distance away was a temple where Smith and Porcher's excavations yielded so many statuettes of Venus and Cupid that it was impossible not to name it the Temple of Venus. Because their investigations there took place so late in their stay, they unfortunately left no written record of the proceedings.[3]

---

[2] WANIS (1996), 277-280 Figs. 1-4.

[3] The Temple of Venus has rubble foundations, on which sit six courses of ashlar, the uppermost forming the offset on which is a course of isodomic blocks L.1.14 W.0.86 H.0.45m, which have, cut in their upper surfaces, pry holes for manoeuvring them into position. Standing on this course is a double row of orthostats L.1.14 W.0.64 H.1.10m. The side nearer the city is terraced into the slope of the hill, while on the other the orthostats have tumbled outwards. At each side of the cella is a raised aisle bordered by four bases, not the three shown by Porcher, each consisting of two blocks. Beyond the return walls of the cella, much of the sanctuary is occupied by a large dais of isodomic work. The interior dimensions of the building are L.17.60 W.9.00, and the width of the sanctuary is 7.20m.

At last, two weeks after Smith's letter of 14th September was written, the overjoyed Maltese sighted H.M.S. 'Melpomene', a steam frigate with 51 guns, launched in 1857, which arrived to collect the second and final consignment of statuary. The ship's log records the sailmakers making dragbelts – which were canvas straps to go over the shoulders of the men pulling the wagons – and fitting gear *for the Expedition of Cyrene*,[4] and on 28th September a party of 94 seamen and 33 marines was landed by Captain Ewart to go up to Cyrene. They were preceded by a band of ten carpenters to assist Dennison, guarded by ten marines. Some of the bluejackets employed their spare time at Cyrene in a little excavation; their only recorded find was a charming little standing figure of a girl, which they named after their ship.[5]

By this time the whole of the ancient road had been repaired by Smith and Porcher's gang in attempts to protect the sculptures from too much jolting over the rock surface, to make the work of the wagon parties easier and to prevent damage to the wagons themselves, without which none of the large statues could have been moved. The work seems to have been successful, in that no fracturing of the statuary was reported, although the wagon wheels suffered from the journeys. Traces of the final descent of the road to Marsa Sousa had been discovered, where it wound round the contours of the steep hillsides at an easy slope, and this section was cleared of vegetation and quite major restoration work carried out, in places where the retaining wall had collapsed during the torrential winter rains and the road had been carried away.

Shortly before this, there had been an influx of semi-nomadic Arabs from the interior, who had encamped in the vicinity of Cyrene to water their flocks until winter, and were being an insidious nuisance in the background, calling out insults and trying to cause trouble. An incident which was not mentioned in any of the letters concerned the sailors' habit of bathing in the Apollo Fountain, which offended the natural modesty of the Arabs, and prevented their women from fetching water. A group of them began throwing stones at the bathers, and a marine fired some blank shots, intending to frighten them off. Not surprisingly, this had the opposite effect – the Arabs around the fountain set up an alarm call which brought hordes more swarming to the spot from afar, rather like vultures seeing others twenty miles away descending on prey. A serious disturbance was prevented only by a conference with the local sheikhs, with Smith and Porcher giving an undertaking that the sailors should use the fountain only at set times. Nevertheless, the multitude did not go away, but stayed in the area of

[4] PRO ADM 53/7576.
[5] S & P no. 122; Reg. 61 11-27, 24.

the Tomb of Residence and the fountain, and Smith and Porcher doubtless had an uneasy night.

Unfortunately Mohammed el Adouli, who would have had influence over the crowd, had struck his tents and returned to Benghazi, probably wishing to avoid the rains which begin in October on the Jebel, and without his intervention the very large number of camel-drivers which Smith and Porcher needed were able to be insolent and obstinate, even refusing to work altogether if arrangements were not to their liking. During the first two wagon trips a certain Sheikh Said put pressure on Smith, with demands for money under the guise of *'harbour dues'*. On this being refused, he lowered the sum requested, and when this was again refused he asked for some bullock skins which he could use. To this Smith agreed, but the following day the sheikh was back, complaining that the skins were not good enough, and claiming that he would not let the wagons pass without payment. Smith dug his heels in and *'ordered him to leave the tomb'*. Sheikh Said, muttering dire imprecations and giving Smith to understand that they would leave the country feet first, left and barricaded the road on the plateau for two days, cutting off Smith, at Cyrene, from Porcher, who was with the wagons and knew nothing about the bleak future which was promised him.

Smith called for two friendly sheikhs of the Haasa tribe and enlisted their help. They duly went to Sheikh Said and successfully ordered him to clear the road and go. However, the wily bird merely changed his position and waited for Porcher to come up from the coast, then entered the wagon party's camp and repeated his threats and demands. Porcher gave him short shrift, whereupon the sheikh and his men returned to Cyrene with an ultimatum for Smith, who also gave him fighting talk. The two friendly sheikhs were again called on, and again Sheikh Said was driven off, so that Porcher and the wagons could safely return – and learn what had happened. The lieutenants decided to cover their backs by telling the Mudir of Ghegheb of the situation, merely as a formality. As Smith was recovering from fever Porcher mounted his horse and rode to Ghegheb, where in the Mudir's absence he spoke to his deputy, who said he would send some letters to the sheikhs concerned.

Although Smith had decided at the end of the summer that they would leave on the next vessel which called, their departure date was brought forward by the trouble which was brewing with the local Arabs. It was thought best to cut their losses and make the third wagon trip the last, meaning that the statue of Archippe and several inscriptions would have to be abandoned, and the final packing of their personal baggage was a hurried affair, with the Bedouin, among whom nothing is wasted, hovering like hawks to pounce on coveted articles such as empty bottles and any other reusable items which were being left behind. The rest of their luggage was loaded on to camels, and departed as it had arrived.

According to the ship's log, the pinnace was sent ashore on the morning of 5th October to bring off the first statues, and a few days later, for some unrecorded misdemeanours, James Catton and George Ford were put in the cells for seven days, three of them on bread and water, and James Pitts received 48 lashes. Captain Spratt's paddle steamer H.M.S. 'Medina' arrived off Mersa Sousa on her surveying mission on the morning of 13th October. Poor Spratt had just missed Smith and Porcher when he called at Tolmeita in April and now, desperately wanting to visit Cyrene, he appeared as they were leaving. Had another trip with the wagons been practicable he would have achieved his desire, but the situation with the Arabs was considered to be explosive, and that afternoon the last of the statuary was brought aboard, together with the gear from the Cyrene working party, who had lost 28 haversacks, six seamen's bags and four 'belts', presumably the drag-belts mentioned above.

After the sailing of 'Melpomene' and before the safe arrival of the party in Malta there was a short period of alarm and speculation, due to a frantic, horrified telegram sent from the Vice Consul in Benghazi to Consul Herman in Tripoli. This message has not been found, but the telegrams it sparked off reflect its content, which must have been fed by a report brought from Cyrene by word of mouth. The story had been exaggerated along the way, and grew in the telling.

TELEGRAMS:

Col: Herman to Ant° Aquilina   *1861 Oct 17*

Requesting return of British subjects and protegés.

————————

Col: Herman to A. Aquilina   *1861 Oct 17*

Transmits order from the Pacha to Caimacam to send down to Cyrene the Cavalry in aid of Lieut. Smith's party.

————————

Col: Herman to Sir W. Fanshawe Martin, or   *1861*
Rear Admiral Codrington   *October 17*

Lieuts Smith and Porcher with a detachment from the man of war at Marsa Sousa have been attacked by the Arabs near Cyrene on their refusal to com-

ply with a demand made upon them for $1500. Two of the party were wounded and the rest closely invested at Ajn Chahat. The governor general has Telegraphed to the Caimacam of Benghazi to despatch all his disposable force to their relief and Mr. Aquilina H.M. Consul has been instructed likewise to report their position to the Officer Commanding the Man of War at Marza Sousa. Cyrene is 120 miles from Benghasi at least 4 Marches – This Intelligence has been received an hour ago from Benghasi.

––––––––––

Malta and Alexandria Government Telegraph

Dr Whitehouse Malta
    to Mr Aquilina Benghazi

Since transmitting the Government dispatch the 'Melpomene' has arrived having on board the two Officers whose lives were in danger at Cyrene – All further excavations – posponed [sic] –
– The Governor desires me to make You Acquainted with this without delay

                              Bengazi Station Octr 17 1861
                              (signed) Sam E. Phillips
                                    Superintendant

Source: [Public Record Office FO 160/79]

Aquilina must have telegraphed the news to Herman, and followed it up with a letter:[6]

                            Vice Consolato Britannico
                            Bengasi 21. Ottobre 1861.

Signore
    In seguito a ciò che prevenni a V.S. Illma collo mia Telegrafica de 17 Ott. alla voca qui spasso del sinistro avuti gl'Inglesi a Cyrene, al vostro ordine dello stesso Giorno, S.E. il Caimacan la spedizione della Cavalleria di cui ha potuto disporre,... alle stesse sera mi venne battuto Telegrafo per diretto dal Governo di Malta per mezzo di Dr. Whitehouse (che qui.... Copia) ho prevenuto a S.E. d'impedire l'invio delle .... gl'Officinali Arrivati a Malta, ma egli sembra

––––––––––

[6] My thanks go to Professor Mottola for tackling Aquilina's handwriting to give this reading.

che dietro gli Ordini avuti all'indomani dal Musin di Tripoly, lascio continua-
re le... ... onde investigare se hanno lasciato delle statue per necessita.

> *Ho l'onore d'essere d'*
> *V.S. Illma*
> *Ume & Obb. Servitore*
> *Ant. Aquilina*

Source: [PRO FO 160/79]

HERMAN to GOVERNOR OF MALTA – October 18th 1861

Transmits Copy of the Pacha's letter relative to the long stay on a barren place of Lieut Smith's party, where there is No Local Authority to protect them –
And requesting to know whether any Arabs were wounded –

Source: [PRO FO 160/2 fols. 2-3]

رتبتر   كياسنو   محب ولا تكارم   جنابدى

درنہ طرقترہ انفیظ اخراج املك اوزرہ تاریخندہ برك وبا مزو سكنماہ مقدم ایكی انكلیز لو مهندس درنہ طرقترہ عیتماانتمشد ایدی
منكور مهندس مسكوہ اولا بہ وحشی عبدردن بجزم مت طویل اقامت اتلكہ ورار شو قدرك منكور مهندسدن بوزیننی محلد حكومت
محیہ نلك منور لینزہ خلا برلا لیفندہ   مهندسدك بوقدہ اوزرہ مت اورلاہ اقا منهى وهكومنك ضبى اولهہ برہ عبدلر
بعضہ معاملارى بحاردۃ وقوعہ سب اولیفی وقت حكومت مسؤل اولمہ جعننك بانہ وسید ثأكید محبت اولمشدر
٢م ربیع الثانی سنہ ١٢٧٨

Traduction

> *Très illustre et honorable Monsieur*
> *il y a sept ou huit mois à partir de la date de cette lettre, deux ingénieurs an-*
> *glais se sont rendus aux environs de Derna pour y chercher et déterrer des anti-*
> *quités. Ces ingénieurs habitent depuis ce long temps au milieu des arabes sau-*
> *vages et nomades, et it faut remarquer que l'endroit où ils résident est privé de*
> *tout représentant de l'autorité locale. Pour ce motif, et comme les dits ingé-*
> *nieurs ont fait en ce lieu un si long séjour et se sont en quelques circonstances*
> *mélés des affaires de ces arabes sans en avertir l'autorité, s'ils ont occasionné*
> *quelque désagréable affaire, je m'empresse de vous prévenir que l'autorité n'en*
> *accepte pas la responsabilté, et je profite de cette occasion pour vous renouve-*
> *ler l'assurance de mon amitié.*
> *12 Bebi – ut – tuni 1278.*

Source: [Public Record Office FO 160/79].

My dear Newton

I have barely time to let you know of my arrival here yesterday in the "Melpomene" with 63 cases on board. They leave next week for England in the "Supply". We had great difficulty in getting away from Cyrene without bloodshed. The Arabs cut us off and wanted to levy black mail or kill us. I got the matter settled by a little diplomacy with the Sheikhs of other tribes who drove the enemy off. For this service Capt. Ewart was pleased to thank me and report the affair to the Admiral.

I got a passage for Dennison yesterday in the 'Himalaya' which was leaving the harbour as we entered it. It will save the expense of a passage. I had no time to settle his account before going, but I have made him no payment at all in money you may tell Panizzi. What I have paid for him for messing I do not yet know. He was employed every Sunday with us. Mr Panizzi may therefore pay him his 15/– a day for the whole time leaving the 2/6 to cover the expenses on his messing When I have made out how much they amount to, I will let Mr Panizzi know. Dennison was exceedingly useful at the packing up. We had 10 Carpenters from the ship.

A telegram came here from Tripoli yesterday to the effect that we were killed by the Arabs. Should it reach England you will know it is not correct.

I am still suffering from the effects of the Fever, I can hardly write I am so shaky. I was confined to bed nearly continuously for six weeks, and the Doctor of the "Melpomene" tells me it has left me with a liver for some time to come. [7]

Capt. Ewart was exceedingly kind in every way, and took the greatest pains in getting every thing done well. All his arrangements were excellent, so that we made three trips of three wagons, and the ship was only three weeks away from Malta. He was at the Xanthus work before. All the men, too, exerted themselves in the most laudable manner and their good behaviour and discipline enabled me in a great measure to get the party off without serious loss of life, and loss of statues.

I hope to be home and see you in the course of a few weeks.

Yours ever sincerely
R.M. Smith

Source: [Original Letters and Papers Vol. LXXI Sept-Dec 1861 fol.146 (B.M.stamp P.9882 26 Oct 1861; copied 9th November 1861)]

It was the morning of 17th October when 'Melpomene' entered the Grand Harbour at Malta, where H.M.S. 'Himalaya' was preparing to leave, [8]

---

[7] See letter written to Newton Sept 14 1861.
[8] PRO ADM 53/8360.

and there was just time to arrange with Captain Seccombe a passage to England for Dennison before she sailed at 1.45pm. Consul Herman's official despatch No.37 from Tripoli on the subject of the *'late attack on Lt. Smith's party by the Nomad tribes at Cyrene'* reached the Foreign Office the following month, and on November 8th a copy was sent to Panizzi. [9]

HERMAN to RUSSELL – October 22nd 1861

My Lord,

I have the honor to report to Your Lordship that on the morning of Thursday last Her Majesty's Vice Consul at Bengasi reported to me by Telegraph that Lieutenant Smith's party and a detachment from Her Majesty's Ship 'Melpomene' had been attacked and were closely invested by the nomad Tribes at Cyrene.

The Governor General immediately telegraphed to the Caimacam at Bengasi to despatch all the disposable Cavalry to the scene of action.

On the same evening the Telegraphic despatch from the Governor of Malta reached me reporting the arrival there on the same day of Her Majesty's Ship 'Melpomene' with Lieut Smith and party on board.

Two of our people were reported to have been wounded but I have not yet been able to ascertain if there were any casualties on the side of the Arabs.

The Governor General on the receipt of the second telegram counter ordered the march of the Cavalry and at my request directed the Caimacam of Bengasi to despatch a trustworthy person to Cyrene to collect and protect any objects that Lieut Smith's party might have been compelled to abandon – But under such a contingency I much fear that all may have been plundered or destroyed before this precautionary measure can be carried out.

I have the honor to be
with the highest respect
My Lord
Your Lordship's most obedient
and most humble servant
G.F. Herman

Source: PRO FO 101/48 A duplicate, passed to the British Museum, differs only in minute details: Original Letters and Papers Vol.LXXI Sept-Dec 1861 fol.242 (B.M.stamp P.10,477 11 Nov 1861)

[9] PRO FO 101/48.

Porcher, back in his quarters on H.M.S. 'Hibernia', wrote on 21st October to Dr Hooker at the Royal Botanic Gardens at Kew, carrying out his intention to send him some 'silphium' seed. He says that he is sure Hooker will remember him on the 'Sidon' when he was on his way to India, and walking over the Petrified Forest near Cairo with him, and continues: *'For the last few months I have been employed making Antiquarian Researches in Cyrenaica, and as the Silphium grows there in great abundance I will send you a Box full of the seeds that I picked in the latter end of June, and will send it home with the Antiquities, in the care of Mr Panizzi of the British Museum. You must be aware that this is the only part of the world where these plants are known to grow, and only in the immediate vicinity of Cyrene, extending in an Easterly and Westerly direction for about 25 or 30 miles.'* He hopes that if Hooker can get the seeds to grow, he might be able to find out the plant's capabilities, as the ancients used it to cure all diseases, *'as it seems to be quite unknown at present. A French surgeon a few years ago made some experiments, but I have never heard what they were, and what use he made of them.'*

No record has been found in the archives at Kew of the seeds' arrival, but the sequel is that Porcher wrote again on 7th December from 50 Montague Square, replying to a letter from Hooker which was *'directed to 15 and detained there some days'*. He is very much obliged to Hooker and Professor Oliver for the trouble they have taken. As Oliver has said *'in his paper'* that he found from Schroff's article that the Silphium now growing at Cyrene was the Thapsia, a distinct plant from the Silphium of the ancients, Porcher wonders if the two plants which look so similar might share any of the same properties. [10]

[10] Royal Botanic Gardens, Kew: English Letters 99 (1856-1900) fols. 397 (448) and 398 (449).

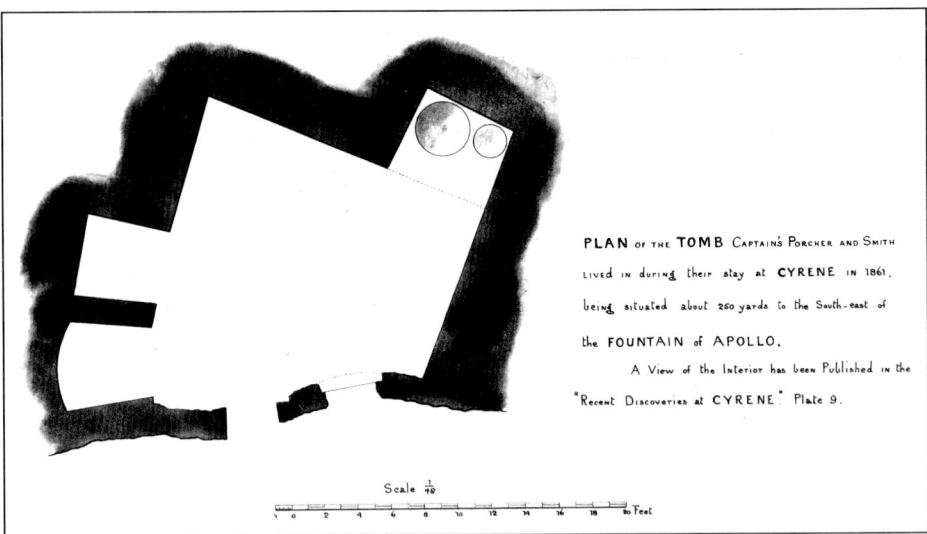

Fig. 17 – Interior view and plan of our Tomb of Residence.

X. DEPARTURE ON H.M.S. 'MELPOMENE'

The final official despatch No.7 from Lieut. Smith with its enclosure was forwarded to Panizzi by the Foreign Office on November 14th with the usual request that *'the despatch may be returned to this Office when done with'*.[1]

Lieut. Smith's Despatch 7 – October 31 1861

Malta, October 31. 1861

My Lord,

I have the honour to report the arrival here of Lieut. Porcher R.N. and myself on the 17th Instant in H.M.S. "Melpomene". The "Melpomene" arrived at Marsa Souza for the purpose of embarking the statues &c discovered at Cyrene since the departure of the "Assurance" in the beginning of June.

We were induced to leave Cyrene by several considerations:

(1) Immediately after the rains set in, the Arabs sow their Crops, which, at Cyrene, cover the greater part of the Ancient City. Having last winter excavated all the promising sites left unoccupied we could this year only have dug in places not likely to yield many specimens of sculpture.

(2) In winter there is great difficulty in obtaining Workmen on account of the severity of the weather. Consisting chiefly of negroes recently brought from the interior they are unable to stand the Intense cold of the Cyrene Winter.

(3) In the course of our residence of nearly ten months at Cyrene we had excavated nearly every attractive site in the City. Further operations must therefore have been conducted more or less indiscriminately.

We should consequently have been obliged to remain seven or eight months doing little or nothing, and should at the end of that period, recommence work with little certainty of success.

---

[1] Original Letters and Papers Vol. LXXI Sept-Dec 1861 fol. 273 (B.M.stamp P.10,629 15 Nov 1861; copied 14 Dec 1861).

I sent your Lordship a report of our proceedings on the 11ᵗʰ of August last. At that time we had nearly completed excavation of the Temple near the Fountain, which proves to be the Temple of Apollo and not that of Aesculapius as I formerly supposed. We afterwards employed the workmen in digging in various parts of the city without any result worthy of note.

*In a previous report to Your Lordship I mentioned the remains of a statue above ground supposed by Captain Beechey to represent one of the Ptolemies [**Pl. 48**]. During the last six weeks of our stay at Cyrene we excavated the building to which this statue belonged, and also a site near the Temple of Bacchus, which, from several sculptures discovered in it, I imagine to be the Temple of Venus.[2] The building in which the Ptolemy was found seems to have been a palace.*

It is unnecessary to give your Lordship a particular account of those buildings, as the enclosed list of cases brought to Malta by the "Melpomene" includes the names or descriptions of everything discovered in them. Both sites proved very fruitful, but chiefly in objects of late Greek or perhaps Roman style. Many of the sculptures are very perfect, some peculiar, and all of considerable beauty.

The operation of getting the statues down to the shore and embarked was, on this occasion, much facilitated by the large number of Seamen and Marines landed from the "Melpomene". Captain Ewart had, besides, made all the necessary arrangements in the course of the passage from Malta, so that not a day was lost before the work was commenced. Before the arrival of the ship we had employed our workmen in making a road from Cyrene to the beach which proved a great service, especially over the first range of mountains, where, on the former occasion, the wagons had to be carried up piecemeal and lowered by means of strong tackle.

Three trips were made to Cyrene with the three artillery Wagons brought from Malta. We intended making four, but were obliged by the hostility of a tribe of Bedouins to leave after making three. By means of the Wagons and Camels however, we Succeeded in embarking all the Sculptures, a few of the Inscriptions only being sacrificed.[3]

At one time the Arabs, for the purpose of levying "black mail", and inspired by simple hatred of Christians, barricaded the road, and cut off communication between Cyrene and the Wagon party. Their Sheikh told me that if we did not give a certain sum of money none of us should be allowed to leave the country alive. His demand being refused, he returned to the position he had

   [2] S & P (1864), 102-104.

   [3] S & P inscriptions nos. 13, 24 Pls. 81 and 84. Left by Tomb of Residence October 1861. Found by Richard Norton in 1911 (ROBINSON (1913), 199).

taken up on the road. I immediately sent for the Sheikhs whom I had to a certain extent befriended in May last by obtaining through the Vice Consul at Benghazi the Pacha's pardon for the seizure of the Castle at Ghegheb. I explained to them the state of affairs, warning them that they themselves would be held responsible for any harm we might receive. They went at once to our enemy Sheikh Seid, and, by threats of annihilating his whole tribe, compelled him to go. Two of the Chief Sheikhs accompanied us to the beach during the last trip.

As only a few inscriptions were at stake we did not consider it advisable to take the Wagons again to Cyrene, thereby running the risk of a serious collision with the Arabs.

I do not believe that Sheikh Seid will however be apprehended or punished in any way by the Government. Nothing has been done in the case of the Sheikh who attacked my caravan and carried off a Negro in July last. In many instances such crimes pass unpunished from the want of good will on the part of the Authorities, but still more frequently from their almost utter want of power. On applying to the Mudir of Ghegheb (the only Government servant within a radius of about 80 miles) for protection from Sheikh Seid and his tribe, two Bashi Bazouks, who never made their appearance, were sent to our relief.

I cannot close this last report on our proceedings in the Cyrenaica without expressing to your Lordship our deep sense of gratitude for the great Kindness and assistance of all the agents of H.M's Government in Barbary, Colonel Herman, Mr. Crowe, Mr. de Fremeaux and Mr. Aquilina, all, as occasion offered, did their utmost to assist and support us.

We are also greatly indebted to Captain Ewart R.N. for the care and forethought displayed in all his arrangements connected with the embarkation of the Statues, as well as for the Kindness to ourselves personally. The Good conduct and perfect discipline of the men had also much to do with the success of the final operations.

I should have sent a report to your Lordship before now, but was prevented doing so by a tedious attack of Fever before leaving Cyrene.

I enclose the list of cases referred to above. They are now on their way to England in H.M.S. "Supply".

I have &c
(sd) R M Smith
Lieut. R.E.

Source: [Original Letters and Papers Vol. LXXI Sept-Dec 1861 fols. 274-275 (B.M.stamp P.10,320 7 Nov 1861; copied 9th November 1861)]

List of Cases of Antiquities
shipped on board H.M.S. "Supply"

1   Minerva – No fragments –

2   Head half of Colossal Female figure (with head Nº. 44) from the Ruins to the N. of T. of Apollo. –

3   Lower half of Dº. with foot. –

4   Colossal female Statue from the Palace where Ptolemys was found. –

5   Lower half of small seated Female figure from Ruins W. of Temple of Apollo with foot. –

6   Large female statue found besides the Minerva, Right arm of Dº. –

7   Small Statue of Apollo(?) from T. to S.W. of Temple of Bacchus. –

8   Upper half of life size Statue (female) from above Temple. –

9   Lower half of Dº. –

10 One of the two Statues (life size), of hunters from Temple to S.W. of Temple of Bacchus. –

11 Other Dº. --------------------------   Dº. ------------------

12 The Philosopher and feet from ruins to N. of Temple of Apollo.

13 Ptolemy – (torso in Armour) –

14 Upper half of the King from Temple of Apollo. –

15 Lower part of Dº. with fragments from Temple to S.S.W. of T. of Bacchus. –

16 Statue of (Pan) –

17 Bust of a Girl from Palace of Ptolemy and small Statuette from Dº. –

18 Bust of a female from palace of Ptolemy

19 dº. ------- dº. ----------- dº. and small Dolphin from T. to S.W. of T. of Bacchus.

20 Statuette of a female fragments from dº.

21 Dº. of a Male (feet separate) from dº.

22 Dº. of Venus.

23 Dº. of a Man and fragments of a Snake belonging to it (Apollo)

24 Bust of a man from palace of Ptolemy

25 Head of Dº.

26 Fragments of Statue in cases Nº. 8/9.

27-29 An Alto relievo of the Nymph Cyrene strangling the Lion and being Crowned by Another Nymph.

30 Upper half of seated figure – the lower being in Nº. 5 with hands.

31 Venus and Cupid in two pieces with small fragments. Life size small head (perhaps that of one of the two Hunters), Three small Statuettes – all from Temple of Venus.

32 Legs of Nº. 10 or 11 also fragments from large Temple near the Stadium.

33   *Legs of N°. 10 or 11.*

34   *Hunters legs with deer skin from ruins to North of Temple of Apollo.*

35   *Small male statue holding a vase in the right hand from d°. –*

36   *Small statue of Bacchus with head & hand And fragments also, one other head. Both from ruins of N. of Temple of Apollo also three small*

37   *Statuettes a small figure of Cupid one d°. asleep in relief and a small figure in relief and fragment of a Statuette all four from Temple of Venus.*

      Small Male statue from Temple of Apollo, head and part of feet – small Statuette, and Animal Crouching from smaller Temple near the Stadium, head smaller than life from Palace of Ptolemy

38   *Small statue from Temple of Apollo & fragment of shoulder.*

39   *Small statue of a Huntress with dog, head and fragments from ruins to N. of T. of Apollo, also small figure of Cupid on a Dolphin, small statuette, head attached to part of body, fragments of statuette all from Temple of Venus – also fragment of Statuette from small Temple near the Stadium.*

40   *Large Male bust from Palace of Ptolemy, head of figure N°. 8 & 9 with fragment of nose attached and neck. Life size Elizabethan looking head & smaller d°. with high conical head dress and small head of Minerva, all from Temple of Venus, Also 4 small heads from d°.*

41   *Small female statuette & fragments (holding a snake) from T. of Apollo. Small female statue with head and neck from T. of Apollo, also*

42   *seated statuette from small building at west end of the platform of Apollo.*

43   *Two inscriptions from ruins to E. of Temple of Apollo.*

44   *Head of Statuette N°. 9 & 8.*

45   *Inscription from large Temple near the Stadium, Terra Cotta, ornamented work from Palace of Ptolemy fragments from excavations of Temple of Apollo and neighborhood. [sic]*

46   *[Pans] head, two statuettes from Temple of Venus and one from smaller Temple near the Stadium.*

47   *Leg and Trunk with grapes &c and fragments from T. of Apollo & neighborhood.[sic]*

48   *Large Male head from palace of Ptolemy.*

49   *Head of the Philosopher (N°. 12) & other head life size from ruins N. of T. of Apollo.*

50   *Bronze male head and marble d°. life size from Temple of Apollo.*

51   *Fragments from excavations at T. of Apollo & neighbourhood.*

52   *One female statuette, in two, with its head. Two smaller d°. also in two, both Venus, one very small Mummy looking statuette, a small hand and two small heads all from Temple of Venus.*

53	*Large head (male) from large temple near the Stadium*
54	*Large head in two from the smaller Temple near the Stadium, Sepulchral bas relief purchased.*
55	*Three heads life size from Temple of Apollo & neighbourhood, two smaller heads and a seated figure from Temple of Venus.*
56	*Head life size with eyes separate in sockets, from the palace of Ptolemy, also two heads and seated statuette from Temple of Venus.*
57	*Head about life size & two smaller ones, with eyes separated from Temple of Apollo & neighbourhood, one sepulchral head with inscription purchased. Broken head from smaller Temple near the Stadium, Four small heads from Temple of Apollo & neighbourhood, two small heads from d°., left hand of a statue of a King (N°. 14 & 15), head went by "Assurance", Dogs head from T. of Bacchus, small hand & fragment from Temple of Apollo. – Rude female statuette from Temple of Venus – fragments of N°. 4.*
58	*Small bust, half of a small male statuette & two other statuettes from Temple of Venus, and small head from Temple of Apollo.*
59	*Sundries fragments &c.*
60	*Small female Statue from Colonnade above the Theatre in street of*
61	*D°. feet Coins &c*
62	*Inscription of M. Antonius.*
63	*D°. of C. Lentulus.*
~~63~~	*One case of impressions of Inscriptions*
~~64~~	*d°. of inscription paper*

R.M. Smith
Lᵗ R.E.

Source: [Original Letters and Papers Vol. LXXI Sept-Dec 1861 fols. 236-238 (B.M.stamp P.10,320 7 Nov 1861; copied 9th November 1861)]

This final despatch was written by Smith where the story probably began – in the Malta Union Club. The explorers had been away for a total of eleven months. They had experienced hardship and discomfort, ill-health and danger, but they had achieved what they set out to do, and as Porcher later wrote, *'it will always be both my pride and pleasure, should an opportunity again offer to devote my energies to the same object'*.

SMITH from Malta to PANIZZI – October 31st 1861

My dear Sir
I have been prevented writing to you before now by an attack of Fever which confined me nearly continuously to bed for six weeks immediately be-

fore leaving Cyrene. I enclose a copy of a report I wrote to Lord Russell this morning. It will inform you of the considerations which induced us to leave Cyrene in the 'Melpomene'. I enclose also a list of the cases shipped on board the 'Supply' & now on their way to England. They are 65 [sic] *in number.*

I enclose also an account of the Expenses of the Expedition since the 30th June last, when the last account was tendered. The balance in favour of the Museum is £8.4.1 – As I have deemed) *this account*
the full account of the grant I now enclose a bill on Cox & Co for) *made a*
£8.4/–) *voucher*

[written slantwise across page: *'This Bill of exchange was not presented, the Trustees being debtors of Lieut Smith to a large amount'*. The Bill of Exchange was attached, similarly annotated.] [4]

I have made out Mr Denison's share of household expenses to be £11. As the whole of the expenses are included in the Enclosed Account the sum which you may place to his debit on account of messing is £11. – I made no payments to him at Cyrene as he did not wish it himself. Through Capt. Ewart I got a passage for him from Malta in H.M.S. Himalaya which was on the point of leaving for England as we entered the harbour. I had not time even to see him before the Himalaya started. He was very painstaking and useful all the time he was at Cyrene especially when we commenced packing. At that time Mr. Porcher had to go with the wagon party I was laid up with fever and had therefore to leave all the superintendence of packing them to Denison. He was employed all the Sundays of his stay at Cyrene being from June 18 to Oct. 14 –

I will not write at further length now as I hope to be home & see you in the course of two or three weeks. Mr Porcher goes home today. In the meantime I am waiting for the Orders regarding me from the Horse Guards.

I am
My dear Sir
Yours most truly
R.M. Smith

Source: [Original Letters and Papers Vol. LXXI Sept-Dec fol. 204 (B.M.stamp P.10,320, 7 Nov 1861; copied 9th November 1861)]

Smith seemed very conscious of the fact that he had been unable to bid farewell personally to Dennison, whose precipitate departure on the con-

---

[4] Original Letters and Papers Vol. LXXI Sept-Dec 1864 fol. 205 (B.M.stamp P.10,320 7 Nov 1861).

157

venient 'Himalaya' was organised by Ewart, but the scene at Malta can be imagined – the arrival of 'Melpomene' and the arrangements which had to be made for transferring her cargo to 'Supply', the paperwork which no doubt was looming in connection with this and with Smith and Porcher's official future movements, the unloading of their personal equipment, the essential visit to their superior officers to report back – with Smith still weak from fever. Panizzi would probably show Dennison this testimonial which reflected the lieutenants' gratitude, and there is no doubt that Smith would make an opportunity to speak to the man when he was next in the British Museum.

On November 12th Lord Paget, on behalf of the Lords Commissioners of the Admiralty, forwarded to Panizzi *'for the information of the Trustees of the British Museum, a copy of a letter from Vice Admiral Sir Wm. F. Martin, dated the 24th Oct^r, No.823, with copies of its enclosures, reporting the proceedings of the officers and crew of Her Majesty's Ship Melpomene in the shipment of Antiquities at Cyrene, and the return of Lieutenants Smith and Porcher to Malta after the successful completion of their excavations.'* [5]

EWART from "Melpomene" at Malta to REAR ADMIRAL CODRINGTON –
October 17th 1861

Sir,

I have the honour to report the arrival of H.M.S. "Melpomene" under my command this day having in pursuance of orders conveyed in your memo of 22nd Sept 1861 proceeded to the neighbourhood of Marsa Sousa on the North Coast of Africa, & thence by land accompanied by 130 men & officers to the cite [sic] of Cyrene, with Artillery wagons, Stores & Provisions transported & embarked 63 cases of marble & have brought them to this Port.

2 – I have embarked the Cyrene expedition, consisting of Lieut. Smith R^l Eng^rs, Lieut. Porcher R^l Navy & 4 Attendants. Their excavation at Cyrene having been concluded they have finally left the site of that ancient City and returned to Malta in H.M.S. "Melpomene" – having accomplished as far as I can judge a great success in the recovery of very fine statuary.

3 – H.M.S. "Melpomene" under my command left Malta on the 23rd Ult: & arrived at the coast near Marsa Sousa on the evening of the 26th. By great good fortune I anchored on the exact spot where measure could be most safely taken for the disembarkation of Waggons &c – a sandy Bay about 3 Miles to

---

[5] Original Letters and Papers Vol. LXXI Sept-Dec 1861 fol. 256-257 (B.M.stamp P.10,553 14 Nov 1861; copied 14 Dec 1861).

the Westward of Marsa Sousa (ancient Apollonia). The same night I sent off a despatch to Lieut. Smith at Cyrene applying for Camels. On the 27th I landed a guard of Marines, ten in number, under Lieut. Sanders, R.M.L.[-]. Carpenters 10 in Number, Provisions for a fortnight for 130 Men, Plank, Stores & despatched them to Cyrene, where they arrived the same night. I also landed another stock of Provisions a guard of Marines & tanks of water to be retained at the landing place, so that in the event of the Ship being forced to put to sea by stress of weather no difficulty would arise in subsisting the party of Men employed in transporting the wagons. No water could be obtained in the neighbourhood, I therefore kept up a constant supply from the Ship. On the 28th at daylight I landed 96 Men & Officers under the command of Lieut. Carter of this ship, & they proceeded at once with their tents & baggage, dragging the three Artillery Waggons, & accompanied by camels carrying water & Tents.

On the morning of the 30th they arrived at Cyrene. Carpenters working with good will kept up a supply of Cases for the Marbles, so that the waggons were constantly on the move.

4 – Between the 28th September & 13th October (inclusive) three trips were made between the anchorage & Cyrene, all the heavy marbles conveyed on board, the smaller cases transported on Camels, & on the 13th Inst. I broke up the encampment on Shore, re-embarking men, waggons, unconsumed provisions, tanks &c. Lieuts. Smith & Porcher having completed their duties at Cyrene embarked with their Attendants.

5 – It affords me very great pleasure to report the excellent conduct of all the Men employed on this really arduous duty. One accident alone has taken place a broken leg, doing very well. Commander Aynesley [sic] in his letter of the 11th June (herewith returned) so well describes the nature of the country between Marsa Sousa & Cyrene, as to make it unnecessary to repeat his description. The Men in dragging the waggons up the Aughbah Mountains, worked with a will & a heartiness admirable in every way. I have the honor to bear testimony to the zealous manner in which Lieut. Carter, assisted by Messrs Jackson & Kane, Mid. & Mr. Wade, Master's Assistant conducted the transport of the Marbles. Mr Ratliffe Assistant Surgeon accompanied the waggon party in all their journeys. Lieut. Porcher of the Cyrene Expedition by his knowledge of the language was of great assistance on these journeys. I am much indebted to him.

Lieut. Smith Rl Engrs who conducted the operations at Cyrene, had a very difficult duty to perform in temporising with the Arab tribe who dwell in that neighbourhood, & who showed unmistakable signs of a wish to have a disturbance. Their hatred of Christians leads them to seek opportunities to plunder & kill. I was myself a witness of the quiet steady conduct of our Men in their encampment at Cyrene, at a period when the slightest indiscretion on *their part would have unquestionably caused a collision. These Arab tribes can muster in very large numbers at short notice. They are quite out of control of the Turkish Authorities. I attribute our having avoided a collision to the judicious measures of Lieut. Smith. I enclose herewith a tracing of the anchorage which was surveyed by Mr Albert, Master of this Ship. It would be of service to any Ship employed on a similar expedition as the rocks are numerous dangerous & not laid down in the Adm^{ty} charts. The anchorage sand & rock would be "untenable" in strong northerly winds.*

Although we had a good deal of swell, rendering it impossible to communicate with the shore for one half the time we were at anchor, still as the Northerly Winds did not blow home we were able to retain our position. At Cyrene itself there is abundance of Water. At Marsa Sousa, the ancient Apollonia none, nor yet at our anchorage. On the 13th in the evening arrived at our anchorage the Medina from Bengarzi, surveying the coast en route to Alexandria. I supplied her with money & Eng^{rs} stores (tallow). On the morning of the 14th I left the anchorage partly under steam with one boiler, & partly under sail accomplished the passage to Malta.

6. I would respectfully suggest that the price of the boots issued to the men landed at Cyrene should be credited to their account, also that a coaling suit of duck be supplied free of expense to replace that torn to pieces by brushwood & hard work. The conduct of the Men well deserves my offering this suggestion for your approval, in addition to the usual payment of Check Money. Herewith are returned Comm^{r} Aynsley's letter of proceedings, also two letters from the British Museum.

I have &c
(signed) C J F Ewart
Captain

Source: [Original Letters and Papers Vol. LXXI Sept-Dec 1861 fols. 258-260 (B.M. stamp none; copied 14 Dec 1861)]

Towards the end of October the British Museum received the following letter from Maclean and Woolley, of 63 Lower Thames Street in the City of London, which is interesting for its extreme economy in the way of punctuation:

Dear Sir,

We have received intelligence from our correspondent at Portsmouth mentioning that the "Himalaya" or "Asmania" will bring some Antiquities for the British Museum coming from the Mediterranean which are shortly expected at the above port at the same time asking what steps we would wish to be taken therefore hasten to send you this information a reply to which we shall feel obliged in order that proper clearance may take Place upon arrival.

We remain
Yrs faithfully
Maclean & Woolley

Please to hand to Mr Panizzi the enclosed note it is regarding a Box of his own we believe for shipment.
Thomas Batler Esqre

Source: [Original Letters and Papers Vol. LXXI Sept-Dec 1861 fol. 178 (B.M.stamp P. 9816 24 Oct 1861)]

The letter refers to a shipment on 'Himalaya' or 'Asmania', whereas the large cases from Cyrene were brought to England on 'Supply', and the antiquities mentioned may have been from another site altogether. However, is it possible that Dennison, who would reach England first, and could see Panizzi, could have been entrusted with the silphium box when he boarded 'Himalaya' to go home? Could the postscript refer not to a box 'for shipment' at all, but to the elusive silphium seeds?

FIG. 18 – Encampment of the Party from H.M.S. Melpomene, near the Head of the Augubah.

FIG. 19 – Eastern City Wall and Ruins of Apollonia.

162

XI. THE CURTAIN FALLS

Towards the close of the expedition all the departments involved dusted themselves down, balanced their accounts and put their paperwork in order. On 26th September the War Office in Pall Mall forwarded to Antonio Panizzi two statements of the stores issued from Malta, to the value of £159.0s.3d, as follows:

Statement for Stores issued at Malta from H.M. Stores for service of Lieutenant Smith R.E. engaged in a scientific expedition on the coast of Barbary

[Da]te of Issue [May] 1861	Articles		Quantity	Rate	£	s	d
	Tents Circular Linen O.P. used		6	£3.15.	22	10	"
	(	Bags Pin	3	1^s/6^d each	"	4	6
	(	Lines Weather	12	1/ "	"	12	"
Tent	(	Mallets Wood	12	6^d "	"	6	"
	(Pins (Iron		24	7^d "	"	14	"
Appurtenances	(	(Wood Small	252	2/6 per 100	"	6	3
	(	Poles circular Tent	6	2/6 each	"	15	"
	(	Valizes	6	3^s/ "	"	18	"
					£26	5	9
	Add Departmental Expenses				3	18	10
				Total £30		4	7

The six circular tents were for the working party of 30 sailors and Lieutenant Luard. This compares with the 19 tents provided for about 100 men from the 'Melpomene'.

Statement of Issues out of H.M.S. at Malta for service of the Scientific expedition to the Coast of Barbary under Lieutenant Smith R.E.

[Da]te of Issue May 2. 1861.	Articles	Quantity	Rate	£	s	d
	Handspikes Common 6f	6	2s/4½d		14	3
Damaged £5.10/- allowed	Gyn triangle 20f complete	1	£31.13s.8d	31	13	8
Damaged £56.6/- allowed	Wagons platform with wheels complete	2	£48.8s	96	16	—
retd	Wheels spare (Fore	2	£3.18s.8d Ea	7	17	4
retd	for ditto (Hind	2	4.9.8 "	8	19	4
	Axes felling 4½ lbs.	6	3s/3d "		19	6
	Barrows wheel elm sides	2	15s/3d "	1	10	6
4 retd	(12 Inch Brass Coggled	8	14s/4¾d "	5	15	2
	Blocks wood (Double (10 Inch not " " with wood (	1	8/4 "		8	4
	shields strapped (Single (not brass coggled	2	2/4½ "		4	9
5 retd 2 useless	(10 Inch(brass coggled	7	2/4½ "		16	7
	Iron Crows 5½ ft	3	10/ "	1	10	"
	Handspikes 7ft Iron shod	12	3s/6½d "	2	2	6
	(Pick Axe	18	8d "		12	"
	Helves (Felling "	6	6½d "		3	3
	(Shovel	3	1/2 "		3	6
	(Spade	3	1/2 "		3	6
	Picks Mins.. 8lb	12	2/6 "	1	10	"
	Rope White 3½ Inch. 226 fms. 475 lbs	475 lbs	10s per lb	19	15	10
	Shovels Iron Common	6	2s/9d each		16	6
	Spades Iron Common	6	2s/9d "		16	6
	Trucks stone with 2 iron trucks	2	£4.19 "	9	18	"
	Wheels wrought iron for barrows	2	5s/ "		10	"
				193	17	~~2~~
	Deduct as per statement overleaf			81	17	4
				111	19	~~10~~ 8
	Add Departmental Expenses			16	16	"
	Total			£128	15	~~10~~ 8

164

Value of Articles returned into store on the 14 June 1861
being "a portion of the foregoing"

	Quantity	Rate	£	s	d	
Blocks wood Strapped with wood shields						
Brass Coggled - Double 12"	4	14ˢ/4³/₄ᵈ	2	17	7	
~ ~ ~ Single 10"	3	2ˢ/4¹/₂ᵈ		7	1	
" "	2					in an unserviceable state - of no value -
Gyn Triangle large	1		5	10 "	"	£5.10. = present value
(Carriages (Hind with bodies	2	₤5.4ˢ --	10	8 "	"	£10.8 = " " of the 2
Wagons (under (Fore	2	₤9.13ˢ "	19	6 "		
platform (Shafts pairs	4	₤1.16ˢ per pair	7	4 "		
incomplete (Wheels (Hind	3	₤3.19ˢ8 each	11	19 "		
((	1	--------		18 "	"	18ˢ/ = present value
(Fore	3	₤2.18ˢ.8 "	8	16 "		
((	1	--------	–	15 "	"	15 = " "
(Fore	2	₤3.18ˢ.8ᵈ. each	7	17 "		The 6 wheels returned
						damaged - the expense of putting
Wheels platform Wagon (Hind	2	₤4.9ˢ.6ᵈ "	8	19 "		them into a serviceable
						condition is £3-
			84	17	4	
		Deduct	3	"	"	
		Total	81	17	4	

Source: [Original Letters and Papers Vol.LXXI Sept-Dec 1861 fol.66 (B.M.stamp P.8840 28 Sep.1861; copied 12 Oct. 1861)]

On November 2nd the War Office wrote to Panizzi, informing him that *'this office has a claim of the following amount, on account of stores supplied for Service of the Exploring Expedition in Cyrene amounting to £279.1.5, as Per Statement annexed'*, and appending the following list:

Statement of Stores supplied by the War Department for Service of the Exploring Expedition in Cyrene.–

Per Letter from Rear Admiral Codrington CB dated 18th Sept 1861 & approved by the Lieut. General Commanding.–

Date of Issue	Articles	Quantity	Rate	£	s	d
1861						
Sept. 21ˢᵗ	(Felling unhelved	6	3ˢ/2ᵈ Ea	"	19	"
	Axes (Pick	12	1/11 "	1	2	"
	Boxes Shot	1	–	"	2	1
	Canteens, Wood	100	1/4 Ea	6	13	4
	(Felling Axe	6)	6³/₄ᵈ	"	16	10
	Helves (Pick "	24)				
	(No 14-2 In	4¹/₂	¹/₂ᵈ lb	"	"	2
	Nails Iron lbs (No 16-2³/₄"	6¹/₄	2ᵈ "	"	1	"
	(No 19-4 "	18¹/₄	1³/₄ "	"	2	8
	(No 15-2¹/₂"	20	2¹/₄ "	"	3	9
	Spades, Iron, Common	62	2/5 Ea	7	9	10
	Straps, Canteen, Brown leather	100	10ᵈ Ea	4	13	4
			£ s d			
	Tents, Circular, Linen, Op. used	19	2.2.6 "	40	7	6
	(Bags Pin	11	1/11 "	"	16	6
	(Lines Weather	38	9ᵈ "	1	8	6
	(Mallets Wood	38	6ᵈ "	"	19	"
	Tent Appurtⁿᶜᵉˢ ((Iron	76	2/3¹/₂ Doz	"	14	6
	(Pins (Wood Small	798	2/6 P.100	"	19	11
	(Poles Circular Tent	19	2/6 Ea	2	7	6
	(Valise dᵒ	19	3/- "	2	17	"
	Wagons (Complete wʰ wheels	3	£48.8ˢ.0ᵈ	145	4	"
	Platform (Wheels (Fore	3	3.18.8"	11	16	"
	(spare (Hind	3	4.9.8"	13	9	"
War Office				£ 242	13	5
Pall Mall	Departmental Expenses			36	8	"
25ᵗʰ October 1861				£ 279	1	5

Source: [Original Letters and Papers Vol. LXXI Sept-Dec 1861 fols. 212-213 (B.M.stamp P.10,183 4 Nov 1861)]

Panizzi was informed of the arrival of the second consignment of statuary on November 16th in a letter from H.M.S. "Fisgard" at Woolwich, stating that *'the "Supply" arrived at Woolwich at 10.0 A.M. this day.'* [1] On November 20th the Foreign Office declared to Panizzi that *'the Inclosures to Lieut. Smith's Letter of the 11th of August may be retained for the use of the British Museum, as well as the Inclosure in Lieut. Smith's No.7 of the 31st of October'.* [2]

That same day, after personally examining the papers which had been

---

[1] Original Letters and Papers Vol. LXXI Sept-Dec 1861 fol.292 (B.M.stamp P.10,642 16 Nov 1861).

[2] Original Letters and Papers Vol. LXXI Sept-Dec 1861 fol. 313 (B.M.stamp P.10,864 21 Nov 1861; copied 14 Dec 1861).

passed to the British Museum, Murdoch Smith as a shrewd Scotsman had some comments to make on the War Office accounts of the previous September, regarding stores supplied from Malta for the use of the expedition, both during and after the embarkation of the first consignment:

SMITH at the British Museum to PANIZZI – November 20th 1861

Sir,

I have the honour to inform you that I have examined the account of stores supplied by the War Department for the use of the late Expedition in the Cyrenaica.

The following items seem to me to require explanation:

The Gyn charged as damaged to the amount of £26.3.8 was never taken to Cyrene at all. It was only used an hour or two for getting the cases into the ships boats.

The charge of £40.10/ – of damage to two wagons seems to me excessive. The wagons were certainly damaged, but I should think that a much smaller sum than £40 would repair them thoroughly.

The white rope (£19.15.10) stone trucks (£9.18) and various other articles issued May 2nd were returned at Malta from H.M.S. "Melpomene" in October last, but the Trustees of the British Museum have not been credited with their value.

The tents issued May 3rd and charged £30.4.7 were drawn by Commander Aynsley H.M.S. "Assurance". Their return into store at Malta is not credited to the Trustees.

The whole of the stores charged £279.1.5 issued September 21st were drawn and returned by Captain Ewart H.M.S. "Melpomene". Their return has not been credited to the Trustees.

> *I have the honour to be*
> *Sir*
> *Your most obed*. *servant*
> *R.M. Smith Lt. R.E.*

Source: [Original Letters and Papers Vol. LXXI Sept-Dec 1861 fol. 318 (B.M.stamp P.10,786 20 Nov 1861)]

Smith and Porcher were also working out their own finances, and the following account was made out, written, as is the letter from Kilmarnock dated 18th December, on Murdoch Smith's personal writing paper, embossed with an oval shape which encloses an oval belt bearing the legend MARTE ET INGENIO, inside which again is a dolphin:

Amount of pay & allowances not paid by the War Office & Admiralty to L¹.
Smith R.E. & L¹ Porcher R.N.

Lt. Smith
316 days @ 8/4   *£131.13.4*

                                        ————

Lt. Porcher
245 days @ 1/-   *£12. 5*
346 " @ 9ᵈ   *£12.19.6*
                                                                                    £25. 4.6

                        R.M. Smith
                        Lt. R.E.
                        Nov.23.1861

Source: [Original Letters and Papers Vol. LXXI Sept-Dec 1861 fol. 355 (B.M.stamp
P.11,039 27 Nov 1861; copied 14 Dec 1861)]

PORCHER from 45 Bryanston Square, London to PANIZZI –
November 29th 1861

Dear Sir,
    *Lieut. Smith and myself calculated the loss of my Navy Pay during the time
I was employed in the Cyrenaica, and made it to amount to £25.4.6, as nearly
as we could reckon without the official papers, which I have not at present in
my possession.*

                                        I remain
                                        Dear Sir
                                        Yours truly
                                        E.A. Porcher

Source: [Original Letters and Papers Vol. LXXI Sept-Dec 1861 fol.357 (B.M.stamp
P.11,194, 30 Nov 1861)]

The first letter after Smith's return to his native Scotland reflects his
true joy at being with his family again, and one can imagine the long
'debriefing' as he remembered and regaled them with anecdote after anecdote, each moment of humour, each time of discomfort and danger. It is
typical of the man that even at this time he remembered to repeat his

request for acknowledgement of the whole crew of 'Melpomene' for their work.

SMITH from Kilmarnock to PANIZZI – December 3rd 1861

Dear Sir

I enclose a cheque on Cox & Co. for £10, the amount of the balance of my account with the Museum. I should have sent it sooner, had I not forgotten about it in the excitement of my first three days at home.

If you have heard anything from Lord Granville in reply to your kind application on my behalf I should be glad to know of it at your leisure.

I hope you are pleased with some of the Melpomene's cargo. I should be very glad if the services of Capt. Ewart the Officers & crew were acknowledged in whatever way you think best as they did their work so thoroughly con amore.

> *Believe me*
> *Dear Sir*
> *Yours faithfully*
> *R.M. Smith*
> "

Source: [Original Letters and Papers Vol. LXXI Sept-Dec 1861 fol.384 (B.M.stamp P.11,364 5 Dec 1861)]

A short while later, the bill *'Receivable order Nᵒ.1977'* for camel hire at Marsa Sousah arrived on Panizzi's desk. The camels employed were those supplied by Mohammed el Adouli in June to carry the water, tents and other baggage of the working party and to transport the smaller cases of statuary. According to the annotation *'repaid 16.12.61'*, this bill was dealt with on the day it arrived.

ADMIRALTY to PANIZZI – December 13th 1861

Sir

Payments, amounting to Twenty-one Pounds, having been made by the Paymaster of H.M.S. "Assurance" to Lieut. Smith R.E., on account of the British Museum, for the hire of camels to convey provisions to a party of men landed from the "Assurance" for the purpose of removing certain Antiquities from ancient Cyrene to the sea-coast, as per voucher enclosed:

I beg leave to request that you will move the Trustees to cause the amount to be repaid to the credit of Naval Services, through Her Majesty's Paymaster General, who has been authorised to receive the same.

I am, Sir,
Your most obedient servant
J Beeby
Dy Acc General of the Navy

Source: [Original Letters and Papers Vol. LXXI Sept-Dec 1861 fol. 410 (B.M.stamp P.11,808 16 Dec 1861)]

The next day, Panizzi wrote individually to Smith and Porcher, passing on to them the British Museum Trustees' reaction to the report which Newton had compiled on the statuary.

PANIZZI to SMITH – December 17th 1861

Dear Sir,
On Saturday last I had the pleasure of laying before the Committee Mr Newton's report on the sculptures, with which the Museum has been enriched through the successful exertions of yourself and Lieutenant Porcher at Cyrene; and I now take the earliest opportunity of communicating to you the high satisfaction of the Trustees in learning that the collections in the Department of Greek and Roman Antiquities have been so largely increased with objects both artistically and historically interesting. In returning you the best thanks of the Trustees for all that you have done to bring about this important result, I am to express the deep sense they entertain of the intelligence, zeal, and persevering labour, which both you and Lieutenant Porcher have devoted to this expedition from beginning to end.
I have further to inform you that the Trustees have authorized me to indemnify
£131.13.4 for the amount of pay which has been withheld from you by the War Office, while engaged in this business, and I am to present you with the sum of
£200. . Two Hundred Pounds as an acknowledgement from the Trustees of the valuable services you have rendered to the Museum.
Enclosed are receipts for these two sums; upon your returning them duly signed, I will pay the amount to your account at Cox & Co's.
£331.13.4
I write to Lieutenant Porcher a letter similar to this, and shall communicate to the Admiralty a suitable acknowledgement from the Trustees for the

effective aid afforded by the officers and crews of H.M.S.s "Assurance" and "Melpomene" in the arduous task of removing and shipping these marbles. The Trustees have approved the accounts of expenditure rendered by you in this behalf, and I enclose a shilling's worth of postage stamps for the difference between the cheque you sent on the 3rd inst. and the amount due on the balance.

The £21 advanced to you by the paymaster of the "Assurance" for Camel Hire has been claimed by the Admiralty and repaid by me.

Believe me, dear sir,
Yours very truly,
A. Panizzi

Source: [NLS ACC 9569 fol. 91]

SMITH from Kilmarnock to PANIZZI – December 18th 1861

Dear Sir

I have just received your very gratifying letter of yesterday's date conveying to me the thanks of the Trustees of the British Museum for my services in the Cyrenaica. I accept with best thanks their very liberal gift of £200. I have also to thank the Trustees and yourself for the support and ready assistance Lieut. Porcher and I received without which we could not have brought our labours at Cyrene to a successful termination.

I enclose the receipts for £200 and £131.13.4.

Believe me
Dear Sir
Yours faithfully
R.M. Smith

Source: [Original Letters and Papers Vol. LXXI Sept-Dec 1861 fol. 418 (B.M.stamp P.11,989 20 Dec 1861)]

PORCHER from 45 Bryanston Square, London to PANIZZI –
December 18th 1861

Dear Sir

I have to thank you for your letter of the 17th instant, conveying to me in most flattering terms the thanks of the Trustees of the British Museum for my excavations in the Cyrenaica, and their intention of presenting to me the sum of two hundred pounds, as well as £25.4.6 withheld by the Admiralty, as an acknowledgement of the service it has been in my power to render.

171

I request you will be pleased to convey to the Trustees my grateful sense of the handsome and unexpected manner they have been pleased to recognize my labour in the field of science, and whilst accepting their liberal donation, assure them that it will always be both my pride and pleasure, should an opportunity again offer to devote my energies to the same object.

Believe me
Yours very truly
E.A. Porcher Lieut. Ret.

Source: [Original Letters and Papers Vol. LXXI Sept-Dec 1861 fol. 420 (B.M.stamp P.11,935 19 Dec 1861)]

Nothing in Porcher's appreciative words reveals the fact that his 70 year old father, Rev. George Porcher, had died at home just two days before this letter was written, about a month after the return of his son from his great adventure. [3]

---

[3] Gentleman's Magazine New Series Vol. 12 Jan-June 1862.

XII. THE PHOTOGRAPHIC APPARATUS

As Smith and Porcher's *'photographic apparatus'* was furnished by the Foreign Office, it initially seemed probable that the model provided would be a 'Fowke' type of folding bellows camera, patented by Captain Francis Fowke R.E. in 1856, which was supplied to the British government by Thomas Ottewill and Co. of London, and was the style of apparatus used by the Sappers trained at South Kensington. This camera was made in teak for use in the tropics, where the natural oils in the wood protected the camera from the excesses of heat and damp. However, the camera in Porcher's illustration of the Tomb of Residence appears unlike the 'Fowke' model, and more closely resembles Ottewill's mahogany double folding camera of about 1853, an example of which is displayed in the Science Museum, London.[1] This was designed as a convenient portable wet plate camera before the introduction of the bellows, and consists of two folding compartments, one sliding within the other, giving movement for focusing. The sides of the outer compartment fold inwards and are held rigid by the lens panel, which is provided with vertical and horizontal movements *'for sky and foreground adjustment'*. The sides of the inner compartment also fold inwards and are held rigid by a light frame at the front end and the ground glass focusing screen at the rear. The camera takes 10"×8" plates, and folds down to a compact 21"×13"×3".

The London Album consists of seven pages of 42 photographs. These are annotated as belonging to Despatches 1, 3-6 and to a letter of August 20th, a date when Smith wrote to General Burgoyne, and include a duplicate set of those sent in Despatch 6, **Pls. 34-41, 43**.

The Edinburgh Album consists of fourteen pages of 38 photographs, containing a miscellany of duplicates known from the London Album, but

---

[1] Inv.No. 1930-343, Source: R.F.C. Teare MBE.

including those which are missing from it, which relate to the Burgoyne letter of August 20th, **Pls. 42, 44-48**. Additionally it contains the only known views of the Apollo Sanctuary **Pls. 19-20** and the Tomb of Residence **Pls. 49-50**. There are also two photographs of sculptures, one of which was described in Despatch 4, **Pl. 29**; the other, of poor quality, showing an unprovenanced figure of Hercules which is now lost, is not included here. Another group is recognised from descriptions of statuary in Lieut. Smith's letter of September 14th to Newton, **Pls. 51-56**.

On 19th November 1872 the photographs enclosed with Despatch 1 of 23rd February 1861 were sent to Newton, but at that stage did not include two of the original photographs, one a near duplicate and the other a study of three young Arabs, **Pls. 2-5, 7-17**. This series has evidently been amalgamated with the photographs mounted in the London Album.

Despatches 1-2

The first photographs to arrive in England, causing a flurry of excitement, were of the statue of Bacchus. The head, **Pl. 2**, was taken against the background of a dark, coarse, hairy blanket which was used as a backdrop in many of the photographs. The bunch of grapes associated with this figure can be seen on the right of **Pl. 3** at the edge of the picture. The following two photographs were taken inside the tomb with the statue reassembled; in **Pl. 4** the figure may be standing at the edge of a recess, with the light coming from the right and the head in shadow. For **Pl. 5** the camera has been moved round to the side of the statue so that the light is now coming from the left, with the arched top of a recess dimly visible above the shadowy head. Smith complained that when taking photographs in the Tomb of Residence it was difficult to get enough light or distance for focusing, but this very fact gives the last two pictures a dramatic and wonderfully mysterious quality.

Photographs of a headless female statuette, **Pls. 6-7** were taken on the upper terrace above the Tomb of Residence, the first showing an opening in the rockface behind filled in with stones. The small statue, now in Istanbul with its head reinstated, stands on an outcrop with a reed mat beside it. In the background a person with bare lower legs and feet lies asleep on another mat. The second view is similar, but with a background of blanket which, as the print in the British Museum shows, has been draped over the reed mat, held up by someone whose left leg can be seen on the right of the shot. Another person can be glimpsed in an entrance to the left.

There follows a photographic mosaic of four consecutive views of the eastern slope of Wadi Haleg Shaloof, showing the impressive loculus tombs which one sees across the wadi from just below the archaic tombs as recorded in **Pl. 12** mentioned below. In **Pl. 8** is the northern end with the plateau visible beyond. Built shrine tomb N.57 can be seen above rock-cut tomb N.58 at the extreme right. **Pl. 9** shows the view further along the slope towards the wadi head, showing the above two tombs at the left and a panorama of rock-cut and built tombs, such as N.62 at the right. A further vista in **Pl. 10** shows part of N.62 on the extreme left, a rock-cut tomb with built façade N.65 in the centre and temple tomb N.52 above on the right. Between are many more tombs partially buried in hillwash and overgrown by vegetation. The final view in **Pl. 11** near the head of the wadi towards the archaic tombs demonstrates best of all the steepness of the wadi side, and shows at the left N.52, the rest of the photograph mainly occupied by rock-cut loculus tombs with built screens above, also showing some of the flights of steps which are frequently seen linking these tombs. **Pl. 12** shows archaic Doric and archaic Ionic tombs beside the ancient road to Marsa Sousah, with an Arab sitting on the projection in front of tomb N.7. The road is very overgrown and covered with hillwash and stone debris.

The beginning of the ancient road along the far side of Wadi bel Ghadir is seen from below the Acropolis hill in **Pl. 13** with a view of the revetment wall. **Pl. 14** shows tombs W.25-30 in Wadi bel Ghadir with two figures outside; the man on the right is Amor Bon Abdi Seyat, and if compared with Pl. 61 in the publication, the other is probably Sheikh Bochlega. In this woodcut the rocky outcrop to the left has been retained, but the figures seem to be transposed.[2] These tombs were called by the Arabs *'el-Suk'* because they appear like a row of little shops.[3] The following **Pl. 15** was taken with the camera at the same position as for the previous plate, and shows Amor again, with three workmen who are probably Saleh, Mohammed and Abdullah.[4] There is a large thumbprint on the photograph. An Arab wearing a barracan appears in **Pl. 16**; this view was used as Smith and Porcher's Pl. 38, reproduced from a watercolour by Porcher, now lost. Two of the Arabs in **Pl. 17** are seated on one of the reed mats bought by Smith and Porcher in Benghazi, while the third man on the right resembles the Arab in **Pl. 12**. A lost photograph is represented by **Pl. 18**, featuring workmen with a shovel and a pickaxe.[5] A shovel turned up during recent Italian excavations in the city, and it was conjectured that it may have been from Smith and Porcher's work.

[2] S & P (1864) Pls. 18, 61.
[3] HAMILTON (1856), 72.
[4] S & P (1864) Pl. 10.
[5] S & P (1864) Pl. 14.

Two photographs of the Apollo Sanctuary which do not appear in the publication were found with the collection in Edinburgh. **Pl. 19** is a view along the Sanctuary, probably taken from the vicinity of the Tomb of Residence. There are no traces of any excavation and it seems to have been too early in the year for any crops. The path leading to the Fountain can be seen, and in the distance is the plateau and the line of the coastal cliffs. **Pl. 20** was taken much nearer to the Apollo Fountain, and shows a group of Arabs at the centre and a pool of water from the Fountain to their right, nearer the camera. Behind them is a built drystone wall which can clearly be seen in Porcher's excellent watercolour of the area.

Despatch 3

All four photographs enclosed with this despatch were taken in the Tomb of Residence. The statue of *'Aesculapius'* [Apollo] features in **Pls. 21-22**. The first picture of the base of the statue, with the light coming from the left front, shows to the left the *'medicine chest'* which after restoration proved to be the sound box to the lyre. Behind it is a large fragment, probably of drapery, turned away from the camera, and on the right is an unidentified rounded object. The second plate shows the head supported on a rock against the dark blanket. The statue of *'Diana'* in **Pl. 23** is standing on the blanket, perhaps beside a recess, with the light from front right. **Pl. 24** shows two statuettes standing on the floor, where there are footprints in the dust, and a head belonging to the small statue in **Pls. 6-7** rests on a folding chair. The light is coming from right front, with the edge of the direct sunlight on the floor and striking the front horizontal strut of the chair. The head and the larger statuette are now in Istanbul.

Despatch 4

All four photographs enclosed with this despatch were taken out of doors. **Pls. 25-26** and **28** feature statue heads placed on the ground or on a blanket, with a backdrop of natural lichened rocks and vegetation. The small statue in **Pl. 27** was photographed on the same outcrop as shown in **Pl. 6**, against the dark blanket which is held up on the left by a disembodied hand.

Pl. 29 shows a statue which, although known to have been found in the excavations of the Temple of Apollo, was not photographed until later, and was taken to England in the second consignment of statuary. The photograph was taken near the end of the terrace, before the arrival there of

Nerva and Archippe. The sun is almost at its zenith and the statue is supported by an iron-rimmed wheel. A blanket lies on the ground in front of the figure and a reed mat is cast aside in the background. An object to the left behind the statue may be a stone truck to which the wheel belonged.

Despatch 5

The first three photographs are of statuary placed on the usual outcrop against a backcloth of two blankets, which in **Pl. 30** can be seen to be hung on a line of whipcord, seemingly attached on the left to the upturned handle of a stone truck. The statue stands with her back to the sea, a turbanned workman holding the right arm in position. Between him and the stone truck is a glimpse of the Apollo Sanctuary in the early afternoon. Pallas Athena in **Pl. 31** was photographed at about the same time, and the date *'July 3, 1861'* is written on the top border of the print. Lying on the right is a cedar branch used in the removal of the Bacchus and the Apollo and behind it is a supine leg, presumably that of the workman in the previous shot. The statue was not moved at all for the enlarged view of its upper part in **Pl. 32**, but another blanket has been held up to screen the figure from the thighs downwards.

Pl. 33 is a photographic portrait of Mohammed el Adouli, Smith and Porcher's friend, helper and guide, seated cross-legged on the dark blanket, his shoes placed neatly beside him, against a backdrop of lichened rock with tufts of grass and wild cyclamen growing in the crevices. A striped barracan or a burnous is flung regally over his shoulders, and he wears light-coloured undergarments with full trousers. On his head, partially covered by part of the barracan, can be seen a cap, probably resembling the dark red tarbush or chechia worn today. His right hand rests in his lap and with his left hand, the fourth finger of which has a signet ring upon it, he holds upright his magnificent long gun with its richly ornamented barrel. Over his left arm hangs his horse's bridle of decorated leather. He presents a magnificent and perfectly relaxed figure as he sits in the sunshine, and although most of his face is in shadow his dark brown eyes and beard can be seen, as can the large nose and generous mouth wearing a half-smile.

Despatch 6

The bronze head in **Pl. 34** is placed on the usual outcrop against a blurred background which may be an out-of-focus Union Jack, and creates an interesting visual effect. If this is correct, it must be the flag which was shown covering a bed in the Tomb of Residence. The female head in **Pl. 35** was photographed on the ground against natural rock, as were those in Despatch 4. The five small heads in **Pl. 36** were photographed in the sunshine, all lying on the dark blanket. The eyes of the head on the right have since disappeared, and the head in the centre, now in Istanbul, was published by Mendel as belonging to a standing Venus. The Young Dionysus in **Pl. 37** was photographed on the terrace against a background of two blankets, which a workman is attempting to hold together for the necessary exposure time. The torso is propped on boulders and holds a bunch of grapes in the left hand, a fragment which was missing until very recently, when it was recognised by Neil Adams at the British Museum, having been confused with finds from Ephesus. On the right, below the blanket, can be seen a pair of white-trousered legs – possibly those of either Porcher or Dennison who is supporting the left arm of the statue in position. The head shown here belongs to another Dionysus statue, while the true head appears on **Pl. 52** and is now united with the correct body in Edinburgh. By the workman's foot is a large unknown fragment of a base.

The two statues in **Pl. 38** are standing on the terrace in front of the blanket. That on the left clearly shows the method of inserting a separate head into the body of a statue. **Pls. 39-41** all show parts of the same colossal female statue on the upper terrace. In the first, the head sits on the torso, which is propped against a stone truck with rocks wedging the wheels to prevent it from rolling away. The second shows the lower part and base against the dark blanket, which must be held up by two people, as the white-trousered left leg of someone kneeling can be glimpsed on the right. The third photograph shows the head against the dark blanket, supported inside the stone truck. The head of Nerva in **Pl. 43** was found after the body.

Two additional photographs **Pls. 42, 44** were sent to General Burgoyne. The first is a late afternoon view of the Nerva statue and the seated figure of Archippe at the end of the upper terrace. A blanket is thrown on the rock behind, and on the right a pole or a handspike rests on another blanket. The second shows the smaller seated figure further along the terrace, propped against a stone block. Its left foot, which is not on display with the statue, was evidently a separate fragment, as it is supported in position by two stones. The fragment of the statue of a hunter is standing before a doorway towards the left, and there may be someone working inside the chamber with a wide entrance to the right. A cedar branch lies beyond the figure and a blanket is thrown over the rock wall behind. If the left foot of the small seated figure had been packed with miscellaneous fragments its identity may not have been realised on its arrival in London. It is stated clearly in the list of antiquities shipped on board 'Supply' to England that Case 5 contained the lower part of the statue and the foot, and fortunately this fragment is believed to have been rediscovered very recently among sundry finds from elsewhere by Neil Adams of the British Museum, who informed me that the marble used and the style of the sandal point to its having a Cyrene origin. The museum number is 1972 8-1, 162, and until now the small foot was thought to have come from Cnidus.

In **Pls. 45-46** the statuary is ingeniously supported. The figure of a *'huntress'*, now in Istanbul, stands against two blocks of marble and limestone, with whipcord passing round the blocks and round the statue in two or three places. The base with the legs of Artemis, which is in two pieces, is supported by a length of whipcord around each leg, fastened to something out of vision. The small head in **Pl. 47** was photographed separately on the ground beside the rocks. The cuirassed torso in **Pl. 48** is seen in full afternoon sunlight near the end of the upper terrace, with its back to the rockface against the blanket, and with a cedar branch in front of it.

Pls. 49-50 are views of the area of the Tomb of Residence. The first is a wide view taken in mid-morning from the opposite hill, showing in the foreground the old road leading up from the Sanctuary of Apollo. Behind and above is the entrance to the Tomb of Residence with a Benghazi mat hung in the doorway (although long before this time a wooden door had supposedly been constructed). To the left is a man in jacket and white trousers, wearing a light-coloured hat which is possibly of straw. To the right Porcher, wearing a foreign service helmet, jacket and white trousers, is starting to ascend the path leading to the upper terrace via the steps they had cut. On this terrace is a large scatter of workmen facing the camera, one of whom, on the far right, appeared in **Pl. 37**. Poles formed from branches of the cedar tree felled when a sledge was needed to transport Bacchus are lying on the ground, or propped up against the rockface. The cuirassed torso of Hadrian stands where it was photographed, as do Archippe and the headless Nerva. Various blankets and mats are draped on the rocks. The photograph must have been taken between August 11th, when Nerva was discovered, and September 26th, when Captain Ewart landed his men. After this date the area would be swarming with mariners, and there would be no leisure for photography. It is more likely to have been taken at the beginning of this period, soon after Nerva and Hadrian were put in place, as Smith was ill during the last six weeks of their stay and spent a considerable time in bed. There do not seem to have been any visitors during this time, so the man standing beside the Tomb of Residence must be either Dennison or one of the Maltese.

The second view was taken late one afternoon, looking along the upper terrace towards the seaward end. Only three or four workmen are on the terrace, but this includes again the man from **Pl. 37**. Two handspikes can be seen leaning against the roughly-built wall to the right of this group. There is an addition to the statuary, the draped female in **Pl. 51**, where she is shown in the same position at the end of the terrace, with Archippe and Nerva at the left and a blanket thrown in the corner. The three heads in **Pl. 52**, placed on the ground, include one where the whites of the eyes are of white marble, the irises missing. The small head on the right is that of the Young Dionysus, now in Edinburgh. A view of three portrait busts photographed against the lichened rocks **Pl. 53** is followed by a separate study of each in the same position **Pls. 54-56**.

No photographs were sent with Despatch 7 from Malta – the statues themselves were already in transit to London, where they would be seen by all the interested parties, but in any case Smith had probably run out of the equipment necessary to process any more photographs. He mentioned to Newton on July 5th that he was *'nearly out of printing materials'* – although he managed to produce at least thirty-three more prints after that date – but he had recently received a new supply of *'glasses'* from Malta, and so would be able to bring back to England the negatives of all the photographs which were taken. Transporting these irreplaceable glass plates must have required infinite care, and how many survived the journey is unknown. In the view of the Tomb of Residence, there is a handled box or either tin or wood in the recess behind the camera, which may be where they were stored at Cyrene, with the processing chemicals.

A larger box containing a *'wet plate collodion outfit'* of about 1855 on display at the Science Museum, London is hinged so that one long side opens downwards, and is fitted with compartments for bottles and a folding metal frame for supporting a dark cloth and even contains a collapsed tripod. A later catalogue of 1864 by Frederick J. Cox of 26 Ludgate Hill, London shows a *'Set of Apparatus for taking Portraits by the Collodion process.'* This wooden box, with a lifting lid like Smith and Porcher's, contained a small camera, achromatic lens with rack and pinion, camera stand, gutta-percha bath and dipper, glass plates and thirteen bottles of chemicals and varnish.

Considering the lengthy and cumbersome processes involved in preparing, exposing, developing and fixing just one glass plate, requiring nitric and sulphuric acids, ether, alcohol, powdered pumice, potassium iodide, silver nitrate and pyrogallic acid, it is surprising that in 1861, at least in theory, it would have been possible for the lieutenants to produce coloured pictures, panoramic views and even sets of stereo photographs – had such novel gewgaws been required.

XIII. PORCHER'S WATERCOLOURS

In his very first despatch to Lord John Russell, dated 23rd February 1861, Murdoch Smith wrote: '*Since our arrival Lieut Porcher has made a large number of drawings of the different objects of interest here particularly the tombs. I have also made plans of some of the more Characteristic of them, so that we hope before leaving to be able to furnish such detail as will give a pretty accurate idea of this remarkable Necropolis.*'

The range of colours used by Porcher is fairly small, and could easily have been achieved with a limited number of pigments, but the occasional use of a brilliant emerald green hints that a greater spread of colours was at his disposal. He probably had a japanned tin paint box, with places for brushes and for mixing colours, which would be lighter for travelling and more practical for the conditions in which he was likely to need it than a beautiful mahogany one. Winsor & Newton and Rowney produced these boxes in various sizes containing moist water colours, and the smallest one to include the emerald green was the 16 cake box which held twenty colours. Alternatively, Porcher could have chosen his own range of colours by fixing replacement pans into an existing smaller box, as in the Cyrenaica he would not need all the colours provided by the manufacturers. The artist's pigment would be mixed with the cool, sweet water flowing from the Apollo Fountain; this he would carry in a japanned water bottle with a cup which fitted over the end. The limited colour range used by Porcher shows his skill in rendering the hues and tones of the countryside, and his deftness with the brush created the freshness and vigour captured in his watercolours.

The watercolours on Whatman paper fall into three basic sizes, some of which have been trimmed down. The first is 4to Imperial, the second 8vo Imperial and the third 16mo Imperial. These sizes and the material used probably indicate that Porcher took with him solid drawing blocks of Whatman thick paper, each of 32 sheets with half-bound covers. The number of surviving watercolours show that he must have had two blocks of the largest size and one each of the other sizes. A letter from Malta in June mentions that the writer was sending to Cyrene via the 'Scourge' six sheets of Royal, six of Imperial and 12 of Cartridge drawing paper. This ties in with the fact that cartridge paper was used for Porcher's duplicate watercolour plans Nos.88-96.

Porcher's watercolour work formed the basis for the engravings and lithographs in the publication, and in 1865 he presented the originals to the Trustees of the British Museum. A folded sheet of blue foolscap summarises that 'In Portfolio of Cyrene' there were 87 originals, broken down into 23 sketches on large mounts, 35 sketches on 32 small mounts, 29 in a small sketch book which has not been traced (see Epilogue), and additionally 3 plans of temples, 17 plans of tombs, 2 plans and elevations of tombs and 3 plans of the country, giving a grand total of 112 watercolours. Of these, 43 views and 11 plans were published. He also enclosed a paper portfolio containing 10 plans on cartridge paper and 5 views on Whatman paper, none of which had been published. All the watercolours are signed 'E A Porcher', but only the Frontispiece and Pls. 17, 31 are dated '1861'. Although forty-seven tombs were explored, only eleven were described and eight plans and an internal elevation published, leaving another fifteen and vignettes unused. Porcher's study of tombs not surprisingly overlapped most of those explored by Pacho, but in comparison he produced more plans. Twelve of Pacho's tombs were not included in Porcher's survey but he added a further twelve tombs himself.

In the following assessment, where an unnumbered watercolour exists in the British Museum and also appears in the publication as a plate, I have given the watercolour a zero number and included the published plate number, all in bold text, e.g. '**Watercolour 0; Plate 123'**. Where a published plate has been engraved from a watercolour which no longer exists I have followed the same process, but added '(missing)' to the watercolour, and only the published plate is in bold, e.g. 'Watercolour 0 (missing); **Plate 123'**. Where a watercolour exists but has not been used in the publication it is in bold, whether or not it is numbered, e.g. **'Watercolour 123'** or **'Watercolour 0'**. Abbreviated plate numbers, e.g. **[Pl. 68]** refer only to plates in this publication. The numbers applied to tombs are those given by John Cassels in his register, compiled in 1953-54.

Studies around the Northern Necropolis

Watercolour 0; Frontispiece This is the last view to record in its complete state Tomb N.180, overlooking the ancient road to Apollonia and dominating the picture, with Tomb N.165 deeply terraced into the hillside beyond. The distant hills are now slashed through by the deep cutting for the new road to Shahat. Porcher has painted horsemen and camels passing along the road through a countryside in early spring, indicated by a faint green wash, with the Mediterranean on the horizon. Dated '1861'. W.353 H.252mm. B.M.Neg. PS.351138.[1] **[Pl. 77]**

Watercolour 0 view; Plate 11 The Fountain of Apollo is on the left with the ruins of the Apollo Sanctuary lying in front of it, mostly covered in hill-wash. The built stone wall at one side of the Fountain, where two people are watering a camel and a horse, can be seen in **Pl. 29**. Again, a thin green wash seems to indicate a spring scene, with four or five distant figures carrying out excavations in the Sanctuary beyond the cisterns, with the sea in the background. W.354 H.228mm. B.M.Neg. PS.351132. **[Pl. 60]**

Watercolour 0 view; Plate 12 The Fountain of Apollo, with an Arab standing at the entrance. The view is inaccurate, as Porcher has depicted the cliff descending abruptly on the left to show hills beyond, whereas the rockface actually continues. W.256 H.177mm. **[Pl. 61]**

Watercolour 0 view; Plate 13 A view showing the eastern slope of Wadi Haleg Shaloof, done in yellow ochre and green. Ashlar-built Tomb N.77 is in silhouette on the left, with shrine Tomb N.57 immediately above loculus Tomb N.58 to the right. Flights of steps can be seen in two places, leading down to sarcophagus enclosures, and rock-cut triple-loculus Tomb N.62 is also shown in this view, which compares with **Pl. 10**. The line of the ancient road above is marked by the tombs cut in the rockface beside it. To the left is the plateau with the blue of the sea beyond, and in the foreground is a herdsman with brown, black and white goats. W.354 H.252mm. B.M.Neg. PS.289232. **[Pl. 66]**

Watercolours 0 view, 88 plan; Plate 14 Tomb N.165 has a large square forecourt and a plain, rock-cut façade, partly built at the top. The single entrance has funeral bust niches on either side. Above are two recesses for stelai and a rectangular recess for an inscribed panel. The former entablature, which was probably Doric, has fallen and the strong shadows thrown on the façade indicate that the forecourt is deeply rock-cut. Three Arabs with a laden camel and donkey are passing, and a horseman is seen further along the road. W.251 H.176mm. B.M.Neg. PS.346618.

The plan of the tomb interior shows a chamber with two facing rows of five loculus entrances, with a section given through one loculus. A Late Roman arcosolium is cut at the end and a cubiculum with three arcosolia is

---

[1] THORN (2005), 32, 403 Fig. 245.

cut at the end of two adjacent loculi whose separating wall has been truncated.[2] W.459 H.314mm, B.M.Neg. PS.241772. (Also Porcher unnumbered duplicate plan where the section is annotated *'ceiling'* and *'floor'* W.335 H.280mm).[3] **[Pl. 67]**

Watercolours 0 view, 89 plan; Plate 15 Tombs N.90-92 have an open forecourt with rock-cut boundaries, and consist of three rock-cut tomb entrances along the main façade. The central Tomb N.91 has a plain door surround within a façade of false ashlar with recessed quoins on either side, referred to by Cassels as *'Slots for entirely built flank walls'*.[4] The Doric entablature has fallen, but there are indications of a defined area above. In the foreground Porcher depicts two armed Arabs, the head covering of one making a splash of vibrant red. The ground is yellow ochre and the low scrub above the tombs is green, while the distant hill is given a dry appearance by the use of grey/brown. W.257 H.168mm. B.M.Neg. PS.346614.

Porcher shows the central tomb with a chamber and eight loculi. The others are of a similar type but smaller, with monument N.89 on the hillside above Tomb N.90. W.454 H.315mm, B.M.Neg. PS.241773. (Also Porcher unnumbered duplicate plan W.382 H.312mm).[5] **[Pl. 75]**

Watercolour 0 view; Plate 16 The range of archaic Tombs N.2-10 previously recorded by Pacho have been given a false foreground for dramatic effect, as in reality the ground drops steeply away from the ancient road in front of their façades, and they could never be seen from this angle. Also incorrect is the way in which the ground above Tomb N.10 on the right descends – in reality the line of the hilltop continues – and the hill on the left has been heightened and dramatised. The rock-cut projection shown clearly in front of Tombs N.6-7 is still there. Grey clouds are driving over the blue sky. W.252 H.176mm.

A view of archaic Doric tristyle and Ionic distyle Tombs N.7-9 was included as Photograph 11 sent with Despatch 1 of 23rd February, photographed subsequently by Weld-Blundell.[6]

Watercolours 0, 117 interior views, 0 plan; Plates 17, 31 In the first interior view of Tomb N.83 Porcher has lengthened the appearance of the 11ft high cubiculum, and at this date the arcosolia seem to be undamaged.

---

[2] Pacho (1827) Pl. XLVIII. 2.
[3] Thorn (2005), 32, 42-43, 350, 359-360. Figs. 30, 229, 236.
[4] Cassels Arch. Blue Book fol. 19.
[5] Thorn (2005), 42, 354 Figs. 28.
[6] Pacho (1827) Pls. XXXVII, XXXVIII; Weld-Blundell (1896) Fig. 6.

He shows swallows nesting near the ceiling on the west side, in the place where they still nest today. An Arab is seated on a reed mat and another is standing nearby, his gun leaning against an arcosolium case. The colours are subdued but true. W.354 H.253mm. B.M.Neg. PS.289234.

A second view, again showing the swallows on the west wall, shows part of the built grave of Demetria on the northern side next to the entrance. Hillwash conceals the steps down into the tomb and covers the floor. W.251 H.177mm. B.M.Neg. PS.346634.

The annotation on the plan and section states: *'CYRENE, PLAN of an ornamented and painted tomb in the Northern Necropolis'*. W.480 H.329mm.

The decorated arcosolia with conches and the painted arcosolium by the entrance were described, but the painted inscription to Demetria and other inscriptions cut in the walls were unmentioned, although recorded by Pacho.[7] The forecourt and façade remained unrecorded, probably also obscured by hillwash.[8] **[Pl. 71]**

Watercolours 0 view, 0 plan; Plates 20, 32 A view of the twelve triple-level loculus Tomb N.86 appears by the colouring to have been painted during the summer, with the ground ochre and the scrub above it green against a dry grey hill. The built balustrade is missing, a block sarcophagus stands at the back and there are two funeral bust niches in the entablature. Two Arabs with their horses are depicted, their saddle-cloths providing splashes of colour, one blue and yellow, the other red. In the distance is a glimpse of the deep blue sea. W.251 H.177mm. B.M.Neg. PS.351139.

The interior of this tomb was planned, the type being described as *'without chambers'*[9] and the loculi as *'sarcophagus recesses being cut directly into the face of the rock'*. . *'separated from each other by thin partitions.'* The plan bears the comment *'Capable of holding 105 Sarcophagi'*, which the lieutenants must have calculated on the basis of eleven loculi containing three burials one behind another at the three levels, and the remaining shorter loculus having burials only two deep, although still at three levels. This tomb is now filled nearly to the gunwales with hillwash, and to produce the plan and section that he did, Porcher must have employed an extremely small Arab to squirm along beneath the roof to obtain measurements. How he came to the conclusion that the entire tomb was triple-level is unknown, as it does not seem ever to have been cleared. W.443 H.302mm.[10] **[Pl. 74]**

[7] Pacho (1827) Pl. LV; S & P (1864), 31.
[8] Thorn (2005), 30, 41, 245-248, 344, 358 Figs. 170-174, 294.
[9] S & P (1864), 32.
[10] Thorn (2005), 41, 344 Fig. 27.

Watercolours 0 interior view, 90 plan; Plate 21 This tomb was apparently located on the eastern side of Wadi Haleg Shaloof, near the quarry behind the Kenissieh, and is reported to be now walled up.[11] The view of a painted chamber shows a vestibule with plain dado and frieze, between which, around the walls, is lattice decoration in light red including roundels at intervals, also hinted at on the ceiling. Broad bands of light red run round the top of the walls, down the corners and enclose the decorated area at top and bottom. Cut into the walls are cinerarium niches which may originally have been concealed by slabs painted with the same lattice design. Three goats are depicted in the chamber, a brown and white, a white and a glossy black and brown. W.153 H.142mm. B.M.Neg. PS.351136.

The unpublished plan shows a forecourt with two loculus entrances and another doorway in a corner, probably once a loculus which has been much widened, leading to the painted chamber. This in turn leads into a small cubiculum with two arcosolia and three formae. At the right-hand side of the plan is a section taken through the painted chamber, two of the formae and the rear arcosolium. W.480 H.318mm, B.M.Neg. PS.241774. Also duplicate unnumbered plan W.481 H.321mm. **[Pl. 70]**

Watercolour 0 interior view; Plate 22 The rock-cut façade of Tomb N.226 has twenty-three funeral bust niches above and around the entrance. Porcher's interior view of the chamber, which originally had pairs of loculi on three sides, is painted in subdued browns, grey and blue. It shows on either side the two remaining pairs of loculi, while the pair opposite the entrance have been cut away to form a cubiculum containing three arcosolia with sculpted shells within their conches.[12] The front wall of the rear arcosolium case is badly damaged, and the mensae on all three are, unusually, formed of sarcophagus lids which have been cut down to fit, those of the flanking two being smashed but left in place. Among hillwash and debris on the floor lies a fragment of a doorslab with a fillet from one of the loculi; also in the dust are various bones and a skull. Porcher was unaware of the 'rainbow' mosaic lying concealed under the hillwash. The tomb was unplanned. W.252 H.176mm. B.M.Neg. PS.289224.[13] **[Pl. 80]**

Watercolours 0 interior view, 91 plan; Plates 23, 41 Porcher portrayed here a lost tomb in the area now called locally 'El Mawy land', described as being *'Cut in the side of a quarry'*.[14] There are five funeral bust niches

---

[11] S & P (1864) Pl. 41; Information Dr Joyce Reynolds.
[12] S & P (1864), 31; MAIOLETTI (1930), 577 Tav. F.
[13] THORN (2005), 41, 346, 360 Figs. 27, 224, 237.
[14] S & P (1864), 32.

in a row inside the antechamber, above an inserted barrel-vaulted arcosolium, indicating that the original six-loculus tomb was the host for later burials. A neat row of six small niches is shown in the wall adjacent to the entrance, while opposite, above the loculi, are other assorted niches. A cone of hillwash has poured in from the entrance and a snarling wild dog is unearthing a skull. The green wash over the damp earth-covered floor probably represents lichen; the other colours used are predominantly blue and brown. Only the interior is published, the antechamber being 27½ ft long by 13ft wide (8.39 by 3.96m). W.252 H.161mm. (Porcher Watercolour no.91 plan with elevation and section through arcosolium, W.480 H.321mm, B.M.Neg. PS.241775, duplicate plan W.488 H.328mm).[15]

Watercolours 0 interior view, 0 plan; Plates 24, 35 The view of Tomb N.131 shows four double-level loculi on each side. Through a doorway opposite can be seen floor graves, beyond which, cut in the end wall, is a barrel-vaulted arcosolium. The overall scene is painted in subdued browns and blue-purple, enlivened by splashes of green and yellow in the clothing of two groups of Arabs on woven mats. W.253 H.176mm. B.M.Neg. PS.351137.

The plan, with its three sections, reveals the true extent of this tomb, which appears foreshortened. On the other side of the first doorway the chamber has been extended laterally to form a spacious area edged with floor graves, and through the next doorway is a chamber which, in addition to the rear arcosolium, contains in the side walls an uncommon feature in Cyrene, banks of square entrances to small chambers on two levels. W.320 H.471mm.[16] **[Pl. 76]**

Watercolour 0 view; Plate 25 Built loculus façade Tomb N.178 is recorded only in a view with the neighbouring Tomb N.179, which has a forecourt enclosed by a dwarf rock-cut wall with chamfered coping. W.453 H.320mm.

It was previously recorded by Pacho and subsequently in ca.1915 was photographed by the Italians and in 1943 by the Germans; it was eventually cleared in 1947 by Burton Brown, who found two female half-figures in the debris.[17]

Watercolour 0 view, (128 missing); Plate 26 This range of tombs with unprepossessing entrances *'called by the Arabs the Kenissieh'* overlooks the

[15] THORN (2005), 348-349 Figs. 226, 239.
[16] THORN (2005), 42, 350, 354, 361 Figs. 29, 228, 233, 238.
[17] Ant. Dept.Cyr. Ph. 3757-1781; HORN (1943), 198 Abb. 28; BURTON BROWN (1948), 78.

ancient road, whose level was later raised by the Italians under General Tassoni. For this work they probably made use of the stone from the built boundary wall of Tomb N.84 shown by Porcher, as this wall no longer exists. In Porcher's view there are steps cut in the road, where at that time it still climbed up and round the shoulder of the hill, with the sea just visible to the right. The entrance to Tomb N.84 is seen low down to the right of the boundary wall, and above is Tomb N.416, reached by some narrow steps in the corner behind the wall. The entrance to the 'Kenissieh' catacomb complex N.66 is one of the openings to the left. W.251 H.177mm. B.M.Neg. PS.346612.

A 1908 photographic view, reproduced here, must have been taken from a point just a few feet to the north of where Porcher had been sitting, and illustrates the artist's accuracy. Here again we see the line of tomb entrances and the road descending from the rising ground, with the mud-filled ruts of chariot wheels clearly visible in the foreground.

The interior of the Kenissieh, planned by Pacho, represents a maze of interconnecting burial chambers and cubicula *'128 feet by 68 feet'*. . *'In the interior we found a large marble sarcophagus, and two marble pedestals'* with inscriptions previously seen by Bourville and later by Norton.[18] Porcher's Watercolour no.128 of marble pedestals, perhaps those from this tomb, is missing.[19] **[Pls. 72a-b]**

Watercolour 0 view; Plate 27 Jean-Raimond Pacho's Tomb of Residence, the enormous hypogeum Tomb N.398, whose portico may have been damaged in an earthquake and is now somewhat concealed by vegetation, stands out in Porcher's view because of his use of dull colours for the foreground. To the right of the picture are the cisterns, seen in Pl. 11, and scattered across the area is a flock of goats, with the line of the sea on the right. W.251 H.166mm. B.M.Neg. PS.346630.

The façade was *'originally ornamented by a colonnade of six pillars, 75 feet in length'*. The hypogeum representing *'The principal room measured 41 feet by 37 feet, with a height of 15 feet, and in it were found fragments of marble sarcophagi, with elaborate bas-reliefs'*. It was then used by the Arabs as a granary, but in 1852 James Hamilton mentions that it was *'inhabited'*, and he was invited to see *'marble boxes, the fragments of two very elegantly carved sarcophagi'*. I was able to locate only the one originally recorded by Pacho.[20] **[Pl. 62]**

---

[18] *C.I.G.* 5153; S & P (1864), 33; Gregory (1909) Pl. to face p. 10.
[19] Thorn (2005) Fig. 10.
[20] Pacho (1827) Pl. LVIII; Hamilton (1856), 71; S & P (1864), 34; Thorn (2005), 23, 28-29 Figs. 7-8, 234.

188

Watercolour 0 (missing); **Plate 29** *'Ruins of the Christian City of Cyrene'* A burnous-clad Arab carrying a gun is leading his mare and her foal towards Cyrene along a track between hummocks strewn with ancient debris, beside the remains of the Byzantine East Church. The ruins of the apse can be seen, and also the distinctive springing of the nave arches. Further along the track is another Arab with a camel, and among the vegetation are some examples of *thapsia garganica*. [21] [Fig. 16]

Watercolours 101 view, 0 plan; Plate 34 The view of rock-cut tombs unregistered by Cassels on the northern face of the eastern hill bounding Wadi bu Turchia [22] shows on the left a plain four-entrance loculus system, a false panelled door in the centre and a pedimented façade on the right. Behind on the hill can be seen the Zawiyah, and in the forecourt are three goats. Also unnumbered duplicate. W.252 H.150mm, W.252 H.147mm. B.M.Neg. PS.346635.

The plan illustrates how the tomb at the far left has been expanded and developed to include a cubiculum with arcosolia. The entrance is now partially blocked with stones and the interior filled with debris and hillwash. With the aid of a torch, a small arched recess can be seen facing the entrance, and a blank wall immediately to the left. The cubiculum Porcher planned is not evident, but the entrance to it may be concealed by the large amount of debris inside. The rest of this side of the complex is also obscured by debris and the loculi are very much buried in hillwash. The almost buried, pedimented open portico at the other end of this group has on the left an entrance with a primitive cymatium to a primary loculus, to which the false door may relate. On the right is a completely plain entrance to another loculus. The main entrance, again with primitive cymatium, leads into a chamber loculus system where the pairs of loculi appear to be raised high above the floor, which is hidden by a deep layer of debris and hillwash, suggesting that they may be of several levels, the right-hand loculus at the rear being unfinished. This tomb's cornice mouldings are identical to those on the nearby Tomb N.364, but the portico is not so deep. In addition to the wide and wonderful vista over the lower plateau to the sea, there is an impressive view from these tombs of the rock-cut tombs on the next hill, one of which appears in Watercolour 118. W.443 H.321mm. [23] **[Pl. 63]**

---

[21] BEECHEY (1828), 404; HAMILTON (1856), 46; STUCCHI (1975), 364-365, 392-395 Fig. 397.

[22] This valley and headland are farmed by Faraj Abdulrheem, who grows apples and very good grapes.

[23] THORN (2005), 345 Fig. 27.

Watercolour 0 plan; Plate 57 is the plan and section of the *'Temple of Venus at Cyrene'*. W.458 H.320mm. **[Fig. 14]**

Watercolour 0 (missing); Plate 58 *'Encampment of the Party from H.M.S. "Melpomene" near the head of the Augubah'* In the foreground stands an armed guard, apparently in Turkish dress, and a few yards in front of him, where the road curves, can be seen the large wheels of the artillery wagons. A group of camels are couched below the road, and beyond them are eleven bell tents of the wagon party. **[Fig. 18]**

Watercolour 0 view; Plate 59 The view of the Tomb of Residence area shows Smith and Porcher's servants in front of the entrances to the chambers on the upper terrace, [24] the blocked entrances on that level and the lower doorway to their living quarters. Groups of Arabs are moving up the road, but the track in front of the Tomb of Residence is concealed by the shoulder of the Acropolis hill. On the left are the cisterns seen in Pls. 11 and 27. The terraces of the hill are a pale green, with the bare rockface light ochre. The view across the plateau makes the sea seem very close, and one is reminded of Smith's comment in the publication that towards the end of their stay, when they were waiting for a ship, the Maltese servants were watching for sight of a sail. W.251 H.176mm. B.M.Neg. No.PS.351135. **[Pl. 59]**

Watercolour 87 plan Interior of the Tomb of Residence. Porcher's 1865 list states: *'Plan of the Tomb Captains Porcher and Smith lived in during their stay at CYRENE in 1861, being situated about 250 yards to the South-east of the FOUNTAIN of APOLLO'*. The interior view, its original watercolour unfortunately lost, is shown in Plate 9. W.480 H.313mm. B.M.Neg. PS.241771. **[Fig. 17]**

Watercolour 92 plan Plan and section only of Tomb N.228, with three loculi to the east, while an antechamber loculus system to the west, now inaccessible, has two loculi in the rear wall, the first extending back underneath the chamber. [25] W.475 H.322mm. B.M.Neg. PS.241776. Also duplicate W.453 H.320mm. Porcher stated on the plan, wrongly, that a view of the exterior had been published as Plate 25. [26] **[Fig. 46]**

Watercolours 98 interior view, 94 plan, Porcher plan 2 Porcher painted an interior view of the earlier antechamber with two cinerarium niches

---

[24] STUCCHI (1975) Fig. 520.
[25] BACCHIELLI (1980), 11-18 Figs. 1-13.
[26] THORN (2005), 346 Fig. 224.

cut in the left wall. The antechamber shows signs of having been Romanised, as it is decorated with a broad centrally-placed red band on a yellowish-white background, and through the doorway opposite chamber loculi are visible, three on each side with two entrances at the rear. An armed Arab with water jars has built a bright fire on the left, while three sheep are gathered in a corner. W.252 H.177mm. B.M.Neg. PS.346621. (Porcher Watercolour plans and sections no.2, W.410 H.320mm and no.94, W.465 H.322mm. B.M.Neg. PS.241778). **[Pl. 82]**

This tomb below El Mawy land was unregistered by Cassels, but was planned both by Pacho[27] and Porcher. Distinctive downward-sloping rock-cut walls flank the forecourt, heightened by inset courses of ashlar blocks. The entrance was cut to receive a stone surround, now missing, and the antechamber, with a chamfered step W.43cm running round three sides, leads into a wide passage with three loculi on each side and two at the rear, all with completely built door surrounds. At the rear, the loculus on the right is double-level, the lower level being longer than the upper one, which has two deep rectangular niches cut at the end with 19cm between them, that on the right H.69 W.38 D.38cm. Their sills slope down approx. 3 cm towards the viewer, while their backs form a cove at the top. The corresponding left loculus has a finely cut inscription recorded by Pacho on the lintel,[28] the characters with serifs, suggesting a 4th to 3rd century B.C. date. This loculus was converted into a chamber, the original slabs left in situ in the floor, and a later triple-level loculus cut additionally at the right side of the rear wall.

Parts of this tomb were coated with a 2cm thick layer of plaster and decorated in Roman times. The antechamber has a painted red band 72cm deep running round it, beginning 59cm above the step, with a clearly visible scribe line at the top. The plaster appears yellowish, with the area above the band generally darker, being blackened by Bedouin fires. Two square niches are cut into the decoration on the left wall, the right H.38 W.34 D.34cm with a 5cm offset at the sides and top, and the left H.36 W.33 D.25cm. Also plastered are the chamber conversion and the loculus with niches at the rear. The niches contain red decoration which exists again as a band H.94cm above the sill.[29]

Watercolours 99 interior view, 95 plan, **Porcher plan 3**. The interior view shows two dogs digging in a vestibule with a cubiculum chamber beyond. To the right the walls have collapsed to reveal two adjacent loculi,

---

[27] Pacho (1827) Pl. XLVIII, 4 plan.
[28] Pacho (1827) Pl. LXVI, 7 inscription; *C.I.G.* 5152.
[29] Thorn (2005), 349-350, 401, 406 Figs. 228, 243.

where another dog, facing the light flooding in from the entrance, is barking. Also duplicate. W.253 H.158mm, W.252 H.175mm. B.M.Neg. PS.346617.

The plan shows several loculus tombs, one of which is altered by the addition of a cubiculum with arcosolia, and another with burial chambers. B.M.Neg. PS.241779. (Porcher Watercolour plans and sections no.3, W.424 H.326mm and no.95, W.460 H.322mm). **[Pl. 83]**

Watercolours 100 view, 96 plan, Porcher plan 4. The exterior view of this untraced tomb shows a rock-cut façade with three entrances and four funeral bust niches, above which is a heavy isodomic built screen. A further entrance with two funeral bust niches is in the right-hand wall of the forecourt, which is a dull pink, stepped at the top, with a large *thapsia garganica* growing on top. The foreground is in dull green and brown and the tomb is blue/grey. An Arab is standing in front of the tomb and another is seated beside a waiting horse. Also duplicate. W.252 H.147mm, W.253 H.174mm. B.M.Neg. PS.346613.

The plan shows three loculus tombs, two with square antechambers, and there is a later burial chamber on another side of the forecourt. W.454 H.311mm. B.M.Neg. PS.241780. Also duplicate W.332 H.251mm. **[Pl. 84]**

Watercolour 112 *'Appearance of the Ruins of 2 Temples and the Stadium'* This is a sunrise picture of the stadium area. The sky is a luminous pale blue and oyster, with a low thin strip of pink cloud and another of pale purple. A small mound catches the first rays of the sun while the rest of the picture is in shadow. In the foreground is an Arab sitting in his tent with a smoking fire, his tethered camel nearby. W.354 H.223mm.

Watercolours 0, 0 plans; Plates 55, 56, the latter including a section, feature the plans of the Temple of Zeus and the small temple near the stadium. W.480 H.321mm, W.461 H.312mm respectively.

Watercolour 113 *'Partial View of the tombs and Sarcophagi in the Northern Necropolis'* In the foreground are six goats on the hill to the east of El Mawy land, which is in shadow beyond. The view is looking towards the Kenissieh, which is below at the right of the picture, with distant figures walking along the road beside it. The western sky is treated in a similar way to 112, but this time portraying sunset. However, the angle of the shadows reveal that the time is early afternoon. This is a lonely place, rarely visited, high above the road, with Tombs N.215-216 cut around the sides of an ancient quarry which is awash with thistles, and a haven for wild life. W.355 H.234mm. B.M.Negs. PS.289232; PS.346625. **[Pl. 73]**

192

Watercolour 114 *'View of the tombs on the Scarped hill below the Fountain of Apollo'.* On the left the northernmost extremity of the Acropolis hill slopes steeply downwards, and the rest of the picture is devoted to the eastern slope of the hill above Wadi bel Ghadir, with its tombs along the ancient road and the natural limestone terraces above. W.353 H.220mm. The same view was published as a photograph by Ghislanzoni. [30]

Watercolour 115 In this view Porcher has pictured himself, with his gun and his dog, strolling past two rock-cut loculus tombs. On the left, Tomb N.224 has a built pediment and four intended loculi entrances, two of which were cut, the one on the right being primary and that on the left secondary with two unrecorded inscriptions: [31]

    i.   L.ΟΓΩΓΛΙΟC   ii.   ΑΓΑΘΩΝΕΜΟC

        P] .... [MA   ...... [ΛΝΗ

In the adjoining two-entrance Tomb N.225 the façade was cut as far as the cornice and the surface dressed for a screen which was never put in place. In the foreground is a monolithic sarcophagus which appears to be slipping down the hill, but is still in the same position today. W.250 H.177mm. B.M.Neg. PS.346633. [32] **[Pl. 79]**

Watercolour 116 This is the first record of six-loculus Tomb N.183 with an isodomic built screen, [33] described as *'Capable of holding 54 Sarcophagi'*, unplanned. In front is an Arab family, the man with a gun and red tarbush, the woman with green headscarf, blue and white striped dress with a red sash and a baby on her back, and a small boy. W.250 H.175mm. B.M.Neg. PS.346616. [34] **[Pl. 78]**

Watercolour 118 This view of Tomb N.276 with its deeply recessed rock-cut façade shows a single central entrance surrounded by numerous funeral bust niches of various sizes, with broken statuary lying in front.

The tomb lies halfway up the north-west face of a hill which is across the valley east of the tombs shown in Watercolour 101. The interior has a small square antechamber, beyond which is a long gallery with low loculi opening off all three sides. Some of the dividing walls between loculi have been

[30] GHISLANZONI (1915) Fig. 75.
[31] Cassels Arch. Grey Book fol. 71.
[32] THORN (2005), 43, 342 Figs. 29, 219.
[33] GHISLANZONI (1915) Pl. 54; CASSELS (1955), 28 Pl. VIId.
[34] THORN (2005), 43, 406 Fig. 220.

removed, probably in the Roman period, making it ideal for Bedouin occupation in recent times, as indicated by a rusted hurricane lamp hanging from a hook in the roof. [35] W.177 H.118mm. B.M.Neg. PS.346623. **[Pl. 85]**

Watercolour 119 This rock-cut temple tomb with two compartments is also unregistered, and is situated towards the bottom of the terraced western slope of the unnamed valley to the east of Wadi bu Turchia. To its left is a similar temple tomb, now very much obscured by hillwash which partially covers the roof, and on the other side is a loculus tomb with a recessed façade. The three sarcophagi above have lids consisting of thick plain slabs. [36] W.177 H.121mm. B.M.Neg. PS.346628. [37] **[Pl. 64]**

Watercolour 120 *'Interior of a small Painted Tomb in the Northern Necropolis'*. This unregistered *'tomb'*, in fact a triclinium recess, has a monochrome decoration in light red. The frieze shows a swag pattern, with a wide border above the wall decoration which is a lattice design with small honeysuckle motifs inside each lozenge. There are two vertical bands near the centre of the far wall, with a plain area between, marking the position held by a former dividing wall between two loculi. On the floor a saddle and a gun leaning against the left wall demonstrate the lack of height in the chamber caused by the depth of hillwash, which may conceal a dado. The *'tomb'* lies in the curve of the ancient road, west of Tomb N.131, below the area of El Mawy land. W.253 H.155mm. B.M.Negs. PS.289222; PS.346636. [38] **[Pl. 86]**

Watercolour 121 *'Interior of a small Painted Tomb in the Northern Necropolis'*. The upper part of this rock-cut triclinium recess, identified recently in the long, narrow forecourt of Tomb N.258, has a painted decoration of light red ribbons and swags of green or red leaves. On the lower half of the walls is a design of bordered panels counterchanged in light red and yellow. W.174 H.107mm. B.M.Neg. PS.351133. [39] **[Pl. 87]**

Watercolour 122 *'Interior of a small Painted Tomb in the Northern Necropolis'*. This rock-cut triclinium recess appears to belong to Tomb N.259 which has an Ionic façade. It has no frieze but the walls are painted with bordered panels of colour in red, yellow and blue. The façade of Tomb

---

[35] THORN (2005), 339 Fig. 28.
[36] This may indicate that the sarcophagi are uncut blanks.
[37] THORN (2005), 43 Fig. 27.
[38] THORN (2005), 357-358, 360-361, 430 Fig. 235.
[39] THORN (2005), 358 Fig. 235.

N.258 can be seen beyond the recess, set back to the left, and two stelai stand on the right. W.175 H.131mm. B.M.Neg. PS.351134. Like the recess shown in Watercolour 120, this one has also been formed from a two-loculus tomb, converted by the removal of the dividing wall. The interior was covered with a coat of limewash at some time during the first half of the last century, obliterating the decoration, but as a result of the sea wind and weather this layer is now wearing away, and enough can now be seen of the colours to identify it from Porcher's recording. [40] **[Pl. 88]**

Watercolour 123a Built façade Tomb N.36 has two entrances for loculi, only one of which was fully cut, and is partly buried in hillwash, with a stepped wall to the left and indications of a defined area among the undergrowth. It was reused in Roman times, as cut around the entrances are numerous niches for the insertion of funeral busts and marble inscription panels which have not survived in situ. The tomb overlooks the site of Norton's 1911 excavations, where Porcher must have been sitting sketching, and it was shown in a view by Pacho, [41] but no plan is known to have been made by either Pacho or Porcher. W.177 H.104mm. B.M.Neg. PS.346624. [42] **[Pl. 68]**

Watercolours 123b view, 0 plan; Plates 19, 33 Described are the façade entrances of Tomb N.17, the rock-cut statuary above and the peculiar form of the chamber, dependent on the rock formation. In his view Porcher recorded this sculptured tomb with the façade partially buried in hillwash and topped by two rock-cut sarcophagi above the entablature, as shown by Pacho. [43] An Arab is sitting by the loculus sarcophagus to the right of the entrance. W.177 H.126mm. B.M.Neg PS.346627.

It was possible to gain access to plan the interior, Plate 33, showing a cubiculum with four barrel-vaulted arcosolia, but due to hillwash in the chambers the evidence for the original loculi was hidden. W.485 H.326mm. (Porcher Watercolour no.123b view). [44] **[Pl. 69]**

Watercolour 0; Plate 44 Captioned in the publication as '*Wady Lebaiath, between Cyrene and Apollonia*', and looking towards the sullen, pewter-like sea, this view shows the interlocking folds of the rugged landscape seen, not only by the lieutenants, but also by the wagon parties. Also duplicate. W.354 H.253mm, W.253 H.183mm.

---

[40] Thorn (2005), 358 Fig. 235.
[41] Pacho (1827) Pls. XXXIII, XXXIV. 2.
[42] Thorn (2005), 31, 42, 344, 355, 403.
[43] Pacho (1827) Pl. LXXXVIII; S & P (1864), 29 Pls. 19, 33.
[44] Thorn (2005), 31, 40, 48-49, 102, 344, 361 Figs. 8, 225, 237, 254.

Watercolour 111 *'The Wady Labouatha about 2 miles to the Eastwards of the city'*. Despite the similarity in the name, this is a different location from that shown in the publication as Wady Lebaiath (above). Pines cover the hilltops and no sea is visible beyond the steep, winding wadi. Three young camels stand on the right, and a herd of goats is shown in the foreground and on the hill to the left. Hamilton describes *'Wady Leboaitha'* as a ravine about a mile south of the town, and running nearly due east, filled with tombs and flights of wood-pigeons. [45]

Studies around the Southern Necropolis

Watercolours 0 view, 0 plan; Plates 28, 36 The main subject of this view is the large built Tomb S.186 with three Arabs on top, bristling with arms, and three more on the ground. Beyond it is the similar Tomb S.185. The foreground is a dull, light olive green with streaks of brown representing tufts of grass, and the hills behind are a light purple/grey. W.252 H.162mm.

This temple tomb has a stepped base supporting one orthostat course and four isodomic courses. There are no entrances into the double-level compartments, and Porcher erroneously shows it with a flat roof. W.465 H.322mm. Weld-Blundell subsequently recorded the tomb, and Maioletti's survey drawing of the longer Tomb S.185 led Cassels to believe that Porcher's drawing represented the latter. [46]

Watercolours 93 plan, 97 interior view, Porcher plan 1 *'Tomb on the S.E. side of the City, 1861'*. The interior, in dull brown and blue tones, shows a long chamber housing two cows and a goat, with six loculus entrances on the left and five on the right, where a four-line Greek inscription appears above the second loculus entrance, gaining this tomb the name *'Tomb of Aristoteles'*. Alterations have been made at the rear, where there is a late Roman hypogeum with side-annexes. Also duplicate. W.253 H.177mm, W.252 H.176mm. B.M.Neg. PS.346615.

Only the two inscriptions found, which had previously been seen by Pacho, were published. However, the Aristoteles inscription had been recorded as far back as 1811 by Agostino Cervelli, who described the tomb as Porcher saw it. [47] Despite reports of this tomb being traced, it remains

---

[45] Hamilton (1856), 78-79.
[46] Maioletti (1931b), 327 Figs. 4-8; Cassels (1955), 35 Pl. I.
[47] S & P (1864), 116 Pl. 85 inscriptions, nos. 27 *C.I.G.* 5154 and 29 *C.I.G.* 5166; Cervelli (1825), 26 Pl. I. 3; Pacho (1827), 382 Pl. LXV, 9-10.

elusive in spite of exhaustive searches by several people. It is thought that the entrance may possibly now lie concealed beneath the tumble of masonry belonging to Tomb S.4 below. (Watercolour 93 plan and section W.469 H.325mm B.M.Neg. PS.241777; also duplicate plan and section W.370 H.320mm). **[Pl. 81]**

Watercolour 0 stele Within the walls of the old Muslim cemetery near the ancient road to Balagrae are the remains of a tomb whose exterior was published in 1915, later registered as Tomb S.4 by Cassels. [48] Porcher painted a watercolour of the massive ΚΛΕΑΡΧΟΣ stele found in the ruins of the fallen façade, captioning it: *'This inscription was on a large block of marble, and found amongst the ruins of the Tombs, in the Southern Necropolis of CYRENE. Size 8'10" x 2'7" x 1'8". By Commander E.A. Porcher R.N.'* A pale blue wash has been used as a background for the white stele, with the lettering and wreath decoration done in grey. Deep grey shading is used to represent the thickness of the slab at the right-hand side and the bottom. At the left side, written vertically, is *'8 feet 10 inches'* and across the top *'2ft. 7 ins'*. Unnumbered, W.274 H.208mm. The inscription had been transcribed in 1848 by Vattier de Bourville, but it is not known whether he was able to venture inside the tomb itself. [49]

Watercolour 129 (missing) is captioned in Porcher's 1865 list as: *'Sepulchral Tables of White marble, found on the South side of the Necropolis'.* 'Tables' may be inscribed marble panels, such as those once inserted into the façade of Tomb N.36 above, or even small slab stelae, but Porcher could alternatively be referring to the small limestone three-legged tables sometimes found standing against rock-cut tombs or sarcophagi, such as those found by Alan Rowe in 1957 during his excavations in the Northern Necropolis. Porcher in his wanderings may have seen another table, now somewhat battered, outside Tomb N.184 beside the ancient road. He would definitely have passed it with the wagon party. A further example stands near Tomb N.354. [50]

Studies around the Western Necropolis

Watercolour 110 This view of Wadi bel Ghadir shows on the right the Acropolis hill, criss-crossed with goat-tracks, dropping steeply. On the left side the even more dramatic hillside, cloaked with grass and pines, plunges

---

[48] GHISLANZONI (1915), 166 Fig. 82; CASSELS (1955), 3, 34; TOMLINSON (1967), 251 Pl. 46c.
[49] BOURVILLE (1850), 584-585; Stele *C.I.G.* 5147; MASSON (1974), 263-270 Figs. 1-2.
[50] THORN (2005) Fig. 258.

precipitously to a vertical face which is in deep shadow. Arabs in the fore-ground are scooping water from a stream. W.354 H.253mm. B.M.Neg. PS.346626. **[Pl. 65]**

Watercolour 0 (missing); **Plate 37** Placed between two archaic tombs is an adapted Hellenistic open antechamber loculus tomb, W.16, the colours existing on its internal façade resembling those shown on Watercolour 124.

Watercolour 124 interior view This shows an antechamber loculus tomb, W.20, first seen by Beechey in 1822 and subsequently by Pacho in 1825. The triglyphs and mutules are shown in blue, with red used for detailing, such as the vertical line at each side of the pilasters.[51] W.427 H.302mm. B.M.Neg. PS.289233. Unnumbered duplicate W.493 H.321mm. Scratched into the plaster on both sides of the antechamber are the remains of Greek graffiti, and on the limewashed pilasters of the façade are many pencilled names and dates from the Second World War.

Watercolour 0 (missing); **Plate 38** The view somewhat resembles Photograph 15 which was sent with Despatch 1 of 23rd February, **Pl. 16**. The view is taken further down the wadi, showing surroundings of archaic Ionic tristyle and distyle tombs, W.48-50. A similar view was taken subsequently by Maioletti.

Watercolour 125 (missing) was referred to in Porcher's 1865 list as: *'Grotto on the Heights – (In small sketch book to the end)'*. This echoes the way in which the Tomb of Altalena and its apparently remote location were described by Beechey, Pacho and Hamilton, raising the possibility that this was the tomb pictured.[52] If so, it is ironic that although watercolours such as no.123 were obviously from this small book, the watercolour sketch no.125 is missing – as was the tomb itself until 1993, when it was rediscovered by the Italian Mission high up in Wadi Halag Stawat, a branch of Wadi bel Ghadir.[53]

Smith and Porcher wrote: *'we were disappointed to find the beautiful front completely destroyed, the whole of the entablature being roughly cut away, evidently for the purpose of obtaining the paintings.'* Footnote: *'We were informed by some Arabs that these paintings were quarried out by M. Bourville.'*[54]

---

[51] MAIOLETTI (1931a) Fig. 8.
[52] BEECHEY (1828), 451; PACHO (1827), 210; HAMILTON (1856), 76.
[53] BACCHIELLI (1995), 163.
[54] S & P (1864), 36.

Watercolour 126 (missing) featured, according to Porcher's 1865 list, a *'Marble Pedestal with a Quadriga on each side'*. This cube-like block with four chariot scenes was noticed in 1852 by Hamilton, who referred to it as an altar, and photographed in 1904 by Hogarth, who, like Porcher, called it a pedestal; it is now located in the new Cyrene Museum. [55]

Watercolour 127 (missing) *'Torso of a Roman Emperor.'* [56]

Watercolour 130 (missing) *'A Cippus found in excavation round the Colonnade of the Temple of Apollo'*

Watercolour 131 (missing) *'Inscription found among the ruins of a building adjoining the Temple of Apollo'*

Watercolour 132 (missing) *'Ornamented slab of sandstone'*

More Distant Locations and Miscellaneous Studies

Watercolour 0; Plate 2 A view of the town of Tripoli from the other side of the bay. The square red tower of the Castello is visible, as are the minarets of mosques on the skyline and shipping in the harbour. W.353 H.222m.

Watercolour 0; Plate 3 *'Town and Castle of Benghazi (Euesperides) from the north'*. The view is striking in that it shows the sparse distribution of the buildings of Benghazi at that date. W.354 H.214mm.

Watercolour 103 *'Appearance of the coast to the North^d of the town, with the only Windmill in the country'*. The sails of the Benghazi windmill very much resemble those at Mykonos, and Porcher pictured two Arabs leading a line of donkeys past it. An annotation on the reverse includes the date *'December 8th 1860'*. W.354 H.218mm. **[Pl. 57]**

Watercolour 104 A view of the British Consulate in Benghazi. In the garden, under a date palm and among some young orange and banana trees, are two small marble sarcophagi found by Vice-Consul Frederick Crowe, now in the British Museum. W.253 H.177mm. B.M.Neg. PS.239231. **[Pl. 58]**

Watercolour 0; Plate 5 (given as 62 by the typesetter) In a boulder-strewn landscape yawns the supposed entrance to the River Lethe, which

---

[55] Hamilton (1856), 45; Hogarth (1905) Pl. facing p. 94, 98; Luni (1976), 265-266 Fig. 36.
[56] Pacho 1827 Pl. LIX, Huskinson no. 70.

leads down to a shallow underground lake inhabited by crayfish. [57] Visitors are relaxing outside the chasm, which was one of the local sights four miles south of Benghazi, but has now reportedly lost any charm it once had. W.252 H.176mm.

Watercolour 0 (missing); **Plate 6** *'Castle and Village of Merdj'*. One Arab tent stands on the flat Plain of Merdj, in front of the spread of low buildings forming the village. Smith and Porcher's bell tents have been erected close to the castle walls. **[Fig. 3]**

Watercolour 0 (missing); **Plate 7** *'Mudir's Room in the Castle of Merdj'*. The Mudir is seated on a long divan in what Smith and Porcher claim was his only room, decorated with columns and Corinthian capitals taken from the remains of an earlier building near the castle. **[Fig. 4]**

Watercolour 0; Plate 8 Encampment near a Roman fortress (Gusr Bili-gadem), 22 miles south-east of Cyrene. Smith and Porcher's two bell tents have been erected in front of the fort, which is situated on high ground, and four hobbled horses are grazing nearby in addition to several camels beside the Arab camp. W.355 H.226mm.

Watercolour 0 (missing); **Plate 30** Wady Muchgun, two miles to the westward of Cyrene. The road plunges down into the deep wadi, which is thick with olive trees. An Arab on foot is leading two laden camels up the road out of the wadi, followed by his companion on horseback with another camel. This may be the way taken by Smith to Benghazi. **[Fig. 5]**

Watercolour 0 (missing); **Plate 42** *'Interior of Mohammed El Adouly's Tent'* This watercolour is unfortunately not present in the collection. It shows Adouli sitting cross-legged on a rug in the spreading shade of his tent, with his Turkish-style slip-on shoes parked neatly outside the rug's border. In the centre of the tent are the household's economical belongings – bedding bound up with a leather strap, water jars, a shallow wooden bowl, a strongbox near Adouli – and a camel saddle frame, one of which is shown by Weir and another pictured in use by Pacho with blanket, camel bag and sheepskin. A very long gun and other weapons are slung from one of the pair of tall centre poles, easy to hand, and burnouses or barracans are hung over a line between the poles. Someone is sitting where the sun floods into the tent, perhaps the ubiquitous Amor. Taking into account the dimensions of bedouin tents given by Weir and those which Hamilton saw in the

[57] THWAITE (1969), 62-64.

200

Cyrenaica, Adouli's tent is probably about 20 feet long and 15 feet wide, with a space of 3 feet between the centre poles. [58] **[Fig. 7]**

Watercolour 0 (missing); **Plate 43** '*Arab Arms of the Cyrenaica*' Another missing watercolour pictures weapons which are probably those of Adouli, a long gun, this time with a spear-like bayonet, a pistol, a dagger and a blunderbuss.

Watercolour 0 (missing); **Plate 45** '*Eastern City Walls and Ruins of Apollonia*' In the distance is the line of the Jebel Akhdar running into the distance. The foreground consists of a mass of tumbled ruins by the sea, difficult to determine in the engraving. **[Fig. 19]**

Watercolour 134; Plate 46 '*State of the Ruins of Imghernis, 10 miles to the Eastward of Cyrene*'. In the distance are several standing sections of the Roman fort walls, with the bath buildings towards the right. In the fore-ground is a well-preserved circular isodomic-built burial plot, apparently containing two built rectangular tombs with gabled roofs. Adjacent to this is another rectangular tomb, this time with panelled sides, raised on a stepped base, also with a gabled roof. An Arab crouching by the first tomb has fired at, and hit, a wild dog, whose companions are fleeing. In the far distance is a line of blue hills. W.354 H.217mm.

Watercolour 136; Plate 47 '*Coasting vessels at anchor off Derna*' shows the old road leading down to the town, which is emphasised by a spread of green, Derna's famous gardens, with some small vessels on the calm sea. W.355 H.320mm. B.M.Neg. PS.289226.

Watercolour 0 (missing); **Plate 48** '*Castle of Derna*' The Turkish flag is flying from the nearest squat circular corner tower, where a cannon can be seen in an embrasure, and camels are passing under the walls.

Watercolour 0 (missing); **Plate 49** '*Arab Camp near Teuchira*' The encampment pitched here on level ground exemplifies the Cyrenaican type of tent which has pairs of centre poles, as opposed to those from Jordan il-lustrated by Weir, which have a spine of single poles. [59] The tents are made from woven strips of wool and black or brown goat hair which the women sew together, resulting in a striped appearance. **[Fig. 8]**

---

[58] S & P (1864) Pl. 42; PACHO (1827) Pl. XCIV; HAMILTON (1856), 150; WEIR (1976), 3 Fig. 28.
[59] WEIR (1976) Fig. 1.

Watercolour 0; Plate 50 Ruins of Ptolemais, an extensive ancient site near the sea. Dogs are baying to the moon which is striking on three columns standing on a podium, part of the Square of the Cisterns. A similar view was shown by Hamilton. Only two columns, out of the original six, are standing today. [60] W.354 H.226mm.

Watercolour 0 (missing); **Plate 51** *'Gateway in the Western Wall of Ptolemais'* The engraving shows the remains of the two massive gate towers, with a horseman galloping past. This is the exterior of the central gate on the western side of Tolmeita, known as the 'Teuchira Gate'. [61]

Watercolour 0; Plate 52 *'Tombs to the westward of Ptolemais'* This shows Porcher sketching while his chestnut horse waits, with a bag hanging behind the saddle for his equipment and another bag lying on the ground beside the artist. The object of his attention is the *'conspicuous built tomb'* whose plan appears in Pl. 53 following. [62] Now running past it is the main road from Benghazi which branches away from the village of Tolmeita to strike up through the escarpment in the direction of Merdj and Beida, and through the rolling red and green hills to Cyrene. W.354 H.233mm.

Watercolour 0; Plate 53 Plan of the built monument at Ptolemais. W.477 H.327mm. **[Fig. 9]**

Watercolour 105 Smith and Porcher's camp at Teuchira – a bleak landscape by the sea, with their bell tent in a quarry to escape the wind, and the city wall visible. W.354 H.228mm.

Watercolour 106 Two individuals are tending a cauldron over a healthy fire in a painted chamber at Teuchira, which bears slight resemblances to the decoration seen at Cyrene, but more especially in the red and green used. W.253 H.157mm. B.M.Neg. PS.289228

Watercolour 108 The Wadi Derna is shown lush with palms and tall vegetation, beside which runs a wide road. A group of houses stands on the hillside to the left. Painted on 14" × 10" paper. W.355 H.253mm. B.M.Neg. PS.289227.

Watercolour 109 The view of the market place at Derna with its Custom House shows low white buildings around a square, where there are Arabs

[60] HAMILTON (1856) Pl. opp. 144; KRAELING (1962), 62, Pl. XX,C.
[61] KRAELING (1962), 57-60, Pl. VI, A.
[62] KRAELING (1962) Pl. XIX, A.

with horses, donkeys and camels in the light shade of two large trees. The feathery tops of palm trees are seen above the buildings. Clean, clear colours have been used – blue, green, brown, purple and ochre, with the central figure wearing a vivid red tarbush and a green robe. W.254 H.146mm. B.M.Negs. PS.289229; PS.346629. **[Pl. 89]**

Watercolour 0; Plate 60 Study of several examples of *thapsia garganica*. W.252 H.174mm.

Continuation of the Illustrations of the Cyrenaica, that have not been published [63]

No.	87	Cyrene	Plan of our Tomb of Residence
	88	do.	" of Tomb in the Northern Necropolis of Cyrene
	89	do.	- do -
	90	do.	" Painted Tomb - do -
	91	do.	" " in the side of a quarry - do -
	92	do.	" " in the Northern Necropolis
	93	do.	" Detached tomb on the South-east side of the city
	94	do.	" tomb in the Northern Necropolis
	95	do.	do. do.
	96	do.	do. do.
	97	do.	Interior of a Detached tomb on the S.E. side of the city
	98	do.	do. tomb in the Northern Necropolis
	99	do.	do. do.
	100	do.	Exterior do. do.
	101	do.	do. do.
	102	Benghazi	General view of the town, taken from Giuliana Point
	103	do.	Appearance of the coast to the North of the town, with the only Windmill in the country
	104	do.	The British Consulate
	105	Teuchira	General appearance of the walls
	106	do.	Interior of the only painted tomb
	107	Derna	The town, taken from the roof of the Consul's house
	108	do.	The Wady which divides the town
	109	do.	The Market square, shewing the Custom house, and the Bazaar
	110	Cyrene	The Wadi Bel Ghadir, or the Valley of Verdure
	111	do.	The Wady Labouatha, about 2 miles to the Eastward of the city
	112	do.	Appearance of the ruins of 2 temples, and the stadium
	113	do.	Partial view of the tombs and sarcophagi in the Northern Necropolis

[63] This list, in Porcher's writing, accompanies the collection of watercolours in their large box folder in the British Museum.

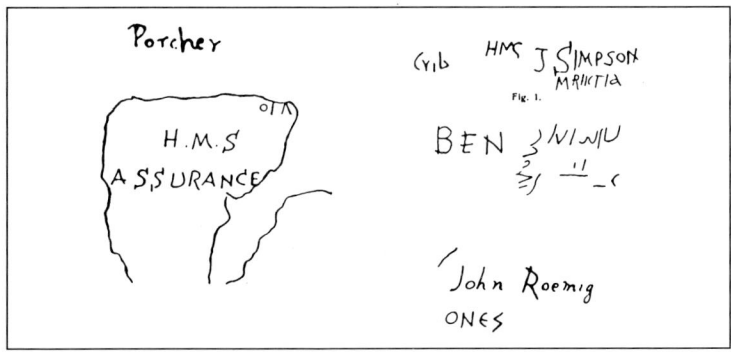

FIG. 20 – Montage of graffiti found on the walls of the Apollo Fountain channel [after Ghislanzoni (1927)].

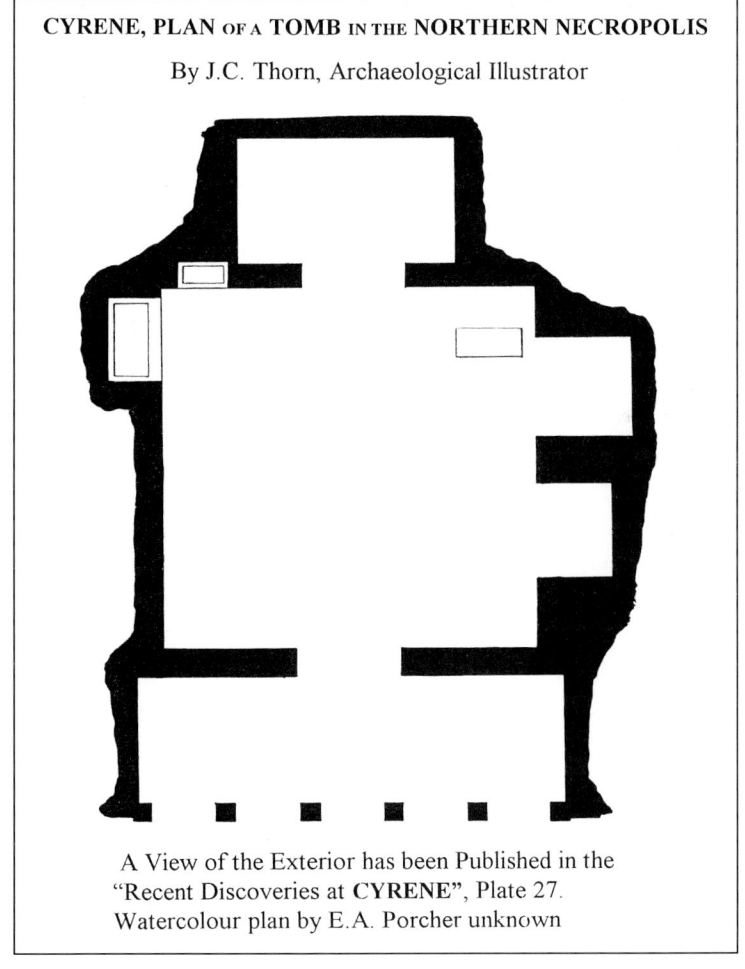

CYRENE, PLAN OF A TOMB IN THE NORTHERN NECROPOLIS

By J.C. Thorn, Archaeological Illustrator

A View of the Exterior has been Published in the "Recent Discoveries at **CYRENE**", Plate 27. Watercolour plan by E.A. Porcher unknown

FIG. 21 – Plan relating to [**Pl. 62**].

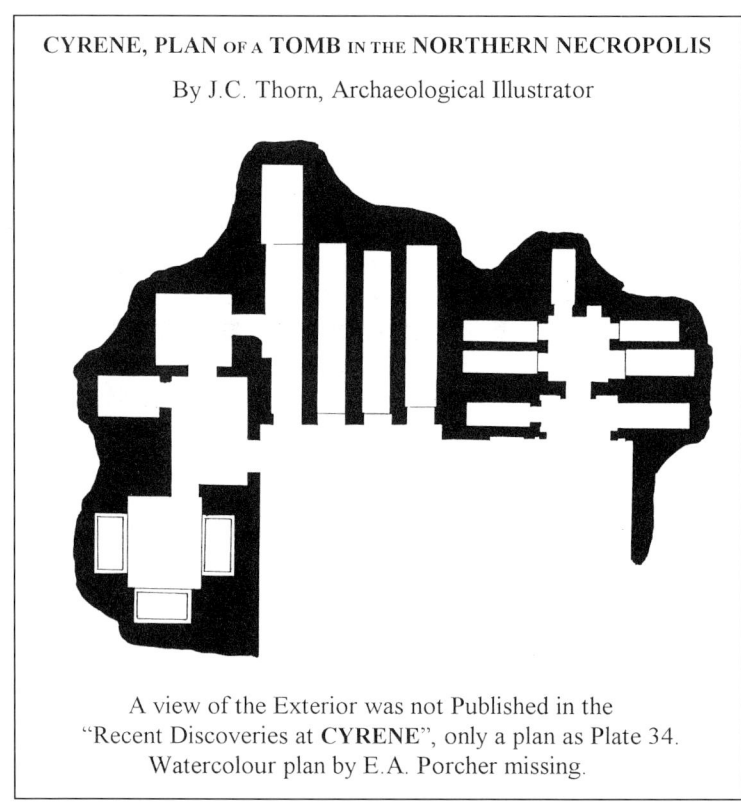

CYRENE, PLAN OF A TOMB IN THE NORTHERN NECROPOLIS

By J.C. Thorn, Archaeological Illustrator

A view of the Exterior was not Published in the
"Recent Discoveries at CYRENE", only a plan as Plate 34.
Watercolour plan by E.A. Porcher missing.

FIG. 22 – Plan relating to [Plate 34; **Pl. 63**].

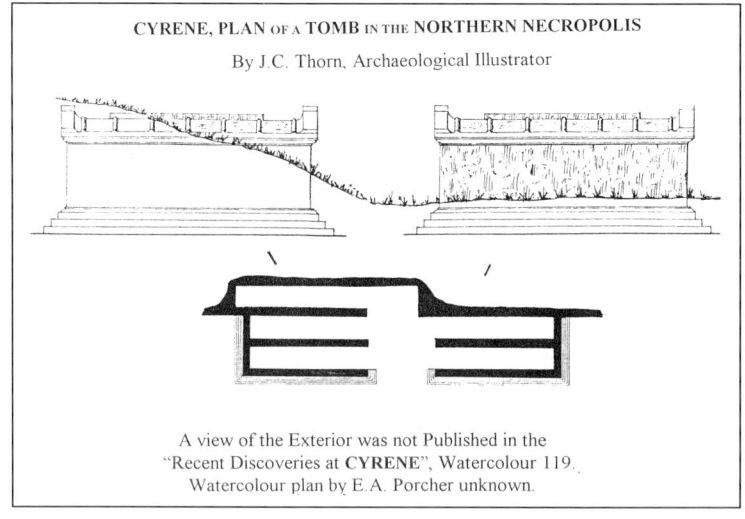

CYRENE, PLAN OF A TOMB IN THE NORTHERN NECROPOLIS

By J.C. Thorn, Archaeological Illustrator

A view of the Exterior was not Published in the
"Recent Discoveries at CYRENE", Watercolour 119.
Watercolour plan by E.A. Porcher unknown.

FIG. 23 – Plan relating to [**Pl. 64**].

206

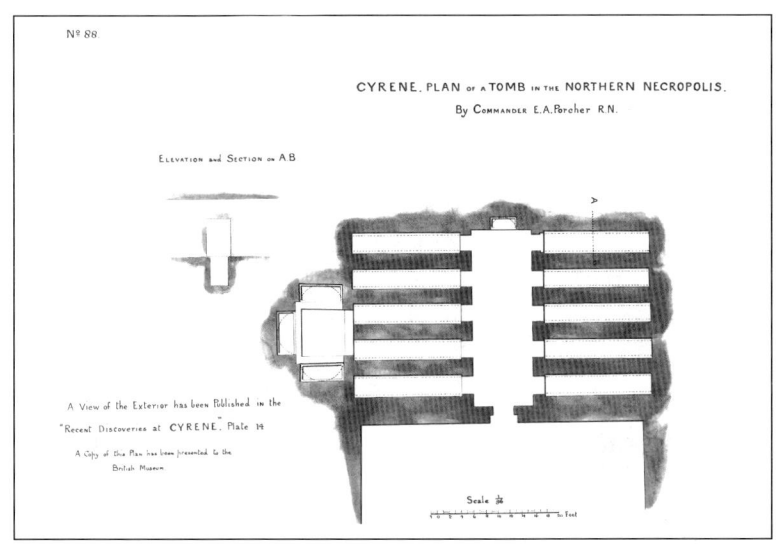

FIG. 24 – Plan relating to [Porcher 88; **Pl. 67**].

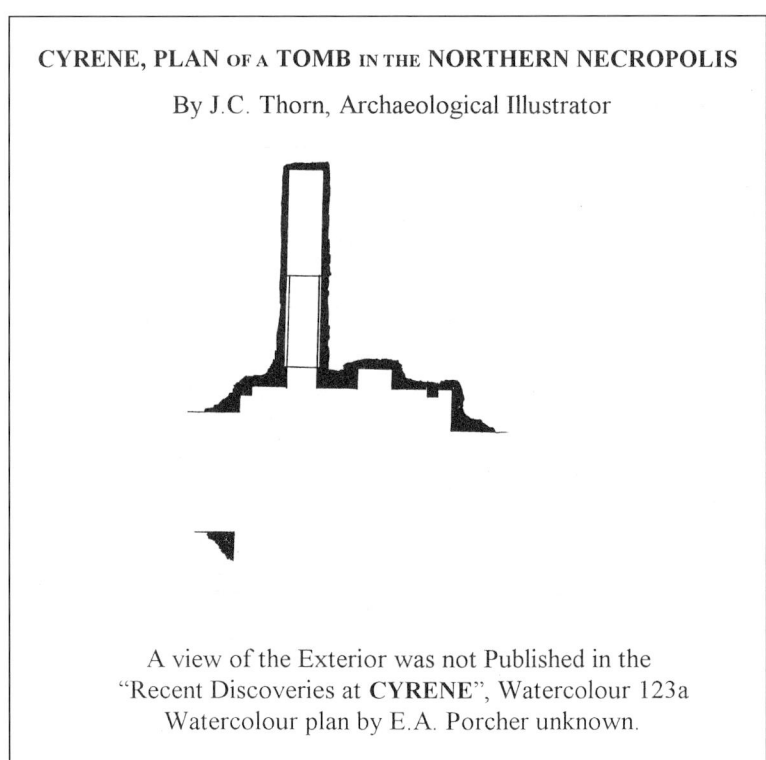

FIG. 25 – Plan relating to [**Pl. 68**].

CYRENE, PLAN OF A TOMB IN THE NORTHERN NECROPOLIS

By J.C. Thorn, Archaeological Illustrator

A view of the Exterior was Published in the
"Recent Discoveries at CYRENE" as Plate 19, Watercolour 123b
with the plan as Plate 33.
Watercolour plan by E.A. Porcher missing

FIG. 26 – Plan relating to [Plate 33; **Pl. 69**].

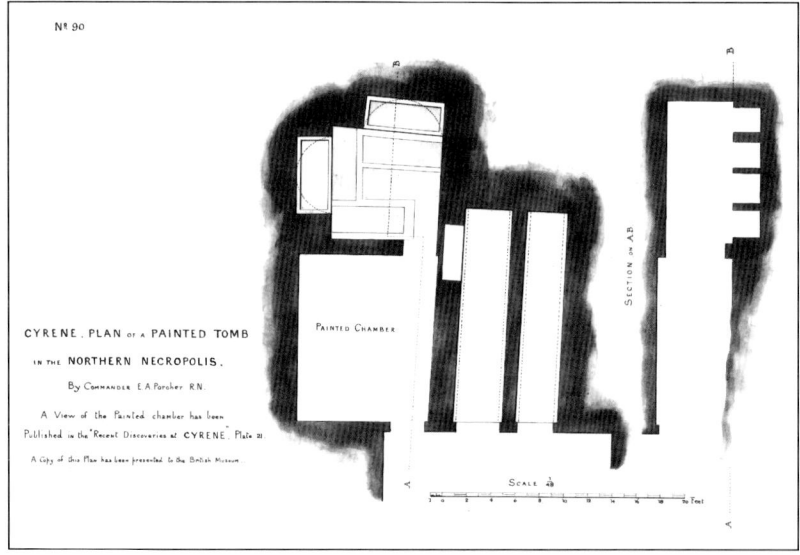

FIG. 27 – Plan relating to [Porcher 90; **Pl. 70**].

208

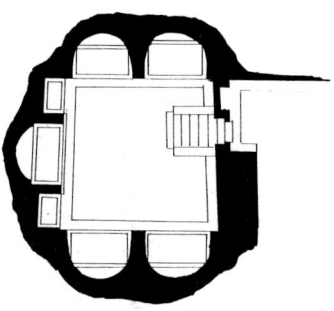

CYRENE, PLAN OF A TOMB IN THE NORTHERN NECROPOLIS

By J.C. Thorn, Archaeological Illustrator

A view of the Interior was Published in the
"Recent Discoveries at CYRENE" as Plate 17, duplicate
unnumbered Watercolour, with the plan as Plate 31.
An alternative view of the Interior is shown here, Watercolour 117.
Watercolour plan by E.A. Porcher missing.

FIG. 28 – Plan relating to [Plate 31; **Pl. 71**].

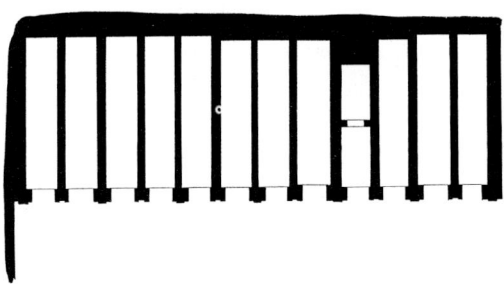

CYRENE, PLAN OF A TOMB IN THE NORTHERN NECROPOLIS

By J.C. Thorn, Archaeological Illustrator

A view of the Exterior was Published in the
"Recent Discoveries at CYRENE" as Plate 20, Watercolour 20
with the plan as Plate 32
Watercolour plan by E.A. Porcher missing.

FIG. 29 – Plan relating to [Plate 32; **Pl. 74**].

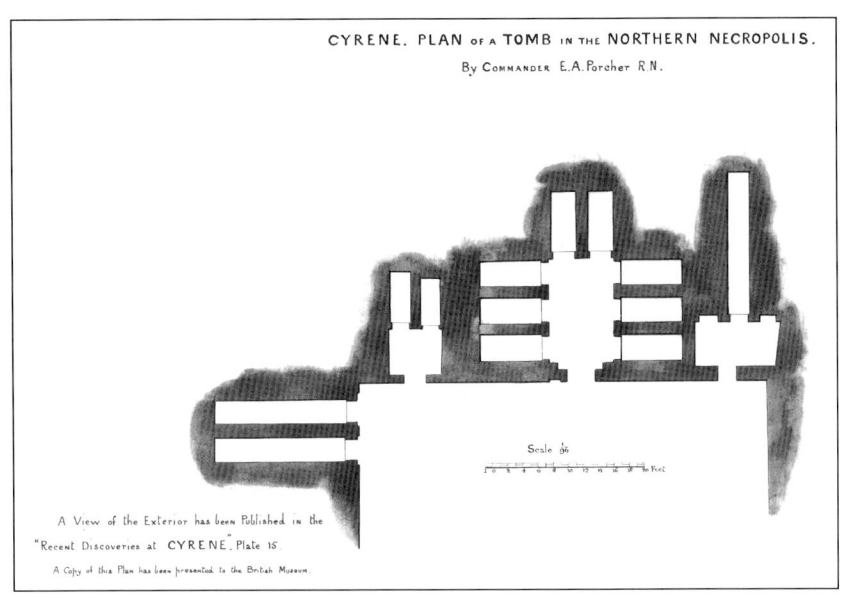

Fig. 30 – Plan relating to [Plate 89; **Pl. 75**].

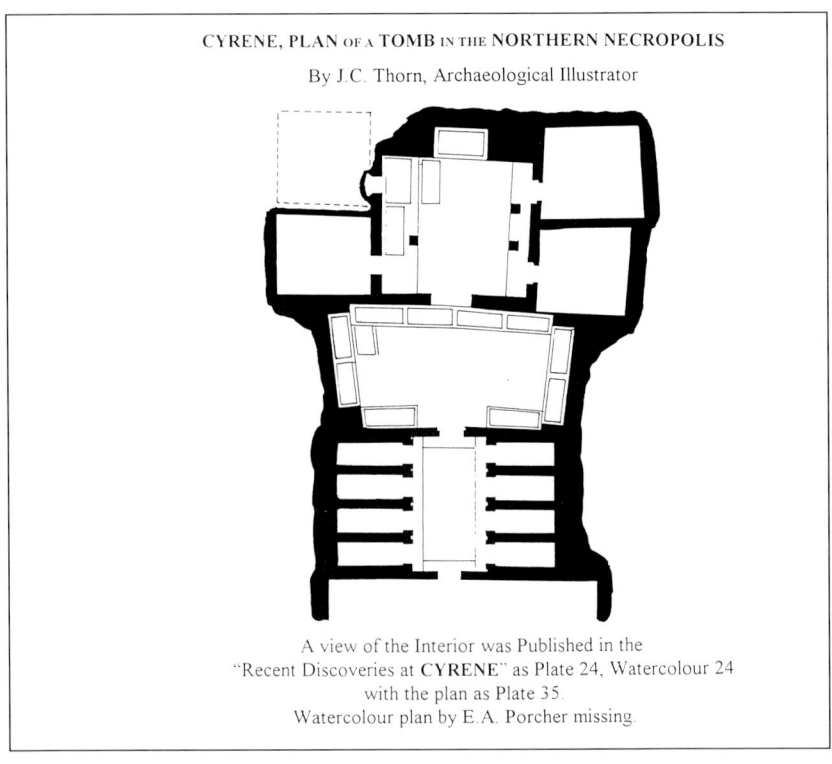

Fig. 31 – Plan relating to [Plate 35; **Pl. 76**].

210

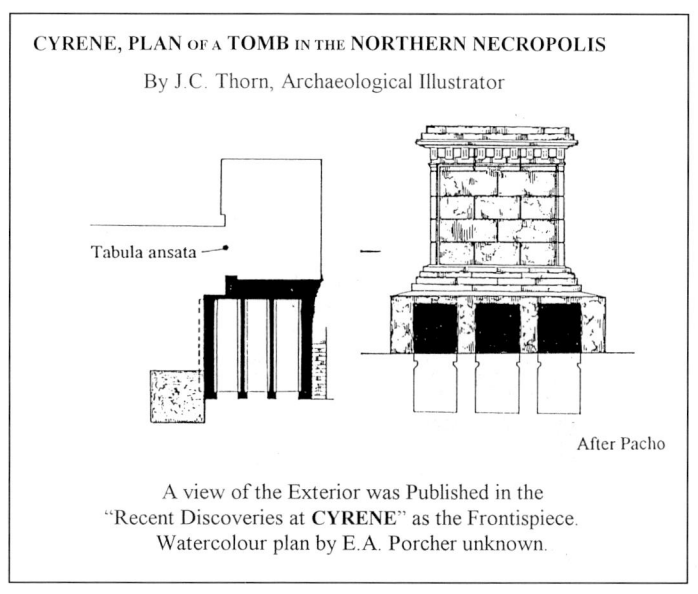

CYRENE, PLAN OF A TOMB IN THE NORTHERN NECROPOLIS

By J.C. Thorn, Archaeological Illustrator

Tabula ansata

After Pacho

A view of the Exterior was Published in the
"Recent Discoveries at CYRENE" as the Frontispiece.
Watercolour plan by E.A. Porcher unknown.

FIG. 32 – Plan relating to [**Pl. 77**].

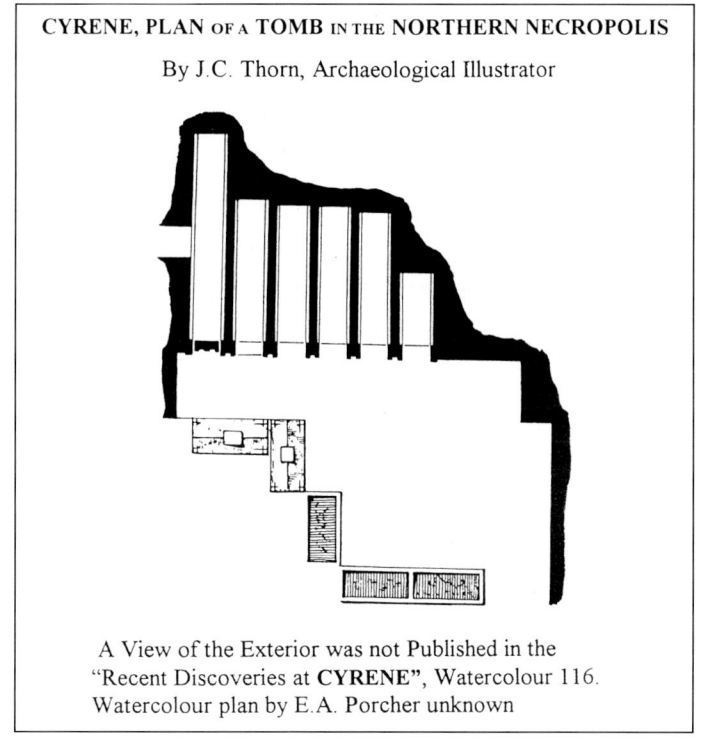

CYRENE, PLAN OF A TOMB IN THE NORTHERN NECROPOLIS

By J.C. Thorn, Archaeological Illustrator

A View of the Exterior was not Published in the
"Recent Discoveries at CYRENE", Watercolour 116.
Watercolour plan by E.A. Porcher unknown

FIG. 33 – Plan relating to [**Pl. 78**].

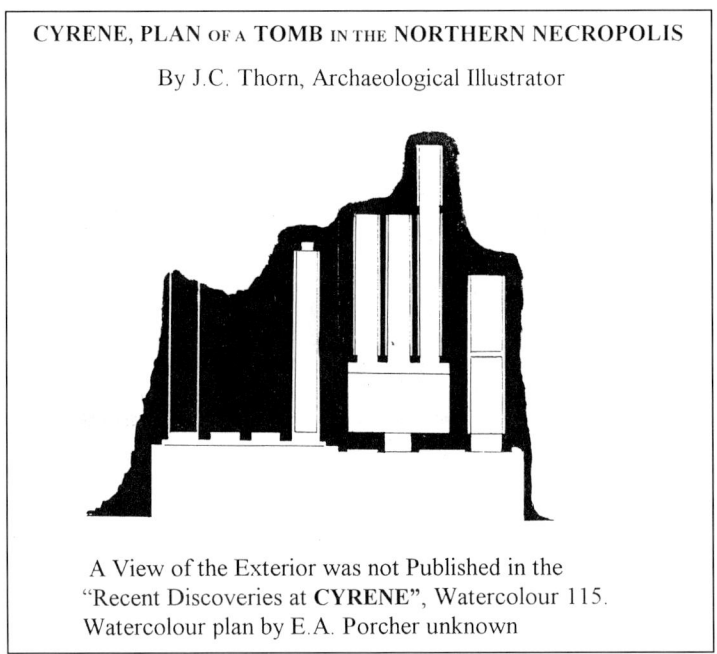

CYRENE, PLAN OF A TOMB IN THE NORTHERN NECROPOLIS

By J.C. Thorn, Archaeological Illustrator

A View of the Exterior was not Published in the
"Recent Discoveries at **CYRENE**", Watercolour 115.
Watercolour plan by E.A. Porcher unknown

FIG. 34 – Plan relating to [**Pl. 79**].

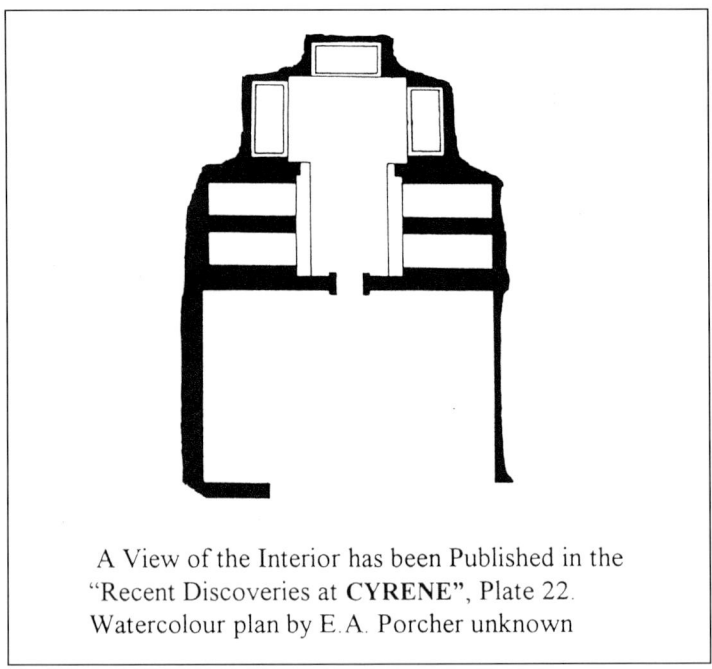

A View of the Interior has been Published in the
"Recent Discoveries at **CYRENE**", Plate 22.
Watercolour plan by E.A. Porcher unknown

FIG. 35 – Plan relating to [**Pl. 80**].

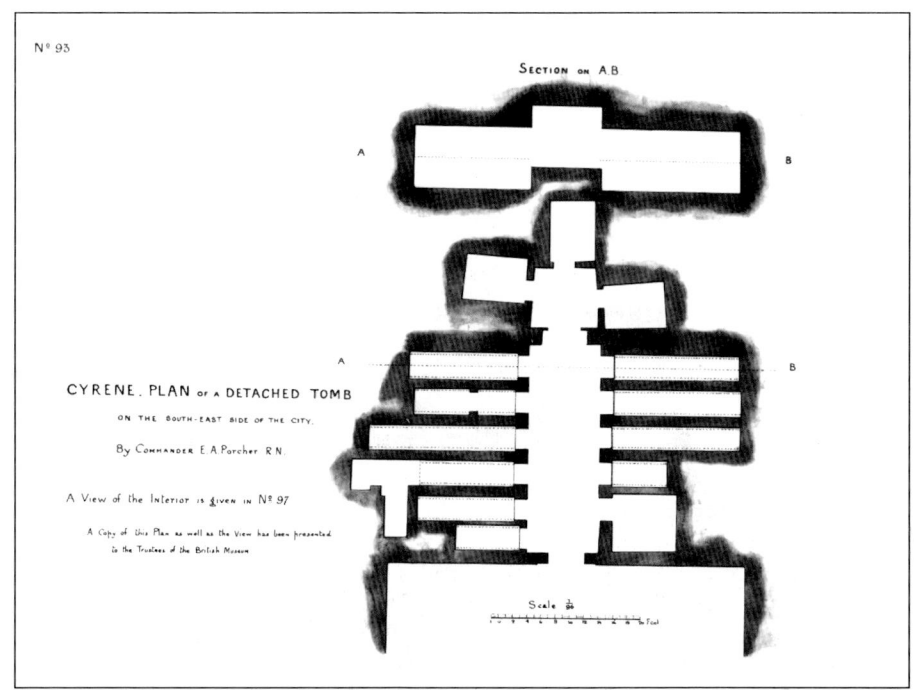

FIG. 36 – Plan relating to [Porcher 93; **Pl. 81**].

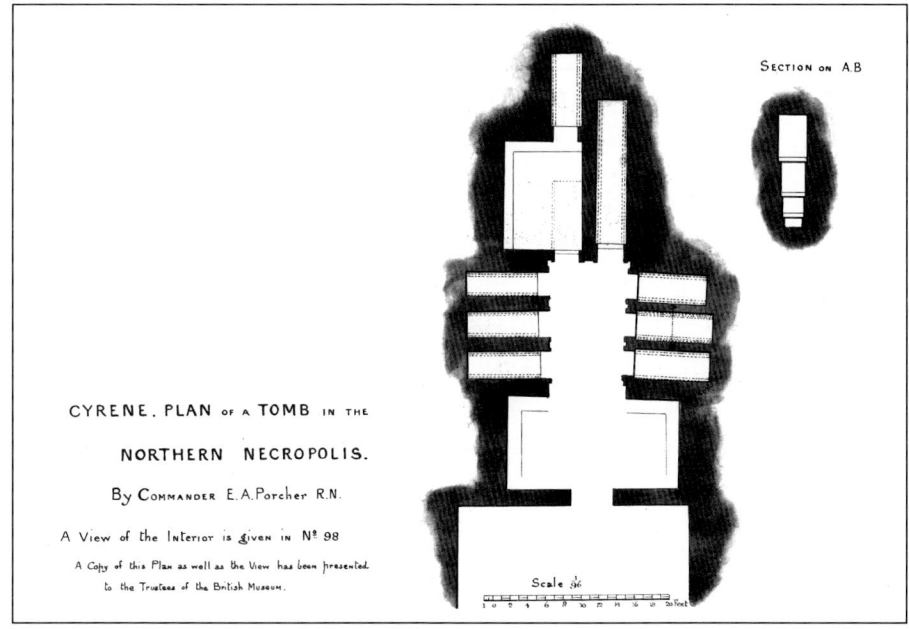

FIG. 37 – Plan relating to [Porcher 94; **Pl. 82**].

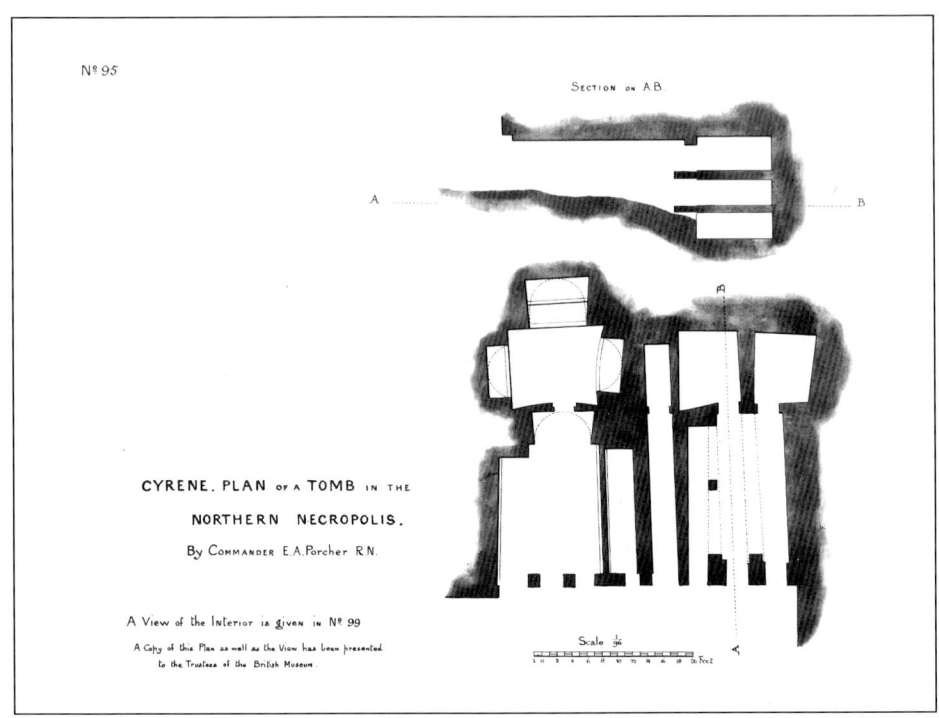

FIG. 38 – Plan relating to [Porcher 95; **Pl. 83**].

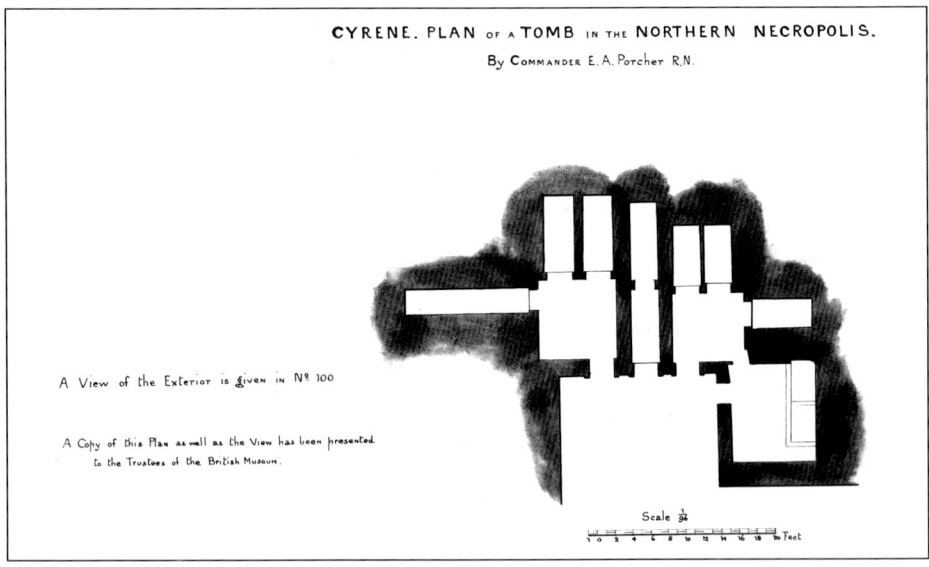

FIG. 39 – Plan relating to [Porcher 96; **Pl.84**].

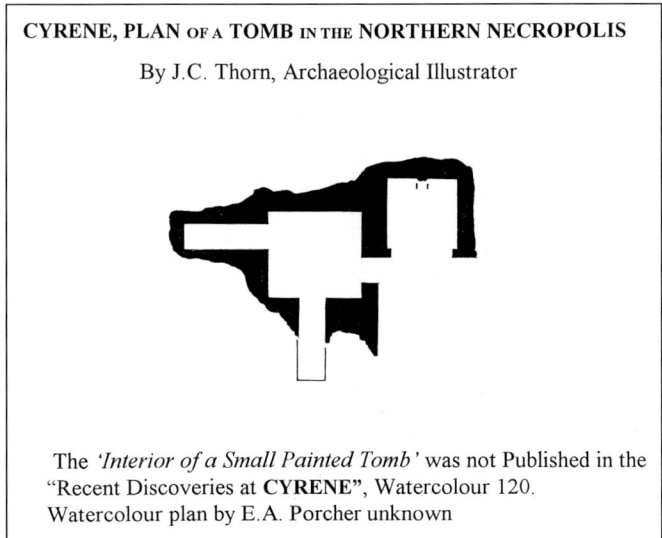

CYRENE, PLAN OF A TOMB IN THE NORTHERN NECROPOLIS

By J.C. Thorn, Archaeological Illustrator

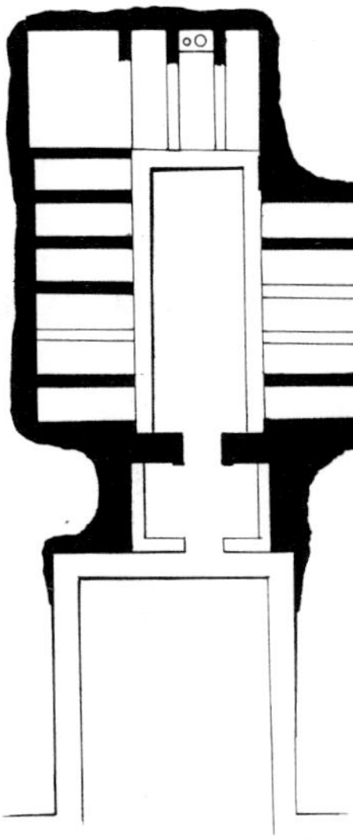

A View of the Exterior was not Published in the
"Recent Discoveries at **CYRENE**", Watercolour 118.
Watercolour plan by E.A. Porcher unknown

FIG. 40 – Plan relating to [**Pl. 85**].

CYRENE, PLAN OF A TOMB IN THE NORTHERN NECROPOLIS

By J.C. Thorn, Archaeological Illustrator

The *'Interior of a Small Painted Tomb'* was not Published in the
"Recent Discoveries at **CYRENE**", Watercolour 120.
Watercolour plan by E.A. Porcher unknown

FIG. 41 – Plan relating to [**Pl. 86**].

The *'Interior of a Small Painted Tomb'* was not Published in the "Recent Discoveries at **CYRENE**", Watercolour 121. Watercolour plan by E.A. Porcher unknown

FIG. 42 – Plan relating to [**Pl. 87**].

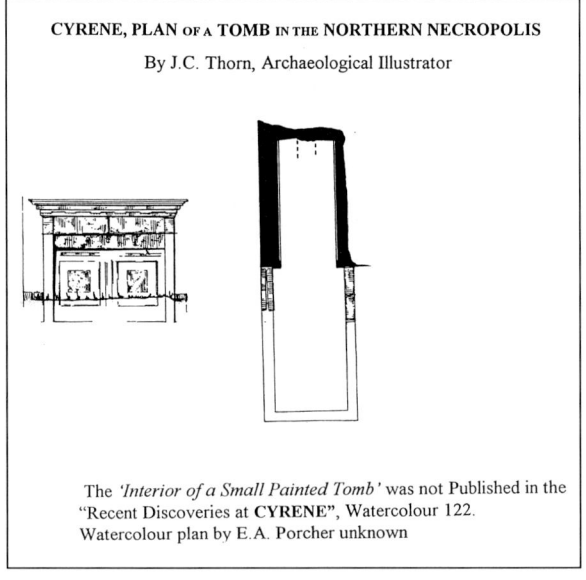

The *'Interior of a Small Painted Tomb'* was not Published in the "Recent Discoveries at **CYRENE**", Watercolour 122. Watercolour plan by E.A. Porcher unknown

FIG. 43 – Plan relating to [**Pl. 88**].

216

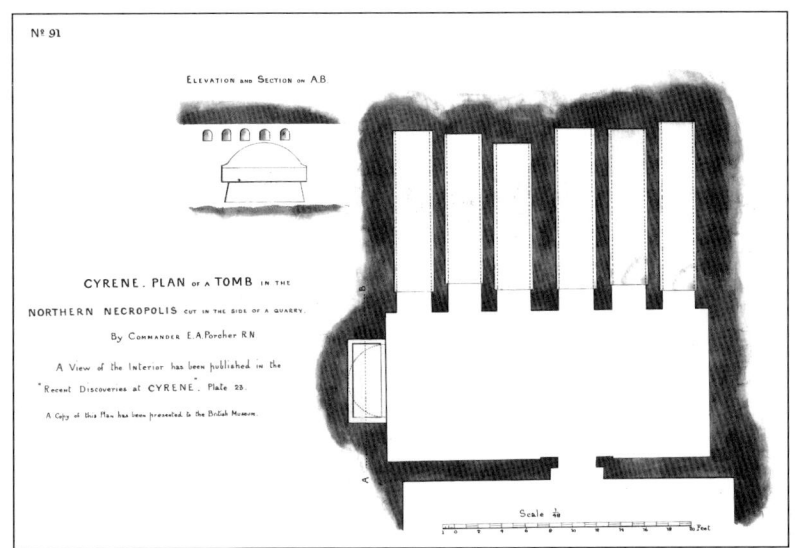

FIG. 44 – Cyrene; Plan of a Tomb in the Northern Necropolis cut in the side of a Quarry [Porcher 91].

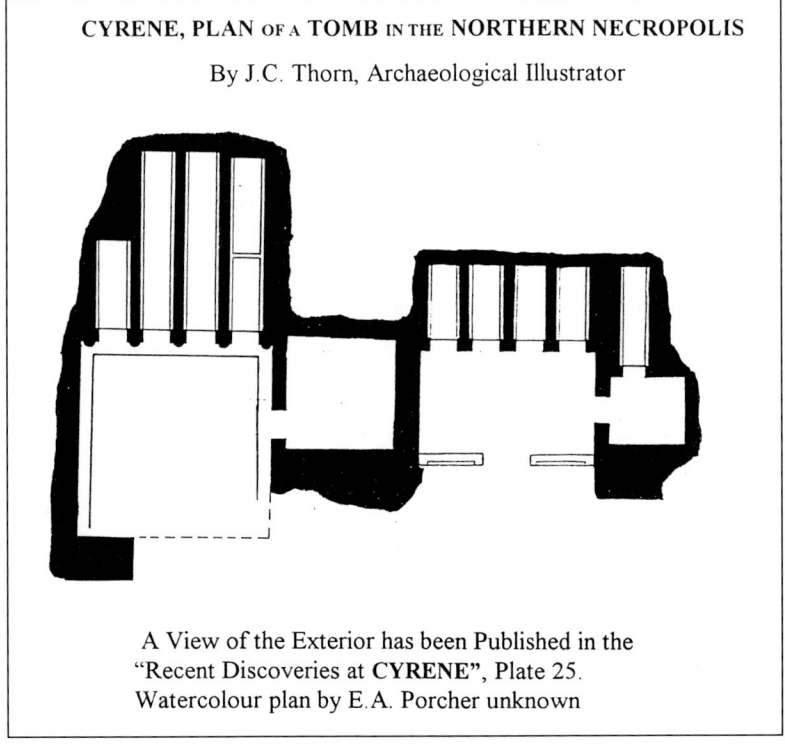

FIG. 45 – Tombs N. 178-179.

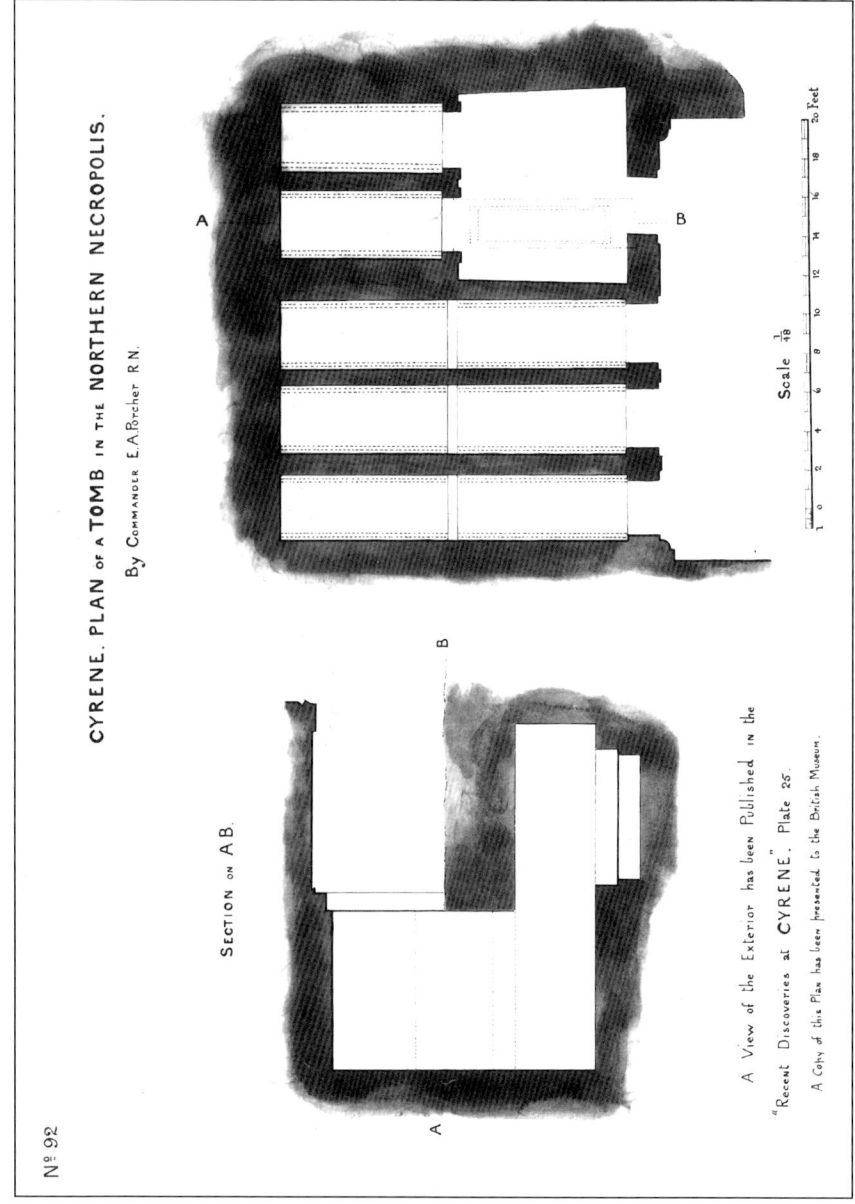

FIG. 46 – The 'tomba della Cariatidi' N. 228.

XIV. EPILOGUE

The Malta Union Club was the stage-set for the opening and closing scenes of the story. It is still in existence, but the present location, a low building covered with bougainvillea, now completely surrounded by hotels, is not contemporary with Smith and Porcher.

An original photograph **Pl. 49** shows the two entrances to the Tomb of Residence, which seem to be just above the level of the ancient road, one hung with Benghazi matting, and the other partly blocked with stones, leaving the top half open for light and air. Although the upper terrace entrances are still recognisable today, the terrace itself is now much narrower, as it has been breaking up and falling into the chambers cut in the friable sandy limestone below. The Tomb of Residence itself no longer survives, and the conclusion must be that the wall and roof have also crumbled and fallen during the intervening years. A photograph taken in 1895 by Herbert Weld-Blundell[1] seems to show the area unchanged from 1861, but views taken in the 1920s, during the time when Libya was an Italian colony, show a row of small shops and houses backing on to the ancient terraces of rock-cut chambers and running the whole length of the Sacred Way, and it has to be considered that the Tomb of Residence may have been cut back when these buildings (called by Goodchild 'post-occupation') were erected.[2] They were later removed in order for the Italians to excavate the area, and another two views taken long after their demolition, one by Derek Buttle in 1952 and the second, about fifteen years later, published by Stucchi,[3] show the dilapidation of the Tomb of Residence area well under way. Nowadays the only sign that the tomb existed at all is a level rock surface representing the floor, with circular features like those shown in Porcher's plan, all concealed behind a well-established, sprawling olive tree.

If four trips had been made with the wagons, as intended, Archippe

---

[1] WELD-BLUNDELL (1896) No. 2.
[2] PERNIER (1927), 149 Fig. 19; GOODCHILD (1976), 312.
[3] Buttle Archive photo; STUCCHI (1975) Fig. 520.

might now be in England, either languishing in the British Museum basement, or on display but standing forgotten in a corner behind more complete exhibits. Instead, she quietly guards the foot of the Sacred Way. This lady was probably moved to her present position during the Italian archaeological activity of the 1920s, but apart from two photographs [4] taken in 1957 she has been incognito since being abandoned in 1861 on the upper terrace by the Tomb of Residence. It was only after seeing a copy of Smith's solitary photograph of her, which he sent to Burgoyne, that I began to suspect that this serene guardian was Archippe, and when in 1996 I found, below the footstool, the two-line inscription published by the lieutenants, this clinched the matter.

If Dennison had not been sent to Cyrene, Smith and Porcher would have found it difficult, during the closing days of the expedition when Smith was ill, to carry out road repairs between Cyrene and Marsa Sousa, look after the workforce, supervise the packing of the statues and accompany the wagonloads. They may have seen some of their hard-won prizes left behind with Archippe and the inscriptions. Even with three wagon trips, if the road had not been repaired, some of the statuary might have been damaged by being thrown from the jolting wagons. In the event, Dennison must have been indispensable.

If the lieutenants had decided to stay in Libya for a further season, they would probably have discovered a great deal of the statuary found by subsequent excavators. One of the statues which escaped Smith and Porcher was found by Italian soldiers in 1913 when, on a cold December day following a torrential storm, they sought to remove a bump in the track at the edge of the Apollo Sanctuary terrace, over which the ration lorries were lurching, and discovered that it was caused by a headless marble Aphrodite, the 'Venus of Cyrene', lying face down in the mud, with the mark of a pickaxe on her left buttock. [5] A great deal of time was subsequently spent by the soldiers in digging holes in search of the elusive head, and a later account of the discovery told of rumours that the Arabs had found *several marble heads in the immediate vicinity*, the writer of the piece being sanguine that one of these might prove to be that of the Venus. [6] However, it has never been found, even after an official Italian government-sponsored archaeological campaign lasting for many years. Many lovely figures were discovered, however, including the famous Three Graces which came to light with other pieces in the Roman baths in the eastern corner of the terrace. The Venus was taken to Benghazi, where it was intended to put her on display

[4] Deutsche Archaeologisches Institut neg. nos. 58. 2644; 58. 314.
[5] GHISLANZONI (1915).
[6] Art and Archaeology (1915), 212 Fig. 2.

220

in a new museum, but orders were received to transport her to Italy, where until recently she has been on view in the National Museum of the Baths of Diocletian in Rome. Rumour has it that she is being returned to Libya. One of the results of all this archaeological activity under the Italians was the construction, near the top of the Jebel Akhdar above the northern necropolis, of the group of buildings which form the Antiquities Department, and the planting of pine and eucalyptus trees. The Department's premises, stark and raw when first built on the bare hillside, are now over eighty years old, and have mellowed to a sandy ochre blending into the landscape, while the grounds, alive with cicadas, are shaded by the gigantic Mediterranean pines and aromatic with the scent of pine and rosemary carried on the warm wind.

The 'Himalaya', on which Dennison came home, was a storeship and troopship built by P & O in 1853 and bought by the government two years later. She was taken over by the Admiralty in 1862 and ended up as a coaling hulk in Portland Harbour, where she was eventually sunk by a Junkers 88 during an air-raid in 1940. Her masts could be seen above water in the harbour until after the war, when a salvage company cleared the wreck, and her figurehead is now in the National Maritime Museum at Greenwich.[7] After his return from Africa, life went on as usual for Dennison, although he must have had some hair-raising tall stories to tell to his family and workmates. I recently learned of an unusual chair of dark wood and canework, possibly a 'smoking chair', now in the possession of the Gristwood family in Sunderland, which on the evidence of a brass plaque fixed to it had been *'Presented by the Workmen of the British Museum to Mr William Dennison, October 1859'*. As there is no official record of this presentation, it was probably a personal gesture by workmen who held him in high regard.[8] In July 1862 Dennison was among forty-one British Museum employees who signed a petition to be allowed time to visit the Great Exhibition.[9]

Murdoch Smith's wish to be involved with this Exhibition, mentioned in a letter to Newton the previous April, does not seem to have borne fruit, but he secured a position in the Fortification Department at the War Office which he held for two years. For some of this time he was engaged in single-handedly drawing up a project for the defence of the upper part of the Bristol Channel.[10] During his time in London his evenings were spent in preparing the text for the publication, with Porcher being responsible for the drawings. He met Henry Layard, the excavator of Nineveh and Babylon, at

[7] ELLIS and WARLOW (1989) I, 32; National Maritime Museum.
[8] Information Barry Gristwood.
[9] Original Letters and Papers Vol. LXXIII April-July 1862.
[10] British Museum Greek & Roman Dept. Original Letters 1861-1868 A-K fol. 715.

the Foreign Office soon after returning from the Cyrenaica, and also at dinner with Newton in 1863, just before starting for a long sojourn in Persia where Smith was in command of the engineers employed on the Indo-European telegraph system. In a long letter to Newton dated March 15th 1865 he described being *'worked almost off my legs'* and spending more time in the saddle than out of it *'in the snows of winter and scorching heat of summer'*. There were 1,200 miles of country to survey and the same distance of telegraph to put up. The Persians he considered to be *'consummate scoundrels... I now regard the Turks as perfect angels altho' somewhat of an Oriental type'*. He had *'heard little or nothing about the Cyrene book which however I believe is now published. I am very greatly indebted to you for yr. invaluable assistance with regard to it. In spite of it however I have no doubt I shall get awfully "slated" by the Athenaeum &c but happily I am thick skinned'*.[11] After Smith's departure Porcher had superintended the final production of the book.[12] The publishers, Day & Son of Lincoln's Inn Fields, wrote to Panizzi in June 1863 seeking permission to photograph the sculpture, considering that this *'would add very much to the authenticity and beauty'* of the book. On the same day the company produced a letter accompanying a prospectus for the book, pointing out that *'the present state of the country. . renders the site of the ancient city all but inaccessible – The remains stand on the edge of a plateau 2,000 feet above the level of the sea, 13 miles from the nearest part of the coast, 50 miles from Derna, and 150 miles from Benghazi, the only villages in existence in a country occupied by lawless fanatical tribes of Bedouin Arabs. A consideration of the circumstances of peculiar difficulty under which the Expedition of Lieut. Smith and Commander Porcher was undertaken, will add to the interest which otherwise attaches to the beautiful specimens of Greek and Roman sculpture by which their labours were rewarded'*. A postscript states: *'The sculptures will be illustrated in photography by Mr Francis Bedford.'*[13]

A collection of Porcher's watercolours in the British Columbia archives chart his travels after his return from Cyrene. In February 1862 he was in Ireland, obviously on the way to the Azores, where his paintbrush was active the following month. During 1863-64 he produced a group of paintings of the British Isles, mostly around the English south coast, and in spring the following year he was in Brazil, around Rio de Janeiro. Moving down the coast of South America, he sailed through the Straits of Magellan and northwards up the coast of Chile, painting near Santiago and Valparaiso in July and August. By mid August he was near Lima in Peru, and at the end of

---

[11] British Museum Greek & Roman Dept. Original Letters 1861-1868 A-K fol. 714-5.
[12] NLS ACC 9569 no. 8; Brit. Mus. MS 39042 fol. 133.
[13] Original Letters and Papers Vol. LXXVI May-Aug 1863.

September he painted *'My Residence at Honolulu, Sandwich Islands'*. Reaching British Columbia, he had command of 'Sparrowhawk', which was stationed at Victoria for three years, and in 1866 he produced four watercolours showing forts and settlements connected with the Hudson's Bay Company at Vancouver Island and Prince of Wales Island. It is intriguing to note that in this area is 'Porcher Island' and 'Burnaby Island' (the name of Porcher's great-grandfather). October saw him at the Hudson's Bay Company's post in Puget Sound, and other watercolours painted in 1867-68 show further views of British Columbia.[14] A photograph from the archives of the Royal British Columbia Museum shows Porcher at around this time, and is reproduced here **[Pl. 90]**. Nearly forty years ago a series of bronze plaques was put up in Victoria, commemorating *'ships and people who made an impact on the marine history of Victoria harbour'*. The plaque to H.M. Gun Vessel 'Sparrowhawk' – *'on this station 1865-1868 with Captain Edwin Augustus Porcher R.N.'* is situated in the Parade of Ships, opposite the statue to Captain Cook.

Porcher returned to England, and on 13th April 1869 was married in Alton, Hampshire to Elizabeth Emmeline Rich. He retired from the Navy in 1872 and went on a tour of the continent, from where news of his death in Germany in 1878 reached his old friend and companion. Smith had also married in 1869, to Eleanor Baker, who lived in Persia with him and produced nine children, unlike Porcher, who remained childless. Tragically, four of Smith's children died young, followed in 1883 by their mother. In the following spring he returned to the British Isles with his remaining family, but on the way three more children died within three days, all from diphtheria, making it a truly nightmare journey.[15] With his two remaining. daughters Smith settled in his native Scotland, and in 1885 became Director of the Museum of Science and Art in Edinburgh. The following February, twenty-five years after his exploits in Cyrene with Porcher, Smith wrote to A.S. Murray at the British Museum, noting that, of the sculptures sent there, *'a considerable number of the less valuable have never so far as I know been exhibited.'* It had occurred to him that as *'the Exploration of the Cyrenaica and the Excavation at Cyrene were undertaken by the late Captain Porcher R.N. and myself, at our own risk and expense, the Trustees might not feel disinclined to transfer those unexhibited sculptures to this Museum, of which I have recently been appointed Director. Or what I should prefer, they might perhaps be pleased to give them back to me and I would myself present*

---

[14] A collection of Porcher's watercolours is lodged in the archives of British Columbia, http:// www.bcarchives.gov.bc.ca.

[15] NLS ACC 9569 no. 19.

them to this Museum.'[16] Murray presented this letter to the Trustees, and reported that several sculptures had been transferred in 1870 to the Museum of the Porte in Constantinople,[17] while other sculptures still unexhibited were of archaeological interest and should be retained, but the exception was the small statue of the youthful Dionysus, which he thought could be spared.[18] Thus it was that this little gem from Cyrene ended its journey in Edinburgh, in the museum where its discoverer was Director.

Porcher's small sketch book used in Cyrene seems to have been dismembered after its deposition in the British Museum, and the individual vignettes mounted for storage. Not all have survived, but the remainder of the twenty-nine sketches in the book are represented by Watercolours 118-119, 121-123a-b, 125 (missing), 126-127, probably 129-132 and perhaps also the unnumbered illustration of *'Arab Arms of the Cyrenaica'*. In 1973 an exhibition, *'Antiquities of Libya'* was held at the British Museum, jointly organised by the Department of Greek and Roman Antiquities and the Society for Libyan Studies. For this occasion some of Porcher's watercolours were displayed, seeing the light of day for a while before being packed away again in their large folder.

Porcher left his papers and remaining paintings to his sister Madelina's only surviving son, Lieut-Col Cecil Du Pre Penton Powney (Thompson) who was born in 1862, the year after her marriage. He in turn left them to his daughter, and eventually, through a family friend, they were sold to a dealer who offered them via Australia House in London to the National Library of Australia in 1972.[19]

If Smith and Porcher were to set out upon such a venture as their Cyrenaican expedition today, they would have a grant from a large company and would test free clothing and equipment supplied by other companies. They would have prepacked convenience foods, high in vitamins, with plenty of plastic bottles and containers. They would have a state of the arts tent, four wheel drive vehicles, a laser-operated theodolite, digital cameras, mineral water in large quantities, all forms of insecticides, mosquito repel-

---

[16] Original Letters and Papers 1886.
[17] Brit. Mus. Dept of G & R Antiquities, Orig. Lett. 1870 fols. 399-403. The sculptures it was suggested might be offered to the Porte were: Duplicate male figure holding a laurel branch (Reg. 61 7-25, 5); Diana, arms wanting (Reg. 61 7-25, 8); Diana Venatrix (Reg. 61 11-27, 159); Draped female figure (S & P no. 14)*; Male figure, headless, attired as a hunter (Reg. 61 11-27, 149); Head of Diana (Reg. 61 11-27, 131); Head of Minerva (Reg. 61 11-27, 60).
* The figure Reg. 61 7-25, 6 was probably substituted, as the description of S & P no. 14 does not tally with the only possible female statue from Cyrene in Istanbul.
[18] Original Papers and Papers 1886.
[19] NLA MS 4602.

224

lants, anti-malarial tablets, first aid equipment and sun protection. They would have radio contact with anyone anywhere, mobile phones, a computer and scanner linked to the Internet, and their own website. They would have a team, made up mostly of students, and would live a homogenised life – not two men on their own in a foreign land. The statuary would not be wrapped in, or cushioned by, old recycled hammocks. Instead, something much less environmentally friendly would be used.

The published description of the old man of Benghazi *'digging small holes at random'* and selling vases and terracottas to Maltese merchants is reflected in the actions of the modern tomb robbers at Cyrene, whose activities have increased dramatically over the last seven years. The difference lies in the fact that today's robbers know exactly where to burrow profitably, leaving small spoil heaps and sad little pieces of discarded, broken pottery as evidence of their digging inside and outside the tombs. On one occasion a shovel and pickaxe were found where the impudent robber had stored them in a tomb, not expecting that it would be visited! These implements were appropriated by the Antiquities Department for official use.

Sadly, the sculptures which have safely stood for many years among the excavated remains of the city are now gravely at risk because of the unscrupulous action of more serious criminals. A few years ago two of the heads of the Three Graces were stolen, and have never been recovered, in spite of hopeful reports to the contrary.[20] A well-known figure of a high priestess which used to stand in the Agora was attacked one night, and unsuccessful attempts made to saw off the head, leaving a pure white scar where the mantle hangs at the side of the neck and a snow of marble chippings on the ground. This statue and many others, even those which used to stand serenely in the sun in the garden of the Antiquities Department, have been taken under cover for safety. However, the precious objects of Cyrene are not always secure indoors, as demonstrated by a recent theft which has involved both Internet and Interpol. In this case, several small heads were stolen and taken to Egypt, where a Cairo dealer, through a Greek intermediary, sent at least two of them to Europe. Through the Internet it was discovered that one was sold at auction in Paris for a very large sum of money to the head of one of the Emirate states, and the second was also recognised.

The ravages of European Consuls and Vice-Consuls such as Vattier de Bourville, Hanmer Warrington, Francis Werry and George Dennis in Cyrenaica were as nothing compared with what is happening today. All

---

[20] After this book went to press, I was again in Cyrene in April 2007, and can report that, happily, my previous statement has been proved wrong. The two recovered heads have been reunited with the Three Graces in Cyrene Museum.

except Warrington, it seems, gained financially by collecting antiquities and selling them openly to museums and connoisseurs, but the amount of artifacts leaving the country was in the nature of drips, and the monetary gain trifling. Nowadays the quantity of smuggled stolen material is more like a steady flow – how large is impossible to judge because of the secret tomb robbing – and the prices paid are enormous. Libya may be an oil-rich country, but the ordinary people are by no means wealthy. The village that Shahat used to be two decades ago is now a town of considerable size which is constantly growing, both in the spread of housing and in population – estimated at 175,000 five years ago. Some of the tomb robbers may be foreigners, but some must be local, and who can blame them? After all, at their doorstep is the necropolis, a source of ready money, the goose that lays golden eggs. If the youngest child of a large brood needs new jeans, having worn out all those passed down from his elder brothers, what could be simpler than for a father to go among the tombs, dig a few holes, find some little pots or terracotta figurines and sell them? That way he can go to the Friday Market and buy what is needed. The Antiquities Department is unable to police the whole vast area of the Cyrene necropolis, and the thieves can slip in and out at all hours, like shadows in the night.

APPENDIX I.
CONCORDANCE OF CASES SHIPPED IN JUNE AND OCTOBER

Cases shipped aboard 'Assurance' in June 1861

Case

1	Torso of Dionysus, its hand and seven drapery fragments	(Reg. 61 7-25, 2; Huskinson no. 32)
2	Legs of Apollo Citharoedus, its right foot, parts of pedestal and snake, three fragments of arm, two drapery fragments	(Reg. 61 7-25, 1; Huskinson no. 12)
3	Lower part of Apollo torso	(Reg. 61 7-25, 1; Huskinson no. 12)
4	Upper part of Apollo torso and five drapery fragments	(Reg. 61 7-25, 1; Huskinson no. 12)
5	Statuette of the nymph Cyrene strangling a lion	(Reg. 61 7-25, 3; Huskinson no. 61)
6	Five pieces - the lower part of Cyrene and the lion	(Reg. 61 7-25, 3; Huskinson no. 61)
7	Head of Dionysus	(Reg. 61 7-25, 2; Huskinson no. 32)
8	Head of Minerva	(Reg. 61 7-25, 12; Huskinson no. 25)
9	Head of Apollo	(Reg. 61 7-25, 1; Huskinson no. 12)
10	Large female statuette and its head	(Reg. 61 7-25, 6; Sent to the Porte; Mendel 628)
11	Numerous small fragments of Apollo and part of snake	(Reg. 61 7-25, 1; Huskinson no. 12)
12	Sound box of Apollo's lyre and fragments	(Reg. 61 7-25, 1; Huskinson no. 12)
13	Female statuette, the head and feet in a separate case	(Reg. 61 7-25, 8; Mendel 621)
14	Statuette with rams horns	(Reg. 61 7-25, 7; Huskinson no. 52)
15	Male statuette, its head and fragments	(Reg. 61 7-25, 4; Huskinson no. 98)
16	Male statuette, its head and fragments	(Reg. 61 7-25, 5; Sent to the Porte, now lost; Mendel –)

17	Large female head	(Reg. 61 7-25, 14; Huskinson no. 133)
18	Two large heads, male and female	(Reg. 61 7-25, 9 and 13; Huskinson nos. 80 and 65)
19	Heads of Hadrian and Cornelius Lentulus	(Reg. 61 7-25, 10 and 11; Huskinson nos. 69 and 63)
20	Two small marble statuettes and a limestone animal (Temple of Bacchus)	(Reg. 61 7-25, 16; Huskinson no. 114, –; The limestone panther of Dionysus (Huskinson no. 35) was shipped in October.
21	Four terracotta lamps, small gold winged figure; one silver coin, twelve copper coins from Cyrene and a silver sphinx and coin from Derna	(by British Museum in November) (Reg. 61 7-25, 17) ... (Reg. 61 7-25, 18) ...
22	Part of a large marble leg	(Reg. 61 7-25, 15; Huskinson no. 107)

Cases shipped aboard 'Melpomene' in October 1861

Case

1	Minerva	(Reg. 61 11-27, 31)
2	Upper half of large female figure and the head	(Reg. 61 11-27, 32; Huskinson no. 72)
3	Lower half of the above large female figure with the foot from ruins to north of Temple of Apollo	(Reg. 61 11-27, 32; Huskinson no. 72)
4	Large female statue from the House of Jason Magnus	(Reg. 61 11-27, 33; Huskinson no. 111)
5	Lower half of small seated female figure with the foot from ruins west of Temple of Apollo	(Reg. 61 11-27, 36; Huskinson no. 117)
6	Large female statue found beside Minerva, with its arm	(Reg. 61 11-27, 39; Huskinson no. 110)
7	Small statue of Apollo(?) from temple to SW of Temple of Bacchus	(Reg. 61 11-27, 62; Huskinson no. 108)
8	Upper half of life-size female statue from above temple	(Reg. 61 11-27, 19; Huskinson no. 71)
9	Lower half of the above statue	(Reg. 61 11-27, 19; Huskinson no. 71)
10-11	Two life-size statues of hunters from temple to SW of Temple of Bacchus	(Reg. 61 11-27, 68; Huskinson no. 97) (One sent to the Porte – Mendel 1111)

12	Nerva and feet from ruins to north of Temple of Apollo	(Reg. 61 11-27, 37; Huskinson no. 67)
13	Cuirassed torso	(Reg. 61 11-27, 35; Huskinson no. 70)
14	Upper half of Hadrian from Temple of Apollo	(Reg. 61 11-27, 23; Huskinson no. 69)
15	Lower half of Hadrian with fragments from temple to SSW of Temple of Bacchus	(Reg. 61 11-27, 23; Huskinson no. 69)
16	Statue of Pan	(Reg. 61 11-27, 28; Huskinson no. 47)
17	Bust of girl and small statuette from House of Jason Magnus	(Not identified) (Not identified)
18	Female bust from House of Jason Magnus	(Reg. 61 11-27, 18; Huskinson no. 81)
19	Female bust from House of Jason Magnus and small dolphin from temple to SW of Temple of Bacchus	(Not identified) (Reg. 61 11-27, 153; Huskinson no. 11)
20	Female statuette fragments from temple to SW of Temple of Bacchus	.....
21	Male statuette, the feet separate, from temple to SW of Temple of Bacchus	(Reg. 61 11-27, 63; Huskinson no. 20)
22	Statuette of Venus	...
23	Male statuette with fragments of snake (Apollo)	(Reg. 61 11-27, 158; Huskinson no. 18)
24	Male bust from House of Jason Magnus	(Reg. 61 11-27, 14; Huskinson no. 73)
25	head of the above	(Reg. 61 11-27, 14; Huskinson no. 73)
26	Fragments of statue in cases 8-9	(Reg. 61 11-27, 19; Huskinson no. 71)
27-29	Relief of Cyrene strangling lion and being crowned by another nymph	(Reg. 61 11-27, 30; Huskinson no. 60)
30	Upper half of seated figure in case 5 with hands	(Reg. 61 11-27, 36; Huskinson no. 117)
31	Venus and Cupid in two pieces with fragments;	(Reg. 61 11-27, 69; Huskinson no. 4)
	life-size small head, perhaps of hunter in case 10 or 11;	(Reg. 61 11-27, 68; Huskinson no. 97)
	three small statuettes - all from Temple of Venus	...

32	Legs of hunter in case 10 or 11;	(Reg. 61 11-27, 68; Huskinson no. 97)
	fragments from Temple of Zeus	(Not identified)
33	Legs of other hunter in case 10 or 11	(Reg. 61 11-27, 68; Huskinson no. 97)
34	Hunters legs with deer skin from ruins to north of Temple of Apollo	(Reg. 61 11-27, 150; Huskinson no. 24)
35	Small male statue holding vase from ruins to north of Temple of Apollo	(Reg. 61 11-27, 126, 80; Huskinson no. 33)
36	Small Dionysus with head and hand,*	(Reg. 61 11-27, 27; Trans. to Edinburgh Museum)

*Hand rediscovered recently in the British Museum by Neil Adams - to be reunited with body

	also another head, both from ruins north of Temple of Apollo.	(Reg. 61 11-27, 92; Huskinson no. 34)
	Three small statuettes;	...
	small Cupid;	(Reg. 61 11-27, 72; Huskinson no. 8)
37	another Cupid asleep in relief;	(Reg. 61 11-27, 74; Huskinson no. 93)
	small figure in relief	(Reg. 61 11-27, 96; Huskinson no. 146)
	and fragment of statuette, all from Temple of Venus.	(Not identified)
38	Small statue from Temple of Apollo	....
	and shoulder fragment	(Not identified)
39	Small huntress with dog, head and fragments from ruins to north of Temple of Apollo.	(Reg. 61 11-27, 159; Sent to the Porte; Mendel 619)
	Small figure of Cupid on a dolphin;	(Reg. 61 11-27, 71; Huskinson no. 7)
	small statuette,	.....
	head attached to part of body;	(Reg. 61 11-27, 81; Huskinson no. 53)
	fragments of statuette, all from Temple of Venus;	(Not identified)
	fragment of statuette from small temple near stadium.	(Reg. 61 11-27, 42; Huskinson no. 28)
40	Male bust from House of Jason Magnus.	(Reg. 61 11-27, 15; Huskinson no. 77)
	Head of figure in cases 8-9;	(Reg. 61 11-27, 19; Huskinson no. 71)

	life-size 'Elizabethan looking' female head;	(Reg. 61 11-27, 17; Huskinson no. 74)
	smaller female head with conical headdress;	(Reg. 61 11-27, 40; Huskinson no. 75)
	small head of Minerva;	(Reg. 61 11-27, 60; Sent to the Porte; Mendel 387)
	four small heads, all from Temple of Venus.	***
41	Female statuette and fragments, holding snake	(Reg. 61 11-27, 25; Huskinson no. 44)
	small female statue with head and neck from Temple of Apollo.	(Reg. 61 11-27, 136 head, 52 body; Huskinson no. 109)
42	Seated statuette from small building at west end of platform of Apollo	(Reg. 61 11-27, 93; Huskinson no. 118)
43	Two inscriptions from ruins to east of Temple of Apollo [?three]	(Reg. 61 11-27, 46-48)
44	Head of statuette in cases 8-9 [already listed for case 40]	(Reg. 61 11-27, 19; Huskinson no. 71)
45	Inscription from Zeus Temple;	(Reg. 61 11-27, 38)
	ornamented terracotta work from House of Jason Magnus;	(Not identified)
	other fragments from Temple of Apollo area	(Not identified)
46	Pans head;	(Reg. 61 11-27, 28; Huskinson no. 47)
	two statuettes from Temple of Venus;	.....
	statuette from smaller temple near stadium	(Reg. 61 11-27, 29; Huskinson no. 27)
47	Leg and trunk with grapes etc.,	(Reg. 61 11-27, 103; Huskinson no. 37)
	also fragments from Temple of Apollo area	(Not identified)
48	Large male head from House of Jason Magnus	(Reg. 61 11-27, 16; Huskinson no. 79)
49	Nerva head and	(Reg. 61 11-27, 37; Huskinson no. 67)
	life-size head from ruins north of Temple of Apollo	(Reg. 61 11-27, 61; Huskinson no. 135)
50	Bronze male head and	(Reg. 61 11-27, 13; Cat. of Bronzes no. 268)
	life-size marble head from Temple of Apollo	(Reg. 61 11-27, 53; Huskinson no. 13)

51	Fragments from excavations in Temple of Apollo area	(Not identified)
52	Female statuette in two with head.	.....
	Two small Venus statuettes in two;	....
	very small statuette;	....
	small hand;	....
	two small heads, all from Temple of Venus	**
53	Large male head from Temple of Zeus	(Reg. 61 11-27, 162; Huskinson no. 78)
54	Large head in two from smaller temple near stadium;	(Reg. 61 11-27, 54; Huskinson no. 136)
	purchased bas relief	(Not identified)
55	Three life-size heads from Temple of Apollo area;	....
	two smaller heads and	**
&	seated figure from Temple of Venus	(Reg. 61 11-27, 94; Huskinson no. 116)
56	Life-size head, eyes separate in sockets from House of Jason Magnus;	(Reg. 61 11-27, 87; Huskinson no. 122)
	two heads and	**
	seated statuette from Temple of Venus	(Reg. 61 11-27, 76; Huskinson no. 55)
57	Life-size head, eight smaller, from Temple of Apollo area;	.....
	purchased funeral bust.	(Reg. 61 11-27, 91; Huskinson no. 86)
	Head from smaller temple near stadium;	....
	left hand of Hadrian;	(Reg. 61 11-27, 23; Huskinson no. 69)
	dog's head from Temple of Bacchus;	....
	small hand from Temple of Apollo;	....
	female statuette from Temple of Venus	....
	Fragments from case 4	(Reg. 61 11-27, 33; Huskinson no. 111)
58	Small bust,	....
	half a small male statuette	....
	and two others from Temple of Venus;	.....

	small head from Temple of Apollo	(Probably Reg. 61 11-27, 131; Mendel 388)
59	Sundry fragments	(Not identified)
60	Small female statue,	(Reg. 61 11-27, 24; Huskinson no. 64)
61	Feet of the above; colonnade above theatre in street of ...	(Reg. 61 11-27, 24; Huskinson no. 64)
	coins etc.	(Not identified)
62	Inscription of M. Antonius	(Reg. 61 11-27, 49)
63	Inscription of C. Lentulus	(Reg. 61 11-27, 43)

One case of inscription squeezes and one of inscription paper.

A number of small heads recorded as coming from the Temple of Venus are impossible to match with their relevant case numbers. These, marked with asterisks, are registered as: 61 11-27, 56-59, 130, 133-135, 139, 140-141, 144. The appropriate Huskinson numbers are: -, 68, 66, 39, -, -, 50, 62, 131, 30, 127, 125.

APPENDIX II.
STATUARY SENT TO THE PORTE IN 1872

1. **Youthful male figure in mantle** (Reg. 61 7-25, 5; Inv. – ; Cat. Mendel –). Of two very similar statuettes shipped to England, one was sent to Istanbul but does not seem to have been available to be studied by Mendel. However, a statuette of this type which may have some relevance was noticed there. The sandalled figure, which lacks a head, stands on a small square base. The broken *'lustral branch'* may have been held horizontally, and the upper and lower folds of the left sleeve differ from those of the extant British Museum example. As Smith claimed that the five statuettes discovered with the one under discussion were *'all perfect'*, and the British Museum register description reads: *'the branch, broken, held straight down'* this may not be the figure sent from England. Its present exterior position makes it difficult to study, being located about thirty feet above ground level in the central bay of the right-hand Ionic pediment on the end façade of the building containing the Museum of the Ancient Orient, overlooking Osmanhamdibey Yokusu. This architecture was modelled on a column sarcophagus from Sidon in Lebanon which is in the Museum collections (PASINLI (1996), 80-84).

2. **Statue of a goddess** (Reg. 61 7-25, 6; Inv.37 T; Mendel 628). This stands on an amorphous base H.5cm with the left leg advanced, its knee slightly bent. The forearms are missing, originally attached by dowels at the elbows.

The head, found separately, [**Pl .24**] has been inserted, a different, whiter marble, and is turned to the right, wearing a diadem. The hair is parted in front in long tresses, deeply drilled, and taken round to back to form a flat bunch of curls, while ringlets fall from the back at each side of the neck where the earlobes are visible. The eyelids are shown, but the pupils are not incised. The nose is straight and the mouth small. The figure is clad in tunic and peplos, the tunic sleeves closed by round buttons – two on the right, four on the left, and the peplos fastened by a round button on the right shoulder, falling away from the left shoulder to reveal the tunic. The right arm was originally extended forwards and to the right, while the left arm must have been nearly vertical, held slightly away from the body and rebated at the elbow. The long, straight, deep folds become much plainer at the back and some of the drapery below the right arm is broken. The toes are exposed on both feet, raised as if wearing sandals, but no footwear is visible.

3. **Statue of Nike** British Museum Register: 'Statuette of Artemis'. (Reg. 61 7-25,

8; Inv. 33 T; Cat. Mendel 621). This figure was once inserted into a square base. Both arms are missing, leaving on the right side three round, deep dowel holes Dia. 20 D. 40mm, one with some lead remaining. On the left side are signs of iron colouration around a former dowel hole, now filled with plaster. At the back, which is roughly worked, an iron rod is embedded in lead on the left scapula. On the right scapula are signs of an iron cramp slightly cut into the marble. The back of the figure has fractured in the upper part by the weight of the missing wings.

The inserted head is turned to the left, with some chips on the left at the base of the throat. The hair is fastened in a topknot, deeply drilled at the top and sides where the locks are drawn back to form a loose bun with a few escaping locks which curl round to the front and one small curl behind the right ear, which is hidden by the hair. The nose is straight, the eyes drilled in the inner corners, while the mouth is small and undrilled. Nike strides forward with the right leg, the left bent back. The body is slightly twisted to the right, and clad in a tunic and mantle fastened with a button on the right shoulder. The right arm was originally raised and the left arm bent, indicated by a small offset in the drapery. The feet are in sandals with a central studded bar and transverse strap behind the toes. A further strap runs diagonally back from both sides of the central bar.

4. Head of Minerva (Reg.61 11-27, 60; Inv. – ; Mendel 387). Untraced.

5. **Hunter** (Reg.61 11-27, 149; Inv.3144; Mendel 1111). This figure, situated in the open at the left end of Istanbul Archaeological Museum old building façade, has been exposed to the elements for many years in recent times. It stands on a completely foreign square base and, like its mirrored counterpart in the British Museum, has always been in two parts, the transition being at the bottom of the tunic which is cramped to the legs, the original holes being reused for the present cramping. The head and both arms are missing, with a rectangular dowel hole for the right arm and a square one for the left arm. The right foot is a separate entity, with the junction at the top of the boot, and a dowel hole in the right side of the heel indicates that a piece of marble was spliced in.

The body is twisted to the left in the upper part and a short tunic falls from the left shoulder, leaving the right shoulder bare. A studded strap crosses the body diagonally and the tunic is held by a cord around the waist. The right arm was originally raised, the left arm originally bent and hanging down, possibly holding an object which continues in the lower part, with the scar of the hand remaining on the hip. The legs are joined by a marble brace at the calf. The figure wears thick-soled boots, the left with a lion's head below the band and two paws hanging. The right boot has no head and only one paw on the inner side. A band of leather runs down the front of each boot with a central square stud, and the toes are exposed.

6. Head of Artemis (Reg.61 11-27, 131; Inv. – ; Mendel 388). Untraced.

7. **Artemis** (Reg.61 11-27, 159; Inv.61 T; Cat. Mendel 619). The base is rectangular H.10cm W.40cm D.30cm, and the right back corner has been spliced in with a modern cramp. A dowel hole under the drapery of the figure may indicate that it once hung lower and had been damaged.

The head is slightly raised and turned to the left. The hair, well worked at the top and sides, is fastened in a topknot and the curls, worked with a small drill of about 2mm, are gathered together and taken up in a roll at the back, where the work is not so thorough. The sides are very slightly abraded. The earlobes are visible. The eyes are large and open, with the ducts drilled and the eyebrows clearly shown. The nose is straight and the mouth small, drilled at the corners. The throat is full and the neck broken with the fracture restored with plaster. The figure stands with the left leg advanced, the knee bent, and the right leg straight. The left arm is bent up at a right angle and the right arm is akimbo, the thumb missing but a scar showing where it met the peplos. The first finger is long, extended downwards. The other fingers are broken at the first joint, but were originally bent, with the scar and remains of the second finger on the peplos. Both hands have been reattached. The left hand originally held something such as a bow (or lance, as Mendel suggested) which would connect with an object at the base by the left foot. The fingernails and wrinkles at the knuckles are clearly shown. Artemis is clad in a peplos with fastening on the left shoulder, the right sleeve showing four diamond-shaped buttons. A cloak thrown over the left shoulder hangs down over the left arm, turned back at the neck/collar in loose folds to the inside of the elbow. Five deep folds on the outside of the left arm fall to the apparently cut-off hem and there is a small tassel at the bottom of the cloak at the back. The legs are booted to mid calf. The soles are thick, and the boot tops have animals' heads suspended from them, with a band running down to the toes. A dog sits by the right leg, its tail curled up the right leg of the figure. Its front legs, the right one broken at mid calf, the left broken at the knee, are extended, slightly parted, the paws remaining on the base and the genitalia indicated. The head has been reattached. The right ear is badly damaged, also the open mouth and jaw with tongue showing. The right eye is incised, with a slight dent for the pupil. The left half of the head is missing. There are traces of a collar around the break in the neck and a hanging ?lead down the back.

DRAMATIS PERSONAE

Adouli   Mohammed el Adouli was a well-known native of Benghazi – in fact the owner of the British Consulate there, which he rented to government for £18 per year – with trading interests throughout Cyrenaica. He acted as guide for several European travellers over the years, his influence with the local Sheikhs proving invaluable (Wanis, Thorn (1995), 27-33 Figs.1-4).

Aynsley   Captain C. Murray Aynsley of H.M. 'Assurance'.

Beechey   Captain Frederick William Beechey of the Royal Navy and his elder half-brother Henry William Beechey, a linguist and talented artist, were the sons of Sir William Beechey, court painter to King George III and Queen Charlotte. They explored Cyrene in 1822 as part of a surveying mission, during which Frederick mapped the whole coastal area of Libya between Tripoli and Derna, and produced the excellent maps of Cyrene which have been adapted for use by many subsequent writers. Their expedition was unfortunately recalled by the Colonial Office as a result of devious actions by the Consul General in Tripoli, Colonel Hanmer Warrington (PRO FO 76/16 fols.7-10). In 1828 their story was published, with the formidable title: *'Proceedings of the Expedition to explore the Northern Coast of Africa, from Tripoly eastward; in MDCCCXXI and MDCCCXXII. Comprehending an account of the Greater Syrtis and Cyrenaica; and of the Ancient Cities composing the Pentapolis'.*

Birch   Samuel Birch was an Egyptologist and Orientalist at the British Museum. At the time of Smith and Porcher's departure he was Assistant Keeper of the Department of Antiquities, and in 1861 became Keeper of the Oriental, British and Medieval Antiquities (Bierbrier (1995), 45-46).

Bourville   Vattier de Bourville was a former French Consul in Benghazi who indulged in the consular pleasure of excavation. The action for which he is always remembered and castigated was the removal of the set of painted metopes from the 'Tomb of Altalena' in Cyrene. These can be seen, by appointment, at the Louvre Museum in Paris, where they are at least protected. Also in the Louvre are collections of terracotta figures and small objects such as earrings and gilded flowers and fruit from funeral wreaths, obtained in the Cyrenaica by Bourville.

Burgoyne General Sir John Fox Burgoyne GCB entered the Royal Engineers on August 29th 1798, where he rose swiftly in the ranks and saw much varied active service abroad, including the Peninsular and the Crimean Wars. He accepted the post of Inspector General of Fortifications in 1845 and later became, in addition, Colonel-commandant of the Royal Engineers. Burgoyne was a man of sensitivity and quick wit, who would hum a tune when he was happy, whatever situation he might be in. Although he attained a considerable age he was still a fit man, except for being, by his own admission, *'deaf as a post'*. He liked to wear a disreputable old hat, which one day a workman picked up and took away with him, thinking it was his, but brought it back when he realised his error. Lady Burgoyne pointed out to her husband *'what a very bad hat it must have been, for a workman to have taken it by mistake for his own, when Sir John interrupted her lecture by saying, "A much better proof of that is his <u>bringing it back</u>".'* (Wrottesley (1873), 463-464). The death of his son, Captain Hugh Burgoyne, when his ship went down in 1870, gave him a shock which affected him physically, although he was still mentally agile. He died in his ninetieth year, about three years after his retirement, and his medals and decorations are on display at the Royal Engineers Museum, Chatham.

Crowe George William Crowe was appointed Consul at Tripoli in 1846, succeeding Colonel Hanmer Warrington following the latter's enforced resignation after thirty-two stormy years in office. On his arrival he found the Consulate empty and in a state of disrepair. It had been uninhabited for a long time, and Warrington had sold all the furniture, except *'some chimney pieces and grates that nobody wanted'* (FO 101/20). Crowe was *'confined to the town'* as the Colonel's family had *'purchased his country house and garden'* which he had built outside Tripoli (FO 101/15 fol.199). Warrington had sunk thirty thousand dollars into this *'delightful place'*, stocking the garden with, among other things, five hundred olive trees (FO 160/64).

Crowe Frederick H. Crowe, son of the above, Vice-Consul at Benghazi (Bailey (1972); (1988)). He left Benghazi on 4th May 1861 on leave of absence and went to Egypt for his health. He was in England during the autumn, and on October 7th wrote from Devizes in Wiltshire, applying for an appointment at Syra. However, on December 18th a new Vice-Consul for Benghazi was being appointed, and he is referred to as *'the late Mr Crowe'* (FO 101/48).

Dennison William Dennison was a British Museum carpenter who lived with his wife Rebecca in Clerkenwell, and to whom the Tomb of Residence must have appeared very much like parts of the Museum basement. He was appointed Clerk of Works at the Museum in 1854 and remained in that post for five years, during which time he was mainly involved with the construction of the well-loved Round Reading

Room between 1854 and 1857 under the architect Sydney Smirke. He is presumably the same *'Denison'* requested on 27th March 1856 by Edward Hawkins to *'Be good enough to remove the two fire engines which you placed temporarily in the basement under the new Greek Room as the space is immediately wanted for the new Assyrian sculptures'* (Brit.Mus.Orig.Lett. Pap.Vol.LIII fol.323). Dennison had a reputation as an excellent supervisor, and it was presumably this which influenced the Trustees when they chose him to go to Cyrene. He delivered to Smith and Porcher a letter from Panizzi written on 7th June, the date when loading of the June consignment was completed, with which Smith and Porcher were helped by two Navy carpenters from H.M.S. 'St Jean D'Acre'. Although arriving too late for this work, Dennison proved himself invaluable in organising the workmen and packing the second consignment. His name appears among forty-one signatures on a petition of 18th July 1862 by *'mechanics and labourers employed at the British Museum'* requesting time to visit the Great Exhibition (Brit.Mus.Orig.Lett. Pap.Vol.LXXIII fol.533).

Ewart Captain Charles Joseph Frederick Ewart of H.M.S. 'Melpomene' had previous experience in the field of embarking marble statuary, as he performed the same service for Sir Charles Fellowes at Xanthus in 1844. The *'man-harness'* used by the bluejackets dragging the wagons was devised by the captain to make their task easier.

Fowke Captain Francis Fowke of the Royal Engineers patented a compact folding camera on 31st May 1856, which was manufactured by the London firm of T. Ottewill and Co. and supplied to the British government. Fowke was well-known in the field of architecture, and was involved in the design of the Natural History Museum and the Royal Albert Hall, both in South Kensington, but the former was revised by Waterhouse and the latter completed by Gilbert Scott as Captain Fowke had died in 1865 of overwork.

Hamilton James Hamilton spent six weeks at Cyrene in 1852 in the course of an extensive tour, guided by Mohammed el Adouli, as a result of which he produced in 1856 his *'Wanderings in North Africa'*.

Herbert Lord Henry Howard Molyneux Herbert was the fourth Earl of Carnarvon, a Member of Parliament with a keen interest in foreign affairs and in archaeology (Dictionary of National Biography). In 1849 Charles Newton had published his *'Notes on the Sculptures at Wilton House'*, the family's country residence. Herbert travelled in 1853 through Syria and Asia Minor, and plunged into politics the following year, making his maiden speech on the eve of the Crimean War. His enthusiasm for archaeology was passed on to his only son, who excavated in Thebes and in the Valley of the Kings with Howard Carter, where they eventually discovered the Tomb of Tutankhamun (Bierbrier (1995), 199-200).

Herman Colonel G.F. Herman, Consul General at Tripoli. Back in 1848, only five weeks after his arrival at Benghazi as Vice-Consul he had written:

'*The whole country between this and Derna in an Archaeological point of view is of the highest interest. .. In about three weeks I purpose pushing a Reconnaissance as far as the Egyptian Frontier – "Inshallah" [when] I return you shall have a Report "De omnibus rebus Cyrenaicis"* ....' Significantly, this was the time when the French Vice-Consul at Benghazi, Vattier de Bourville, had also been exploring the area (FO 101/20). In later years Crowe suggested that the Vice-Consulate at Benghazi should be raised to a Consulate but Herman, who did not agree, wrote on 10th October 1861: '*Neither am I of the opinion that the Archaeological labours of Lieuts Smith and Porcher which in all probability a few months will bring to a close, are at all likely to attract to the shores of the ancient Hesperides and the Cyrenaica the tide of immigration, and in its train the large infusion of rascality from all parts of the Mediterranean, that Mr Crowe appears at once to anticipate, and apprehend.*' (FO 101/48).

H.R.H.   His Royal Highness the Duke of Cambridge.

Martin   Vice Admiral Sir William Fanshawe Martin, Commander in Chief.

Newton   Sir Charles T. Newton began his career in the British Museum in 1840 as Assistant in Department of Antiquities, followed by a period under the Foreign Office in a consular capacity at Mitylene on the Island of Rhodes and at Rome, where he served from June 1859-January 1861, before returning to the British Museum as Keeper of Greek and Roman Antiquities 1861-1885 (Jenkins (1992), 96; Rhodes (1973), 180).

Panizzi   Antonio Panizzi, formerly Keeper of Printed Books at the British Museum, put forward in 1852 his proposal for what was to become the world-famous circular Reading Room. In 1857 he was appointed Principal Librarian.

Russell   Lord John Russell entered parliament in 1814 and was very much involved in parliamentary reform, with literature high on his list of interests. In 1831 after the Government Reform Bill had been at first rejected, Sydney Smith told Lady Holland '*the people along the way were very much disappointed by his smallness. I told them he was much larger before the bill was thrown out, but was reduced by excessive anxiety about the people*'. The Bill was approved the following year. Russell became a skilled orator, and it was stated by Charles Gore: '*He possesses the temper and tact of Lord Althorp, with ten thousand times his eloquence and power.*' For the next thirty years Russell held various important posts, including two spells as Prime Minister, and at the time of Smith and Porcher's expedition he was Secretary of State at the Foreign Office, also one of the Trustees of the British Museum.

Somerset   His Grace the Duke of Somerset K.G., First Lord of the Admiralty.

Spratt   Thomas Abel Bremage Spratt, born in 1811, entered the Navy at the age of sixteen and became distinguished in the field of surveying. His interests also encompassed geology and archaeological research, and he produced such books as '*Travels in Lycia, Milyas and the Cibyratis*' and publications on Greek inscriptions in Crete and in the Levant, which he called 'Inscriptiones Sprattianae'. He also published his opinions on the soundness of de Lesseps' plans for the Suez Canal and a study of wave influence on the Nile Delta deposits. Spratt was consulted from the first by Smith on his project, and showed great interest. He later had orders to give assistance to the expedition, as long as it did not interfere with his duties. Spratt very much wanted to visit Cyrene himself, but to his undoubted chagrin he arrived in the area with his surveying ship 'Medina' too late, just as the 'Melpomene' was embarking the last of the statuary and Lieutenants Smith and Porcher were making a swift escape from a difficult situation on shore.

Warrington Colonel Hanmer Warrington, excessively patriotic but hot-headed and disobedient towards those in government, ruled the roost for 32 years as Consul General at Tripoli, from 1814 until 1846 when he was forced to resign by an exasperated Foreign Secretary. Born in about 1778 at Acton near Wrexham, he joined the army at the age of sixteen, rising to the rank of Lieutenant-Colonel in the Dragoon Guards. During the Peninsular War in Spain, under the future Duke of Wellington, he reportedly had his horse killed under him by a cannon, and two musket balls went through his uniform (FO 101/19). He was appointed by the Prince Regent *'in the name and on the behalf of His Majesty. . as His Agent and Consul General at Tripoli in the room of Mr Langford'*, and after a penniless sojourn at Gibraltar, he arrived at the consulate with his wife and young family, a brood which swelled to ten surviving children, about half of whom were born in Tripoli and baptized by Warrington. They found the building in a parlous state of repair, *'part of it having virtually fallen down.'* (FO 76/7 fols.26-27). According to an account written by his French rival and adversary, and discovered only in 1928, Warrington had married the illegitimate daughter of the Prince Regent. Unlikely as this may seem, there are nevertheless some puzzling links concerning blank patches in Warrington's life story and extremely large sums of money, but the truth of the matter will probably never be known. The Warringtons married in Croydon, with the bride's father being named on the marriage certificate as David Pryce of Northwood Cottage, Isle of Wight. Jane Eliza Warrington was *'striking and dignified, at first rather reserved, but most charming when one knew her'*, according to the wife of de Breughel, the Dutch Consul, who first met her in 1827. She died in 1841 and was buried in the Protestant cemetery near Tripoli, of which her husband was one of the founders; five years later the colonel applied for permission to bring her home to England for deposition in the family vault. This was granted, and instructions were given to the Commissioners of Customs to allow her remains to be landed on their arrival (FO 101/15). On 18th March 1847 Crowe wrote *'I hear that Col. Warrington has received the Order of the Guelf from Hanover, and that he has gone home in the expectation of being Knighted by the Queen for his long service.'* Five months later he reported the *'death of poor old Colonel*

Warrington at Patras' after riding *'for several hours with some English officers.'* (FO 101/18). At the time of Smith and Porcher's expedition some of Warrington's family were still in or around Tripoli. Frederick was an interpreter at the Tripoli consulate, a post he had held since 1827 at £20 per year (FO 101/50), Herbert, an alcoholic, was complaining of ill-treatment from Consul Herman and Vice-Consul Reade, and Osman was in some legal trouble – a civil suit (FO 101/47).

Wodehouse Lord John Wodehouse, later created Earl of Kimberley, was Under-Secretary for Foreign Affairs in 1859-61 and evidently requested official reports to be sent by the expedition, but this document has not been traced.

GLOSSARY OF TERMS USED IN DESPATCHES AND LETTERS

ACHBAR/AUGHBAH   The steep descent from the lower plateau to the coastal plain.

ARTILLERY DRAG   see PLATFORM WAGGON

ARTILLERY GYN/GIN   Three-legged apparatus for hoisting heavy weights by means of tackle and a winch or windlass.

BASHI BAZOUK   Title of a Turkish cavalryman.

BLOCKS   Pulleys with sheaves (wheels) which can be single or double, used in tackle.

BLOW HOME   If the wind "blows home" it continues without ceasing over land and sea. When interrupted by a mountain range along the shore, as here, it cannot blow home.

BUDGET   In this context, the contents of a bag – a bundle.

BY A "FLUKE"   By a piece of unexpected good luck, by chance.

CANTEEN   In this case a wooden vessel with a capacity for holding 3 or 4 pints of water, carried on the shoulders by means of leather straps.

CELLA   Interior body of a temple, housing the deity.

CIPPUS   Small low column, usually with inscription.

CROW/CROWBAR   Iron lever with a sharp point at one end and two claws on a slight bevel bend at the other; for levering heavy objects, drawing spike-nails etc.

DEAL   as PLANK, but of smaller dimensions.

DUCK   Fabric used for the clothing of seamen and soldiers in the tropics.

FIRMAN   Turkish passport.

FRUSTA   Fragments (from the Latin *frustum*).

GUN WAGGONS   see PLATFORM WAGGON

HANDSPIKES   Levers of tough ash used for heaving round the windlass on a vessel or for moving heavy articles. The handle is round but the other end is square for inserting into the holes in the windlass.

HELVES   Wooden handles for implements such as pickaxes and shovels.

HOOP IRON	Flat, thin bar-iron.
HOVE IN SIGHT	Nautical term used when hauling in the anchor, or when a sail is sighted.
KAIMAKAM/CAIMACAM	Ottoman Lieutenant-governor.
MARROW	The vital or essential part, often "pith and marrow".
MUDIR	Local Governor and tax collector for the Ottoman Empire.
OKBER	see ACHBAR.
PACHA	Ottoman Governor-general.
PERIBOLUS	Wall enclosing a sacred area.
PERISTYLE	Colonnade surrounding either the exterior of a building or an open space.
PIECEMEAL	One part at a time.
PLANK	Thick boards at least 18 ft long and $1\frac{1}{2}$ to 4 inches thick, 9 to 10 inches broad.
PLATFORM WAGGONS	In artillery, a carriage on four wheels, fitted for the transport of guns, mortars, traversing platforms, or other heavy stores.
PRONAOS	Inner portico in front of a temple cella.
REVETMENT	Sloping wall supporting the outer face of a rampart.
ROD IRON	The use of rod iron to strengthen packing cases is described in W.K. Dickson's biography of Smith in connection with the Cnidus lion. The case was made of 3" deals, and at the four corners and at every alternate plank of the bottom and the lid, rods of $\frac{1}{2}$" iron were driven through the sides from the bottom. When the lion had been hoisted into the case these bolts were all riveted on the lid.
SPIKE NAILS	Deck nails in the form of spikes 4" to 12" long.
STONE TRUCKS	Carts without sides for carrying stones.
SILPHIUM/SYLPHIUM	The plant which, in Classical times, grew abundantly in the Cyrenaica and was valued both as a delicacy and as a medicine, used to treat a multitude of ailments. In a letter of 1st May 1860, Mr Crowe described experiments which a Dr Saval was conducting on 'Derias' or 'Drias', the Arabic name for the supposed silphium. He extracted a medicinal substance from the brown, carrot-like root by means of alcohol, and used it to treat wounds with, Crowe claimed, satisfactory results. The seeds and the bark of the root formed a strong purgative (Brit.Mus.Porcher Watercolour portfolio). SEE ALSO Chapter 7 n. 17.
TACKLE	Combination of ropes and blocks.
TALLOW	Animal fat used for making candles and soap and dressing leather; in this context more likely for greasing parts of a vessel.
THE PORTE	In full "the Sublime Porte", the Ottoman court at Constantinople = the Turkish Government.

VALIZES/VALISES	Cylindrical cloth or leather cases for kit.
VIZIERAL LETTER	Letter of authorisation from a high Turkish official or minister.
WHITE ROPE	Rope which has not been tarred.

LIST OF FIGURES

LIST OF PLATES

LIST OF PORCHER WATERCOLOURS

BIBLIOGRAPHY

ALLAN 1967	ALLAN M., *The Hookers of Kew 1785-1911* (London 1967)
ANON 1915	ANON, *Recent Discoveries at Cyrene* in Art and Archaeology Vol. I, 5 (March 1915)
BACCHIELLI 1980	BACCHIELLI L., *La Tomba delle 'Cariatidi' ed il decorativismo nell architettura tardo-ellenistica di Cirene*, Quad. XI, 11-34 Figs. 1-31
BACCHIELLI, 1995	BACCHIELLI L., *The Italian Archaeological Mission at Cyrene 1993-1994*, Lib.Ant.n.s. I, 161-164 Pls. LXXV-LXXIX (Rome 1995)
BAEDEKER 1929	BAEDEKER K., *Baedeker's Egypt* (Leipzig 1929)
BAGNANI 1921	BAGNANI G., *Hellenistic Sculpture from Cyrene*, JHS XLI (1921), 232-246 Figs. 1-5 Pls. XVII, XVIII
BAILEY 1972	BAILEY D.M., *Crowe's Tomb at Benghazi*, BSA 67 (1972), 1-11 Pls.1-4
BAILEY, 1988	BAILEY D.M., *Crowe's Tomb at Benghazi - a Postscript*, Libyan Studies 19 (1988), 87-94 Figs. 1-6
BEECHEY 1828	BEECHEY F.W. AND H.W., *Proceedings of the Expedition to Explore the Northern Coast of Africa, from Tripoly Eastward* (London 1828)
BIERBRIER 1995	BIERBRIER M.L., *Who Was Who in Egyptology* (London 1995)
BLACKWOOD 1997	BLACKWOOD R., *The Whitsunday Islands, An Historical Dictionary* (1997)
BLACKWOOD'S 1845	BLACKWOOD'S EDINBURGH MAGAZINE *The Overland Passage* Vol. 57 (352) (Feb 1845)
BONACASA 2000	BONACASA N., ENSOLI S. (eds.) *Cirene* (Milan 2000)
BOURVILLE 1850	DE BOURVILLE, J.V., *Rapport au Ministre*, Archives des Missions Scientifiques et Littéraires, Vol.I, 580-586 (Paris 1850)
British Museum	*Central Archives*: Orig. Lett. Pap. XLI (Oct 1848-Feb 1849) Orig. Lett. Pap. XLII (March-Oct 1849) Orig. Lett. Pap. LIII (July 1855-March 1856)

Orig. Lett. Pap. LXVIII (July-Dec 1860)
Orig. Lett. Pap. LXIX (Jan-May 1861)
Orig. Lett. Pap. LXX (June-Aug 1861)
Orig. Lett. Pap. LXXI (Sept-Dec 1861)
Orig. Lett. Pap. LXXIII (April-July 1862)
Orig. Lett. Pap. LXXVI (May-Aug 1863)
Orig. Lett. Pap. (1886)

Dept. of Greek and   Orig. Lett. I (1860)
Roman Antiquities: Orig. Lett. II (1861-1868)
Ph. Album II, 19-25
Porcher Watercolours

Manuscripts: 38993 fols. 390-393
41411 fols. 95-96

BURTON BROWN 1948   BURTON BROWN T., *Recent Work in the Dodecanese and Cyrenaica*, Antiquity XXII, 75-78

BUTTLE 1957   BUTTLE D., *The Greek and Roman Architecture of Cyrene* Thesis no. 2280, John Rylands University Library, Manchester

CASSELS 1955   CASSELS J., *The Cemeteries of Cyrene* BSR XXIII (N.S.X), 1-43 Pls. I-XIII

Cassels Archive: Blue field notebook
Grey field notebook

CERVELLI 1825   CERVELLI A., '*Explication des dessins d'antiquités de la Cyrénaïque*', Société de Géographie II, 1-30 Pls.I-III (Paris 1825)

C.I.G. III 1853   *C.I.G.*, ed. Franz I., 517-562, nos. 5129-5362b (Berlin 1853)

COOK 1929   BUDGE, Sir E.A.W., *Cook's Handbook for Egypt and the Egyptian Sudan* (London 1929)

DELLA CELLA 1822   DELLA CELLA P., *Narrative of an Expedition from Tripoli in Barbary to the Western Frontier of Egypt, in 1817* (London 1822)

DICKSON 1901   DICKSON W.K., *The Life of Major-General Sir Robert Murdoch Smith* (Edinburgh and London 1901)

ELLIS, WARLOW 1989   ELLIS R. AND WARLOW B., *The Royal Navy at Malta* I (1989)

GARDNER 1920   GARDNER E.A., *The Aphrodite from Cyrene*, JHS XL (1920), 203-205 Fig. 1 Pls. IX-X

Gent. Mag. 1861   Gentleman's Magazine N.S. Vol.11 (July-Dec 1861)
Gent. Mag. 1862   Gentleman's Magazine N.S. Vol. 12 (Jan-June 1862)

GHISLANZONI 1915   GHISLANZONI E., *Notizie Archeologiche sulla Cirenaica* in *Notiziario* I Fasc. I-II del n. 4, 1-175

GHISLANZONI 1927   GHISLANZONI E., *La Fonte di Apollo* in *Notiziario* IV, Anno XII Tav. XXXII-XXXIX, 215-243 Figs. 1-47

GOODCHILD 1958   GOODCHILD R.G., REYNOLDS J.M., HERINGTON C., *The Temple of Zeus at Cyrene*, PBSR (1958), 30-62 Figs. 1-7

GOODCHILD, 1976	GOODCHILD R.G., *Libyan Studies* ed. Joyce Reynolds (1976)
HAMILTON 1856	HAMILTON J., *Wanderings in North Africa* (1856)
HOGARTH 1905	HOGARTH D.G., *Cyrenaica*, Monthly Review Vol. XVIII, 90-106 (1905)
HORN 1943	HORN R., *Kyrene*, Die Antike, 19 Band 197-203 (Berlin 1943)
HUSKINSON 1975	HUSKINSON J., *Roman Sculpture from Cyrenaica in the British Museum*, Corpus Signorum Imperii Romani Vol. II Fasc. I (London 1975)
JENKINS 1992	JENKINS I., *Archaeologists and Aesthetes* (1992)
KRAELING 1962	KRAELING C.H., *Ptolemais, City of the Libyan Pentapolis* (Chicago 1962)
LUNI 1976	LUNI M., *Documenti per la storia della istituzione ginnasiale e dell'attività atletica in Cirenaica in rapporte a quelle della Grecia*, Cirene e la Grecia, Quad. VIII, 223-284
MAIOLETTI 1930	MAIOLETTI B., *Le Fonti dell'Architettura Romana in Cirenaica*, Rivista delle Colonie Italiane, July 1930, 568-588 (Roma 1930)
MAIOLETTI 1931A	MAIOLETTI B., *L'Architettura della Necropoli di Cirene*, Rivista della Colonie Italiane, September 1931, 714-722 (Roma 1931)
MAIOLETTI 1931B	MAIOLETTI B., *Tipi di Tombe nella Necropoli di Cirene*, Architettura e Arti Decorative, Anno II, 321-331 (Roma 1931)
MASSON 1974	MASSON O., *L'Inscription Généalogique de Cyrène (SGDI 4859)*, BCH XCVIII, 263-270 Figs. 1-2
National Library of Scotland	NLS ACC 9569 : published in Dickson (1901), 150-162
NEWTON 1861-63	NEWTON C., *History of Discoveries at Halicarnassus, Cnidus, and Branchidae* (London 1861-63)
O'BYRNE 1849	O'BYRNE W.R., *The Naval Biographical Dictionary*
O'BYRNE 1855	O'BYRNE W.R., *O'Byrne's Naval Annual for 1855* (1969 facsimile)
OLIVERIO 1929	OLIVERIO G., *Campagna di Scavi a Cirene nell'Estate 1927*, Afr.Ita.II 111-154 Figs. 1-65
PACHO 1827	PACHO J.-R., *Relation d'un voyage dans la Marmarique, la Cyrénaïque et les oasis d'Audjelah et de Maradeh* (Paris 1827)
PASINLI 1996	PASINLI A., *Istanbul Archaeological Museum*, 80-84
PERNIER 1927	PERNIER L., *Campagna di Scavi a Cirene nell'Estate del 1925*, Afr.Ita.I 126-155 Figs. 1-23
PESCE 1948	PESCE G., *Il 'Gran Tempio' di Cirene*, BCH LXXI-LXXII, 307-358 Figs. 1-8
PESCE 1949	PESCE G., *La Documentazione del 'Gran Tempio' in*

	Cirene, Bulletin No. 38, Société Royale D'Archéologie (Alexandria 1949), 83-129 Figs. 1-11	
Public Record Office	ADM 53/7101	Ships' Logs - 'Boxer'
	ADM 53/7011-12	Ships' Logs - 'Assurance'
	ADM 53/7122	Ships' Logs - 'Scourge'
	ADM 53/7576	Ships' Logs - 'Melpomene'
	ADM 53/8360	Ships' Logs - 'Himalaya'
	FO 76/6-7	General Correspondence before 1906 - Tripoli
	FO 101/15	General Correspondence
	FO 101/18-20	General Correspondence
	FO 101/47-48	General Correspondence
	FO 101/50	General Correspondence
	FO 160/2	Embassy and Consular Archives Correspondence
	FO 160/18	Embassy and Consular Archives Correspondence
	FO 160/47	Embassy and Consular Archives Correspondence
	FO 160/64	Embassy and Consular Archives Correspondence
	FO 160/78-79	Embassy and Consular Archives Correspondence
	WO 55/1056	Engineers' Letter Books for 1860-1866

RHODES 1973   RHODES D.E., *Dennis of Etruria* (London 1973)

ROBINSON 1913   ROBINSON D.M., *Inscriptions from the Cyrenaica* in *AJA* XVII, 157-200 Figs. 1-40

ROSENBAUM 1960   ROSENBAUM E., *A Catalogue of Cyrenaican Portrait Sculpture* (London 1960)

S.E.Cir   OLIVERIO G., - CARATELLI G.P., - (D. MORELLI), Supplemento Epigrafico Cirenaico, *ASA* XXXIX-XL, 219-375 Figs. 1-171 N.S. XXII-XXIV (1961-1962) (Rome 1963)

SILIOTTI 1998   SILIOTTI A., *Egypt Lost and Found* (London 1998)

SMITH, PORCHER 1864   SMITH R.M., PORCHER E.A., *History of the Recent Discoveries at Cyrene made during an Expedition to the Cyrenaica in 1860-61* (London 1864)

SMYTH 1854   SMYTH W.H., *The Mediterranean* (1854)

SMYTH 1867   SMYTH W.H., *The Sailor's Word-book: an Alphabetical Digest of Nautical Terms* (1867)

STUCCHI 1975   STUCCHI S., *Architettura Cirenaica* (Rome 1975)

THORN 1993   THORN J.C., *Warrington's 1827 Discoveries in the Apollo Sanctuary at Cyrene*, Libyan Studies 24 (1993), 57-76 Figs. 1-14

THORN 1998   THORN J.C., *Explorers of Cyrene 1822-1894* in La Cirenaica in Età Antica, Atti del Convegno Internazionale di

Studi, Macerata 18-20 Maggio 1995, Macerata (1998), 565 Tav. III,1

THORN 2005   THORN J.C., *The Necropolis of Cyrene: two hundred years of exploration* (Rome 2005)

THORN 1999   THORN D.M., *ΑΡΧΙΠΠΑ: A Lost Statue Rediscovered*, Libyan Studies 30 (1999), 69-76 Figs. 1-6

THWAITE 1969   THWAITE A., *The Deserts of Hesperides* (London 1969)

TOMLINSON 1967   TOMLINSON R.A., *False-façade Tombs at Cyrene*, BSA LXII, 241-256 Pls.44-47

VAUX 1862   VAUX W.S.W., *On Recent Excavations at Cyrene* in Trans. Royal Society of Literature Vol.VII (1862), 399-420

WANIS, THORN 1995   WANIS S., THORN D.M., *Mohammed el Adouli*, Libyan Studies 26 (1995), 27-33 Figs. 1-4

WANIS 1996   WANIS S., *Theseus and the Minotaur in Cyrene*, in Scritti de Antichità in Memoria di Sandro Stucchi, ed. Bacchielli L. and Bonanno Aravantinos M., 'L'Erma' di Bretschneider, Studi Miscellanei 29 Vol. I (Roma 1996), 277-280 Figs. 1-4

WARD-PERKINS 1958   WARD-PERKINS J.P., BALLANCE M.H., *The Caesareum at Cyrene and the Basilica at Cremna*, PBSR (1958), 137-194 Figs. 1-23 Pls. XXVI - XXXVI

WARD-PERKINS 1987   WARD-PERKINS J.B., GIBSON S.C., *The 'Market Theatre' Complex and Associated Structures, Cyrene*, Libyan Studies 18 (1987), 43-72 Figs. 1-27

WELD-BLUNDELL 1896   WELD-BLUNDELL H., *A Visit to Cyrene in 1895*, BSA II, 112-140 Pl. IV Figs. 1-8

WEIR 1976   WEIR S., *The Bedouin*, Museum of Mankind, British Museum Ethnography Department (1976)

WHITE 1984   WHITE D., *Background and Introduction to the Excavations, The Extramural Sanctuary of Demeter and Persephone at Cyrene, Libya*, Final Reports I (Philadelphia 1984)

WROTH 1883   WROTH W., *A Statue of the Youthful Asklepios*, JHS IV (1883), 46-52

WROTH 1886   WROTH W., *Imperial Cuirass-ornamentation and a Torso of Hadrian in the British Museum*, JHS VII (1886), 126-142

WROTTESLEY 1873   WROTTESLEY, LIEUT.-COL. THE HON. G., *Life and Correspondence of Field Marshal Sir John Burgoyne* (London 1873)

PLATES

Pl. 1 – Robert Murdoch Smith in 1856.

Pʟ. 2 – Head of the statue of Bacchus, front view [1].

PL. 4 – Statue of Bacchus, front view [3].

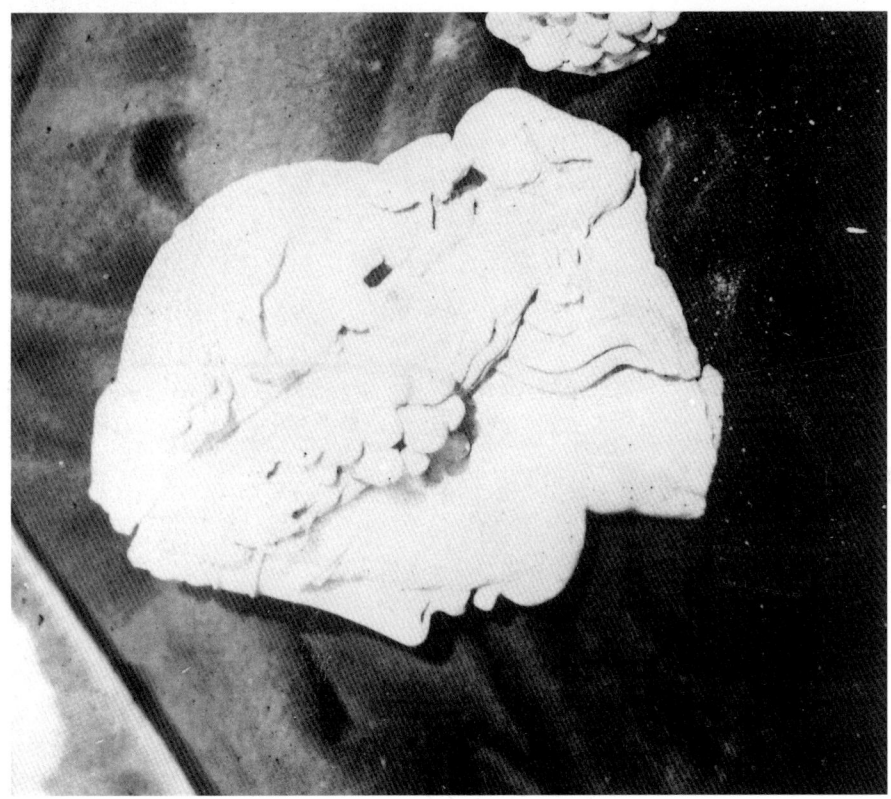

PL. 3 – Head of the statue of Bacchus, profile [2].

265

PL. 6 – Small female statue from the Temple of Apollo [5].

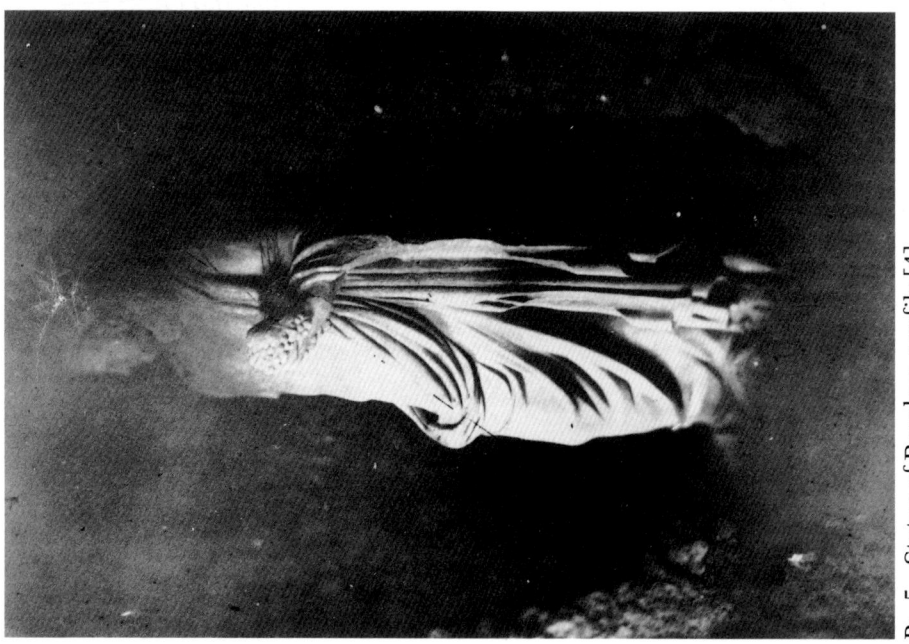

PL. 5 – Statue of Bacchus, profile [4].

266

PL. 7 – Small female statue from the Temple of Apollo [6].

PL. 8 – The face of one of the hills in the Eastern Cemetery [7].

267

PL. 9 – The face of one of the hills in the Eastern Cemetery [8].

PL. 10 – The face of one of the hills in the Eastern Cemetery [9].

268

PL. 11 – The face of one of the hills in the Eastern Cemetery [10].

PL. 12 – Excavated tombs in the Eastern Cemetery [11].

PL. 13 – View in the Wadi Bil Ghadir of the road along the face of the cliff leading to the Western Cemetery [12].

PL. 14 – Excavated tombs in the Western Cemetery [13].

270

Pl. 16 – Excavated tombs in the Western Cemetery [15].

Pl. 15 – Excavated tombs in the Western Cemetery [14].

271

PL. 17 – Group of three young Arabs [16].

PL. 18 – Group of our blacks [17].

272

Pl. 19 – Sanctuary of Apollo looking north-west [ca. January 1861].

Pl. 20 – Fountain of Apollo looking west [ca. January 1861].

PL. 21 – Lower part of the statue of Aesculapius with casket [1].

PL. 22 – Head of Aesculapius, front view [2].

274

PL. 23 – Statuette of Diana strangling a lion [3].

PL. 24 – Two statuettes and head of small statue [4].

Pl. 25 – Two heads viz Cornelius Lentulus and head of colossal statue [1].

Pl. 26 – Head of Minerva and colossal female head [2].

276

PL. 28 – Colossal female head [4].

PL. 27 – Small half draped statue [3].

277

PL. 30 – Larger of the two female statues. The workman is holding on the right arm which is broken off at the shoulder and wrist [1].

PL. 29 – Small female statue – the right hand holds a snake by the head, the body of which encircles the arm. [Only mentioned in this Despatch – photographed ca. August 1861].

278

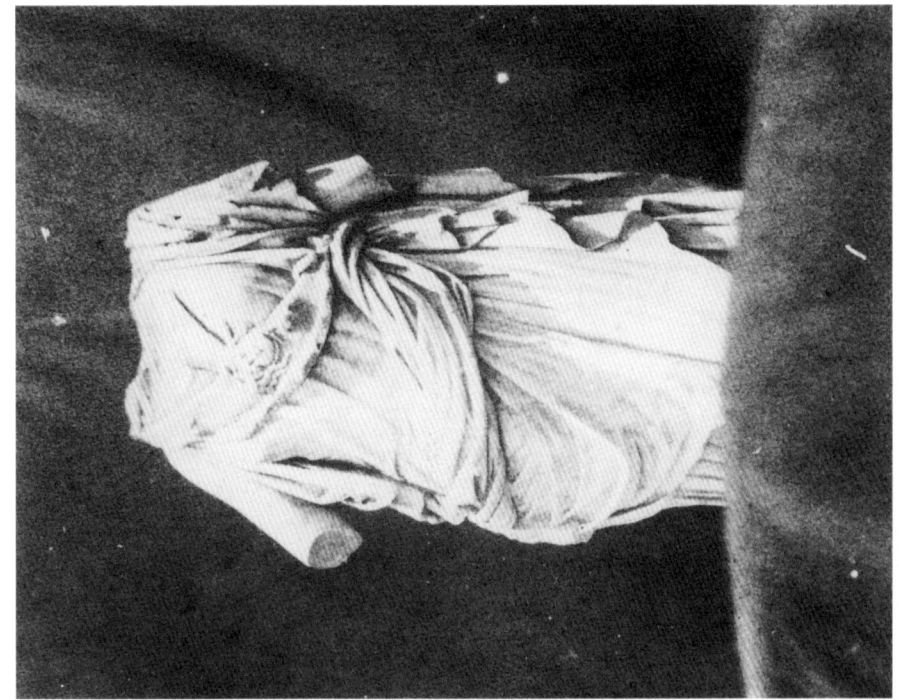

Pl. 31 – Smaller of the two statues, full length [2].

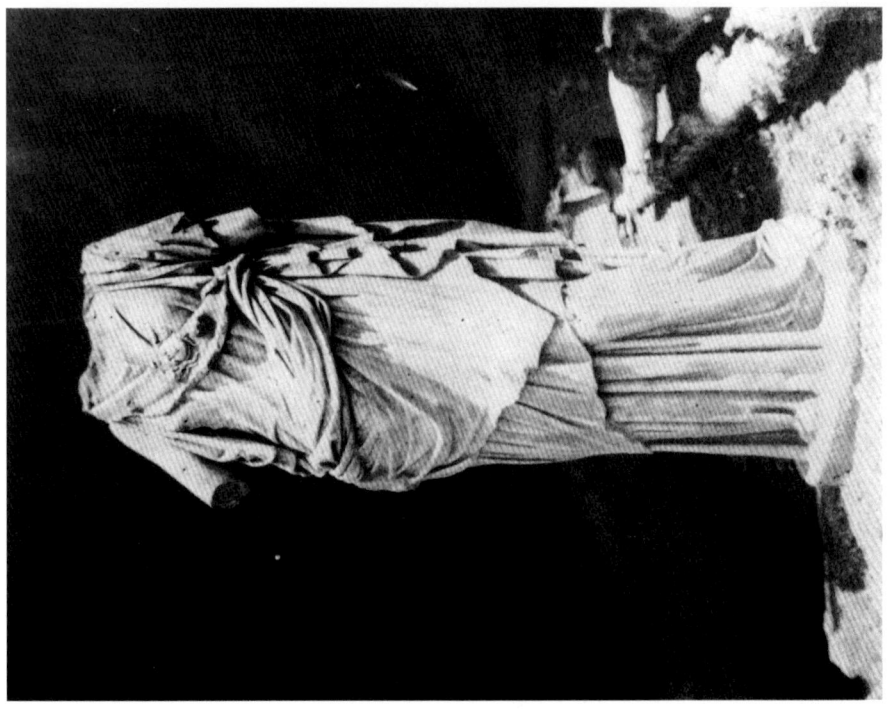

Pl. 32 – Smaller of the two statues on a larger scale, upper part [3].

279

PL. 33 – Portrait of Mohammed el Adouly an influential Arab of the Cyrenaica who has always been a particular friend of ours, and who has often been of considerable service to us [4].

PL. 34 – Bronze head from Temple of Aesculapius [1].

PL. 35 – Female head, life-size, from Temple of Aesculapius [2].

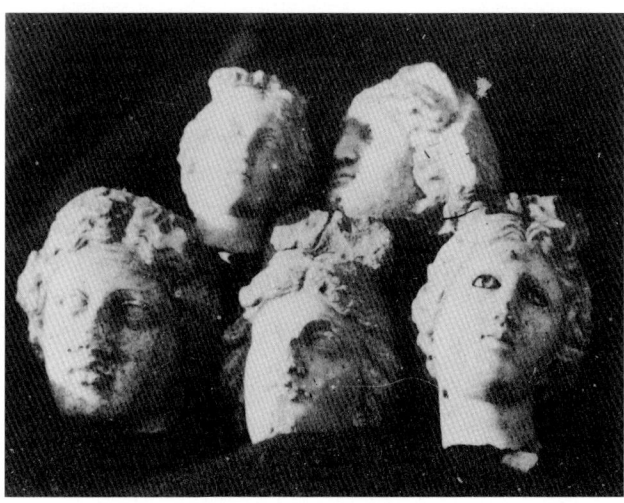

PL. 36 – Group of small heads from the Temple of Aesculapius and the vicinity [3].

PL. 37 – Small statue of Bacchus [4].

PL. 38 – Two statuettes [5].

Pl. 39 – Upper part of colossal statue from near the Temple of Aesculapius [6].

Pl. 40 – Lower part of colossal statue from near the Temple of Aesculapius [7].

Pl. 41 – Head of colossal statue separate on a larger scale [8].

Pl. 42 – Statue of the Philosopher, and large seated figure, Archippe [9].

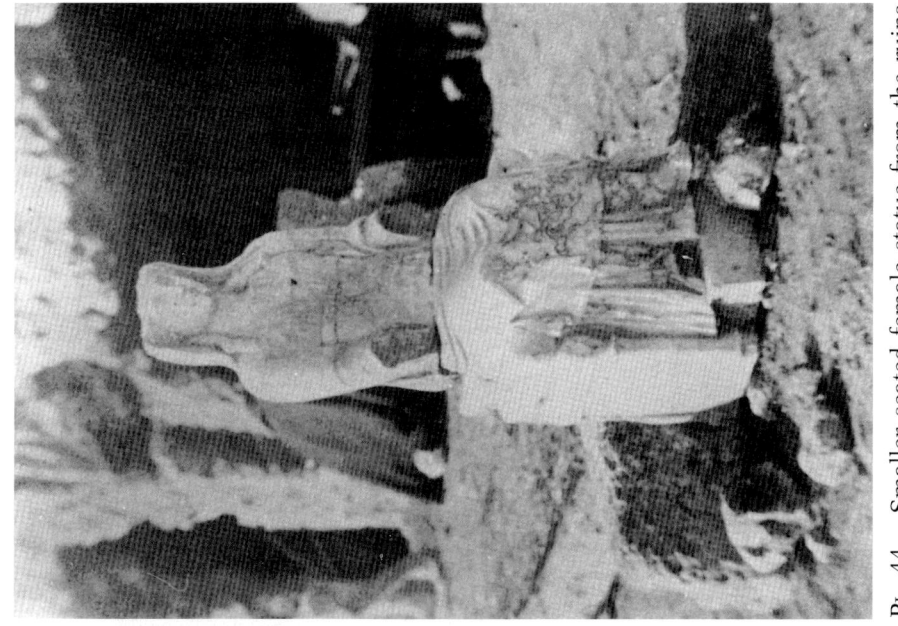

PL. 44 – Smaller seated female statue from the ruins near the Temple of Aesculapius [11].

PL. 43 – Head of the Philosopher, separate [10].

285

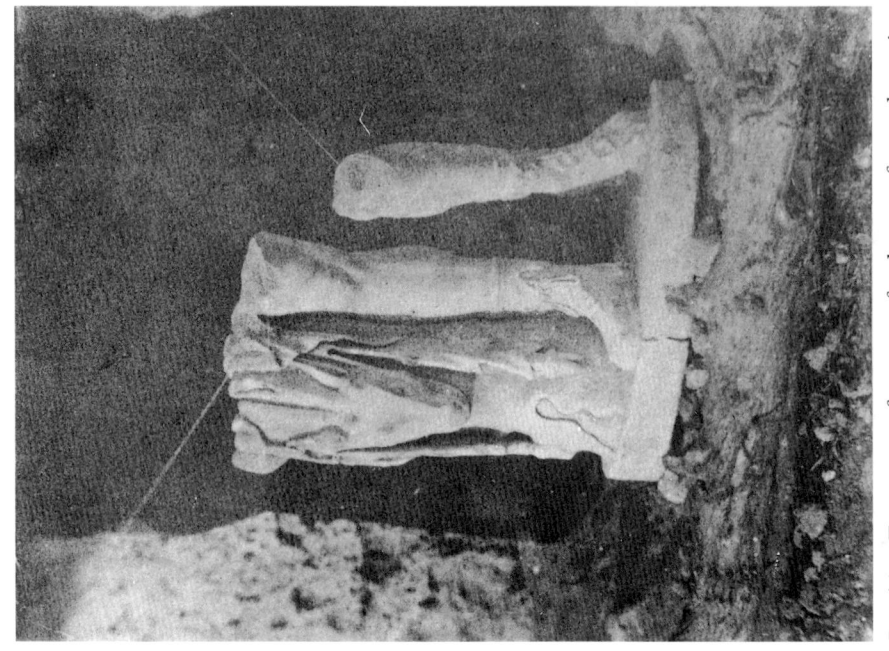

Pl. 46 – Fragment of statue of a hunter from the ruins near the Temple of Aesculapius [13].

Pl. 45 – Statue of a huntress perhaps Diana or Cyrene from the ruins near the Temple of Aesculapius [12].

286

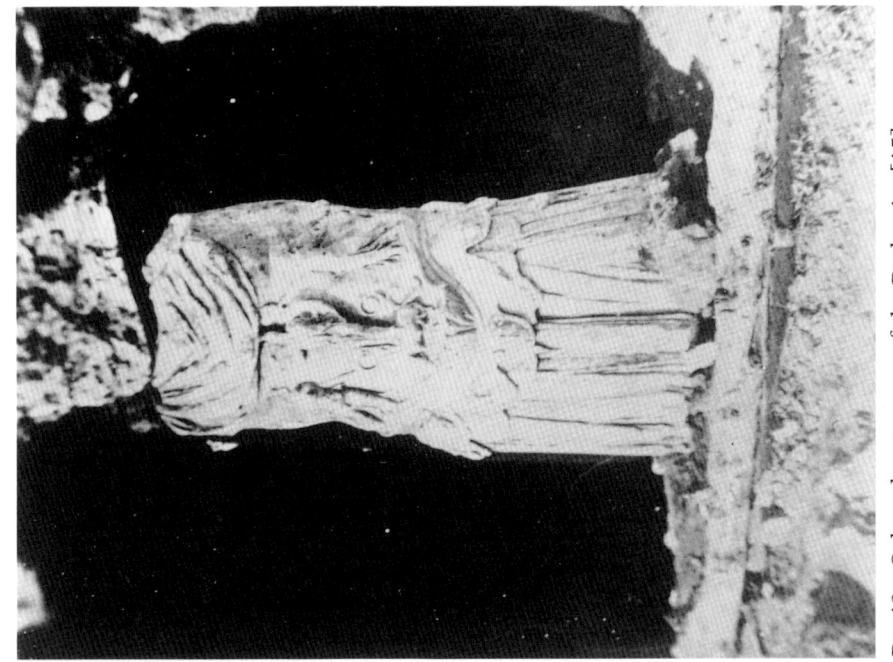

Pl. 48 – Colossal statue one of the Ptolemies [15].

Pl. 47 – Female head from the ruins near the Temple of Aesculapius [14].

287

PL. 49 – The Tomb of Residence from across the 'Central Wady' [ca. August 20th 1861].

PL. 50 – The terrace above the Tomb of Residence [ca. September 14th 1861].

PL. 51 – Colossal draped female statue.

PL. 52 – Group of three heads.

PL. 53 – Group of three busts.

PL. 54 – Bust of a girl.

290

PL. 56 – Colossal male bust.

PL. 55 – Colossal male bust.

291

PL. 57 – Benghazi, appearance of the Coast to the North of the Town with the only windmill in the country [Porcher 103].

PL. 58 – Benghazi, the British Consulate [Porcher 104].

PL. 59 – Central Wadi and Slope of the Eastern Hill of Cyrene [Plate 59].

PL. 60 – Western Hill of Cyrene, with Entrance to the Fountain of Apollo [Plate 11].

PL. 61 – Fountain of Apollo [Plate 12].

PL. 62 – Large Tomb on the Face of the Western Hill of Cyrene [Plate 27].

294

PL. 63 – Exterior of a Tomb in the Northern Necropolis [Porcher 101].

PL. 64 – A Tomb in the Northern Necropolis [Porcher 119].

PL. 65 – The Wadi Bil Ghadir, or the Valley of Verdure [Porcher 110].

PL. 66 – General View of one of the Hills in the Northern Necropolis of Cyrene [Plate 13].

296

PL. 67 – Large Tomb at the Eastern end of the Northern Necropolis [Plate 14].

PL. 68 – A Tomb in the Northern Necropolis close to the one embellished with figures [Porcher 123a].

PL. 69 – A Tomb Embellished with Figures in the Northern Necropolis [Porcher 123b].

PL. 70 – Interior of a Painted Tomb in the Northern Necropolis [Plate 21].

298

Pl. 71 – Interior of an ornamented and Painted Tomb in the Northern Necropolis [Porcher 117].

Pl. 72a – Tombs (called by the Arabs "Kinissieh") in the Northern Necropolis [Plate 26].

Pl. 72b – Photographic version of the same view, taken in 1908.

PL. 73 – Partial view of the Tombs and Sarcophagi in the Northern Necropolis [Porcher 113].

PL. 74 – Tomb for 105 Sarcophagi in the Northern Necropolis [Plate 20].

Pl. 75 – Tomb in the Northern Necropolis [Plate 15].

Pl. 76 – Interior of a Large Tomb in the Northern Necropolis [Plate 24].

302

PL. 77 – Eastern End of the Northern Necropolis of Cyrene [Frontispiece].

PL. 78 – A Tomb in the Northern Necropolis capable of holding 54 Sarcophagi [Porcher 116].

PL. 79 – Tombs in the Northern Necropolis [Porcher 115].

PL. 80 – Interior of a Tomb in the Northern Necropolis [Plate 22].

304

PL. 81 – Interior of a Detached tomb on the S.E. side of the city [Porcher 97].

PL. 82 – Interior of a Tomb in the Northern Necropolis [Porcher 98].

PL. 83 – Interior of a Tomb in the Northern Necropolis [Porcher 95, 99].

PL. 84 – Exterior of a Tomb in the Northern Necropolis [Porcher 100].

PL. 85 – A Tomb in the Northern Necropolis [Porcher 118].

PL. 86 – Interior of a small Painted Tomb in the Northern Necropolis [Porcher 120].

PL. 87 – Interior of a small Painted Tomb in the Northern Necropolis [Porcher 121].

PL. 88 – Interior of a small Painted Tomb in the Northern Necropolis [Porcher 122].

308

PL. 89 – Derna, the Market Square, shewing the Custom house, and the Bazaar [Porcher 109].

PL. 90 – Edwin Augustus Porcher, R.N. [British Columbia Archives A-08358].

INDEX

43 - LIVERANI, P. - *Municipium Augustum Veiens*. Veio in età imperiale attraverso gli scavi Giorgi (1811-13), 1987.

44 - STRAZZULLA, M. J. - Le terrecotte architettoniche della Venetia romana. Contributo allo studio della produzione fittile nella Cisalpina, 1987.

45 - FRANZONI, C. - *Habitus atque habitudo militis*. Monumenti funerari di militari nella Cisalpina romana, 1987.

46 - SCARPELLINI, D. - Stele romane con *imagines clipeatae* in Italia, 1986.

47 - D'ALESSANDRO, L.
PERSEGATI, F. - Scultura e calchi in gesso. Storia, tecnica e conservazione, 1987.

48 - MILANESE, M. - Gli scavi dell'oppidum preromano di Genova, 1987.

49 - SCATOZZA HÖRICHT, L. A. - Le terrecotte figurate di Cuma del Museo Archeologico Nazionale di Napoli, 1987.

50 - UHLENBROCK, J. P. - The Terrecotta Protomai from Gela: A Discussion of Local Style in Archaic Sicily, 1989.

51 - CAVAGNARO VANONI L.,
SERRA RIDGWAY, F. R. - Vasi etruschi a figure rosse. Dagli scavi della Fondazione Lerici nella necropoli dei Monterozzi a Tarquinia, 1989.

52 - RALLO, A. (a cura di) - Le donne in Etruria, 1989.

53 - CALCANI, G. - Cavalieri di bronzo. La torma di Alessandro opera di Lisippo, 1989.

54 - MORANDI, A. - Epigrafia di Bolsena etrusca, 1990.

55 - FAVARETTO, I. - Arte antica e cultura antiquaria nelle collezioni venete al tempo della Serenissima, 1990.

56 - BONGHI JOVINO, M.
(a cura di) - Artigiani e botteghe nell'Italia preromana. Studi sulla coroplastica di area etrusco-laziale-campana, 1990.

57 - STRAZZULLA, M. J. - Il principato di Apollo. Mito e propaganda nelle lastre «Campana» dal tempio di Apollo Palatino, 1990.

58 - BURANELLI, F. - Gli scavi a Vulci della società Vincenzo Campanari - Governo Pontificio (1835-1837), 1991.

59 - JONGSTE P, F. B. - The Twelve Labours of Hercules on Roman Sarcophagi, 1992.

60 - MEDRI, M. - Terra sigillata tardo italica decorata, 1992.

61 - EQUINI SCHNEIDER, E. - Septimia Zenobia Sebaste, 1993.

62 - MILANESE, M. - Genova romana. Mercato e città dalla tarda età repubblicana a Diocleziano dagli scavi del colle di Castello (Genova-S. Silvestro 2), 1993.

63 - DEICHMANN, F. W. - Archeologia Cristiana, 1993.

64 - CIAGHI, S. - Le terrecotte figurate da Cales del Museo Nazionale di Napoli. Sacro stile committenza, 1993.

65 - RENZI, G. C. (a cura di) - Monumenti e culture nell'Appennino in età romana. Atti del Convegno. Sestino, 12 nov. 1989, 1993.

66 - MARCONI COSENTINO, R.,
RICCIARDI, L. - Catacombe di Comodilla. Lucerne e altri materiali dalle gallerie 1, 8, 13, 1993.

67 - SZABÒ, M. - Archaic terracottas di Boeotia, 1993.

68 - CALCAGNI, G. - L'antichità marginale. Continuità dell'arte provinciale romana nel Rinascimento, 1993.

69 - MANZELLI, V. - La policromia nella statuaria greca arcaica, 1994.

70 - SCARFÌ, B. M. - Studi di archeologia della x Regio in ricordo di Michele Tombolani, 1994.

71 - VARONE, A. - Erotica pompeiana. Iscrizioni d'amore sui muri di Pompei, 1994.

72 - POLLAK, L.
(M. M. Guldan ed.) - Römische Memoiren, Künstler, Kunstliebhaber und Gelehrte (1893-1943), 1994.

73 - CHARALAMPIDIS, C. P. - The Dendrites in pre-Christian and Christian Historical-Literary Tradition and Iconography, 1994.

74 - VIACAVA, A. - L'atleta di Fano, 1994.

75 - MODONESI, D. - Museo Maffeiano. Iscrizioni e rilievi sacri latini, 1995.

76 - DOLCE, R., NOTA SANTI, M. - Dai Palazzi assiri, 1995.
(a cura di)

77 - BARBANERA, M. - Il guerriero di Agrigento. Una probabile scultura fronto-nale del Museo di Agrigento e alcune questioni di ar-cheologia «siceliota», 1995.

78 - PUPPO, P. - Le coppe megaresi in Italia, 1995.

79 - AMBROGI, A. - Vasche di età romana in marmi bianchi e colorati, 1995.

80 - CARAFA, P. - Officine ceramiche di età regia. Produzione di ceramica in impasto a Roma dalla fine dell'VIII alla fine del VI se-colo a.C., 1995.

81 - PAVESE, C. O. - L'Auriga di Mozia, 1996.

82 - CAVAGNARO VANONI, L. - Tombe tarquiniesi di età ellenistica. Catalogo di ventisei tombe a camera scoperte dalla Fondazione Lerici in lo-calità Calvario, 1996.

83 - ROSSETTI TELLA, C. - La terra sigillata tardo-italica decorata del Museo Nazio-nale Romano, 1996.

84 - BELLELLI, G. M., BIANCHI, U. - *Orientalia Sacra Urbis Romae. Dolichena et Heliopolitana.*
(a cura di) Recueil d'études archeologiques et historico-religieuses sur les cultes cosmopolites d'origine commagénienne et syrienne, 1997.

85 - CAMBITOGLOU, A., HARARI, M. - The Italiote Red-Figured Vases in the Museo Camillo Leone at Vercelli, 1997.

86 - BETTELLI, M. - Roma. La città prima della città: i tempi di una nascita. La cronologia delle sepolture ad inumazione di Roma e del Lazio nella prima età del ferro, 1997.

87 - GÓMEZ PALLARÉS, J. - Edición y comentario de las inscripciones sobre mosaico de *Hispania*. Inscripciones no cristianas, 1997.

88 - DE CESARE, M. - Le statue in immagine. Studi sulle raffigurazioni di sta-tue nella pittura vascolare greca, 1997.

89 - SPANU, M. - *Keramos* di Caria. Storia e monumenti, 1997.

90 - REBECCHI, F. (a cura di) - Spina e il delta padano. Riflessioni sul catalogo e sulla mostra ferrarese. Atti del convegno (Ferrara 1994), 1998.

91 - BONANNO, C. - I sarcofagi fittili della Sicilia, 1998.

92 - SANNIBALE, M. - Le armi della collezione Gorga al Museo Nazionale Romano, 1998.

93 - DE FRANCESCHINI, M. - Le Ville Romane della X Regio (Venetia et Histria). Cata-logo e carta archeologica del territorio dall'età repubbli-cana al tardo impero, 1998.

94 - CHRZANOVSKI, L., ZHURAVLEV, D. - Lamps from Chersonesos in the State Historical Mu-seum-Moscow, 1998.

95 - GIAVARINI, C. (a cura di) - Il Palatino. Area sacra sud-ovest e Domus Tiberiana, 1998.

96 - DRAGO TROCCOLI, L. - Scavi e ricerche archeologiche dell'Università di Roma
(a cura di) «La Sapienza», 1998.

97 - ZACCAGNINO, C. - Il *thymiaterion* nel mondo greco. Analisi delle fonti, tipo-logia, impieghi, 1998.

98 - BARICH, B. E. - People, water and grain: The beginnings of domestica-tion in the Sahara and the Nile valley, 1998.

99 - CHIESA, F. - Demoni alati e grifi araldici. Lastre architettoniche fittili di Capua antica, 1998.

100 - PENSABENE, P., PANELLA, C. - Arco di Costantino. Tra archeologia e archeometria,
(a cura di) 1999.

101 - PENSABENE, P. - Le Terrecotte del Museo Nazionale Romano. Gocciolatoi e protomi da sime. Appendice: aggiornamento al catalo-go delle Antefisse, 1999.

102 - GENOVESE, G.   - I santuari rupestri nella Calabria greca, 1999.

103 - MORANDI, A.   - Il cippo di Castelciès nell'epigrafia retica, 1999.

104 - MESSINEO, G.   - La tomba dei Nasonii, 2000.

105 - AGOSTINIANI, L., NICOSIA F.   - Tabula Cortonensis, 2000.

106 - DE' SPAGNOLIS, M.   - La Tomba del Calzolaio. Dalla necropoli monumentale romana di Nocera Superiore, 2000.

107 - ACCARDO, S.   - Villae romanae nell'ager Bruttius. Il paesaggio rurale calabrese durante il dominio romano, 2000.

108 - ZAMPIERI, G.   - Claudia Toreuma. Giocoliera e mima. Il monumento funerario, 2000.

109 - TAYLOR, R.   - Public Needs and Private Pleasures. Water Distribution, the Tiber River and the Urban Development of Ancient Rome, 2000.

110 - MONACO, M. C.   - *Ergasteria*. Impianti artigianali ceramici ad Atene ed in Attica dal protogeometrico alle soglie dell'Ellenismo, 2000.

111 - DE' SPAGNOLIS, M.   - Pompei e la Valle del Sarno in epoca preromana: la cultura delle tombe a fossa, 2001.

112 - PENSABENE, P.   - Le terrecotte del Museo Nazionale Romano. II. Materiali dai depositi votivi di Palestrina: collezioni «Kircheriana» e «Palestrina», 2001.

113 - AMBROSINI, L.   - I thymiateria etruschi in bronzo di età tardo classica, alto e medio ellenistica, 2002.

114 - OGNIBENE, S.   - Umm Al-Rasas: la chiesa di Santo Stefano ed il «problema iconofobico», 2002.

115 - LA GRECA, F. (a cura di)   - Fonti letterarie greche e latine per la storia della Lucania tirrenica, 2001.

116 - VARONE, A.   - Erotica Pompeiana. Love Inscriptions on the Walls of Pompeii, 2002.

117 - GIUDICE RIZZO, I.   - Inquieti "commerci" tra uomini e dei. *Timpanisti, Fineo A e B* di Sofocle. Testimonianze letterarie ed iconografiche, itinerari di ricerca e proposte, 2002.

118 - SÖDERLIND, M.   - Late Etruscan Votive Heads from Tessennano. Production, Distribution, Sociohistorical Context, 2002.

119 - DE' SPAGNOLIS, M.   - La villa N. Popidi Narcissi Maioris in Scafati, suburbio orientale di Pompei, 2002.

120 - PIERACCINI , L. C.   - Around the Hearth. Caeretan Cylinder-Stamped Braziers, 2003.

121 - STIBBE, C. M.   - Trebenishte. The Fortunes of an Unusual Excavation, 2003.

122 - ATTANASIO, D.   - Ancient White Marbles. Analysis and Identification by Paramagnetic Resonance Spectroscopy, 2003.

123 - ZAMPIERI, G.   - La Tomba di "san Luca Evangelista". La cassa di piombo e l'area funeraria della Basilica di santa Giustina in Padova, 2003.

124 - AGATI, M. L.   - Il libro manoscritto. Introduzione alla codicologia, 2003.

125 - BARRESI, P.   - Province dell'Asia Minore. Costo dei marmi, architettura pubblica e committenza, 2003.

126 - CORTI, C.   - L'*ager* nord-occidentale della città di *Mutina*. Il popolamento nel carpigiano e nella media pianura dalla romanizzazione al tardoantico-altomedioevo, 2004.

127 - MINETTI, A.   - Orientalizzante a Chiusi e nel suo territorio, 2004.

128 - DE' SPAGNOLIS, M.   - Il mito omerico di Dionysos ed i pirati tirreni in un documento da *Nuceria Alfaterna*, 2004.

154 - CAPRIOLI, F.   - *Vesta Aeterna*. L' *Aedes Vestae* e la sua decorazione archi-
                               tettonica, 2007
155 - THORN, M. D.   - The Four Season of Cyrene, 2007.

Finito di stampare in Roma nel mese di settembre 2007 per conto de
«L'ERMA» di BRETSCHNEIDER
dalla Tipograf S.r.l.
via Costantino Morin, 26/A